Advance Praise For
A Survival Guide to Computer Contracts

Despite the significant number of business technology systems implemented each year, most executives are unprepared for the challenges inevitably created by this process. **A Survival Guide to Computer Contracts** *provides practical and effective guidance for each step of the procurement, negotiation and implementation process.*

This book provides a very necessary and useful tool for anyone facing the formidable task of selecting and contracting for a business computer system. Having experienced this situation, I only wish such a Guide had been available at the time for our use.

> Donald J. Hudson
> President, Vancouver Stock Exchange 1982–1995

A Survival Guide to Computer Contracts *fills a vacuum in a critical yet vulnerable area hitherto largely ignored by managers...The Survival Guide helps managers and legal counsel think through issues in plain English and brings into the open concerns that can no longer be swept under the carpet or allowed to rest on good faith alone as technology becomes the foundation of new business services and growth.*

> Pavan Sahgal, Editor in Chief
> *Global Investment Magazine*
> *& Global Investment Technology*

Monassebian, previously a principal in, and general counsel to, one of the financial industry's leading developer's of global trading systems, brings first hand knowledge from the trenches of Wall Street's demanding securities industry. In my 11 years as a reporter/editor for Wall Street & Technology, it is rare to encounter a resource so lucid and plain spoken about the complex subject of technology contracts.

> Ivy Schmerken
> Editor in Chief, *Wall Street & Technology*

In a world in which new technology is essential for survival, this book allows businessmen and counsel alike to arm themselves with the knowledge necessary to negotiate contracts that will afford full protection from purchase through use. Jeff Monassebian is to be congratulated upon this comprehensive work.

Howard Graff, Esq.
Partner, Baer Marks & Upham LLP

After thirty years in the technology business, I can say with some authority that **A Survival Guide to Computer Contracts** *is the most useful practical guide to technology contracts. It relates, with a businessman's clarity, the legal nuances of contract drafting to the business practices associated with the complete life cycle of technology planning and implementation.*

Alan Grody, Adjunct Professor,
New York University, Leonard N. Stern School of Business

In a step by step process, Monassebian identifies and explains all of the many managerial decision points that a business should consider in configuring its computer systems. Moreover, all of the critical contractual aspects of the process are presented and illustrated with sample legal agreements.

Joseph A. Giacalone, Ph. D., Henry George Chair in Economics & former Dean College of Business Administration, St. John's University

This Survival Guide provides a comprehensive and eminently accessible road map to the successful implementation of even the most complex enterprise-wide investment in systems technology. A must read, not only for MIS executives, but any manager, legal, or financial officer involved in the technology investment decision making process.

Porter Bibb
Managing Director, Ladenburg, Thalmann & Co. Inc.
Author, *It Ain't As Easy As It Looks*

Jeff Monassebian speaks from a position of knowledge and is a true expert in the field of business computer systems.

> Jeffrey E. Lewis, Esq.
> Senior Vice President & Counsel,
> The Chicago Stock Exchange

A Survival Guide to Computer Contracts is a repository of years of knowledge and experience that offers any entity immediate access to information that otherwise can only be obtained by relying on extensive and sometimes costly support organizations. It is not only a step by step guide, but also a reference for anyone who is involved in technology vendor selection and negotiations.

> Michael Abbaei
> Senior Vice President & Chief Information Officer
> Legg Mason Wood Walker, Incorporated

This book is interesting, informative and helpful to both professionals and novices. It is truly a survival guide for those involved in the purchase, sale or development of computer systems.

> Jeffrey M. Slopen, Esq.
> Partner, Wilson, Walker, Hochberg, Slopen

A Survival Guide to Computer Contracts is commendable not only from a businessman's perspective, but also from a litigation counsel's point of view. If one observes the tenets so simply put forth in the book, litigation is itself avoided.

> Arthur M. Lieberman, Esq.

Jeff Monassebian is uniquely qualified to write A Survival Guide to Computer Contracts. He brings extensive legal, business and technology expertise to the task. The world of information technology will benefit greatly from this multifaceted approach. He writes clearly and without excessive jargon making the book accessible to a wide audience.

> George H. Spencer
> Chairman, Heritage Capital Corp.

A Survival Guide

to

Computer Contracts

A Survival Guide

to

Computer Contracts

How to Select & Negotiate for

Business Computer Systems

By Jeff Monassebian, Esq.

Edited By Marcy J. Gordon, Esq.

A Survival Guide to Computer Contracts
How to Select & Negotiate for Business Computer Systems

Published by:
Application Publishing, Inc.
P.O. Box 4124
Great Neck, NY 11023
(516) 482-5796
(fax) 773-4743

Cover design and illustration by Lightbourne Images. © Lightbourne Images, 1996
Interior design and typesetting by The Roberts Group

ISBN 0-9650971-7-X : 24.95
Publisher's Cataloging in Publication Data
Monassebian, Jeff
    A survival guide to computer contracts : how to
select & negotiate for business computer systems / by
Jeff Monassebian.
        p. cm.
        includes index.
        LCCN: 96-83000.

        1. Computer contracts—United States—Popular works. 2.
Computers—Purchasing. 3. Business—Data processing. I. Title
KF905.C6M66 1996   343.73'09'99
                                    QBI96-20160

Printed In the United States
Printed On Acid Free Recycled Paper
    ∞

This book is dedicated to my father who taught me that a person's reputation is mostly a function of their sense of ethics and principles; my mother who taught me the value of knowledge and education and my wife who shares and instills these values in our children.

CONTENTS

APPENDICES

INDEX OF AGREEMENTS

A disk containing an electronic copy of the agreements reprinted in this book can be ordered by completing the order form at the end of this book.

PREFACE

Over the last ten years, friends and business colleagues would call to seek advice on problems with their computer and information systems. After listening to the circumstances of each complaint, I would usually ask:

What capabilities are described in your requirements definition?

What services, functions, training requirements, documentation standards and implementation schedules have been identified in your request for proposal?

What was the result of your due diligence of the vendor's qualifications?

What are the vendor's obligations and your remedies under the procurement agreement?

Invariably, the answer to most of these questions was generally the same—*I don't know.*

It is indeed remarkable that in many cases individuals who are successful business entrepreneurs in their own right do not devote the time to properly identify what they require from the computer system, conduct an organized search and evaluation of available system options, assess the vendor's experience and qualifications or effectively negotiate the terms and conditions of the procurement agreement. *I was too busy—the system looked right—it was the vendor's standard agreement,* are the all too common excuses for not having invested the necessary up-front time. The cost of such distracted management is often lost opportunities and wasted resources of all kinds.

The idea behind *A Survival Guide to Computer Contracts* resulted from this scenario. When my partners and I sold our software development and consulting firm, I finally had the time to put pen to paper (actually fingers to keyboard). This book is intended to provide the business person with a guide to the various issues involved in acquiring computer technology—from requirements definition to implementation. It is my hope that after reading this book you will be in a better position to define and support your system requirements as well as manage your legal services budget.

JM
February 20, 1996

ACKNOWLEDGMENTS

Special thanks to Joseph Rosen for his practical insight and assistance during the preparation of this book; B. Judson Hennington III, Esq. for his contribution on alternative dispute resolution and Steven Yadegari for his editorial assistance.

NOTICE

This book is designed to provide general information in regard to the subject matter covered. Every effort has been made to make this collection as complete and accurate as possible. However, it is sold with the understanding that laws vary from state to state, and if legal advice or other expert assistance is required, the services of a competent professional should be sought. Therefore, this text should be used only as a general guide and not as the ultimate source for the acquisition of computer technology. Computer procurement agreements must be carefully reviewed by an attorney who can make sure that the agreement is consistent with the terms and conditions agreed to with the vendor.

The author, advisors and publisher shall have neither liability nor responsibility to any person or entity with respect to any loss or damage caused or alleged to be caused directly or indirectly by the information contained in this book.

If you do not agree with the above, you may return this book to the place where it was purchased for a full refund.

CHAPTER

OVERVIEW

1. INTRODUCTION

Computer and information technology plays a dominant role in virtually every aspect of the world's economy. Individual businesses, regardless of size, have found having a computer system is now critical to their survival. Once implemented, that system becomes management's vehicle for filing, retrieving, manipulating and distributing the information necessary for daily business operations (hence the term *management information system*). Throughout this book management information systems of all types will be referred to as *System*.

Effective *System* procurement demands detailed planning and requirements definition, comprehensive due diligence (which includes evaluation of vendor proposals and *System* offerings) transaction structuring, contract negotiation and management of the implementation process. An organized and structured approach to *System* procurement will ensure that the *System* supports your business requirements, accommodates future growth and is sold and supported by a reliable organization.

2. EXECUTIVE SUMMARY

In 1994 over $250 billion was spent in the United States on *Systems* development. This figure represents more than 175,000 projects. On average, however, only 16% of software projects were completed on time and on budget; in larger companies only 9% came in on budget. It has been estimated that approximately 30 to 40% of all *Systems* fail in some way. In a 1994 report entitled *Charting the Seas of Information Technology*, The Standish

Group estimates that in 1995 American companies will have spent $81 billion for canceled software projects and another $59 billion for software projects that were completed but exceeded original estimates.

System implementation failures uniformly result from a combination of several factors. The most common are insufficient or the complete lack of: (a) requirements definition; (b) *System* review, evaluation and testing; (c) vendor due diligence and (d) active user involvement during implementation. The trials accompanying a failed *System* implementation are usually augmented by the absence of a comprehensive agreement outlining each party's obligations and remedies. This book will review the steps associated with the *System* procurement process as well as examining contract negotiation strategies. A brief summary of each chapter appears below.

☐ Chapter Two contains a review of the process of preparing a requirements definition that identifies the capabilities needed for your new *System*, along with vendor evaluation criteria. The requirements definition can later be used as the basis for developing a request for proposal to be sent to potential vendors.

☐ Chapter Three evaluates the benefits and disadvantages of pre-packaged, customized and custom computer software so you can determine which is best for you.

☐ Chapter Four reviews non-disclosure, trial use and beta test agreements. Trial use and beta test agreements are quite useful in confirming the proposed *System*'s and vendor's ability to support your requirements. Sample agreements are reprinted at the end of the Chapter.

☐ Chapter Five evaluates the relative benefits of turn-key solutions, outsourcing (which includes service bureau and facilities management services) and *System* leasing as alternatives to the traditional implementation of directly purchased computer hardware and the licensing of computer software. Later in the Chapter, tax and escrow considerations are reviewed in connection with structuring the procurement transaction.

☐ Chapter Six analyzes contract provisions containing the salient rights and obligations in *System* procurement agreements with respect to computer hardware, software licensing, software development and maintenance agreements.

☐ Chapter Seven identifies and reviews dispute resolution mechanisms available as alternatives to litigation.

☐ The appendices at the end of this book contain sample software licensing, development, maintenance and hardware procurement agreements with recommended wording (Appendix A), a sample Request for Information (Appendix B), a sample Request for Proposal (Appendix C) and Glossary.

C H A P T E R

2

REQUIREMENTS and DUE DILIGENCE

1. INTRODUCTION

This Chapter will review the process associated with preparing an effective requirements definition. The requirements definition is probably the most important step in the *System* procurement process. Without a clear definition of what you expect the *System* to do, the vendor cannot help but ultimately fail. The requirements definition can subsequently be used as the basis of a Request for Proposal (RFP). The RFP can in turn be used to compare, evaluate and rate each vendor's proposed *System*.

2. REQUIREMENTS

2.1 Definition

What business functions should the *System* support, how will it be used and by whom, what type of information will be processed, how quickly must it be available and how many physical locations must be supported? These are just a few of the issues which must be addressed in order to prepare a comprehensive requirements definition.

Once implemented, the *System* will materially affect your entire business operation. Therefore, you should have a comprehensive game plan before you begin. In formulating the requirements definition, the first step is to identify and document (a) the flow of information into and throughout your organization; (b) how the information is used and (c) who uses it. Depicting this information in a data flow diagram will allow you to better visualize current operations and devise appropriate adjustments. A sample data flow diagram is included as *Figure A*. The data flow diagram facilitates the next step in the requirements definition phase—operation definition. During the second step, you must define each operation needed to move information through the organization and have it readily accessible when needed.

With the first two steps completed, you can now focus on how the users will interact with the *System*. This section of the requirements definition should define data entry, report generation, search capability and other similar requirements.

To maximize longevity, the requirements definition should include reasonable growth rates in the volume of information and transactions expected in your business over the next three to five years as well as any foreseeable changes in your business operations.

In order to develop a comprehensive requirements definition and achieve the *System's* full acceptance and use, you must solicit participation and input from employees, vendors and customers. These same people, as well as your accounting firm, can also be a valuable source for identifying consultants, available *Systems* and *System* vendors.

2.2 Consultants

Retaining a consultant knowledgeable in your industry and the current state of technology is invaluable to ensuring a successful *System* implementation. The importance of selecting a consultant knowledgeable in your industry cannot be overstated. First, you will avoid having to pay to educate the consultant about your general business practices, and second, the consultant may be able to advise you about available *Systems* and share practical experiences of dealing with various vendors.

As with any professional you employ, make certain to validate the consultant's credentials. Request references and copies of studies or reports prepared by the consultant; how many years experience and how many other clients the consultant has in your industry. A list of consulting firms can be found in *Consultants & Consulting Organizations Directory*, published by Gale Research Inc. (800-877-4253).

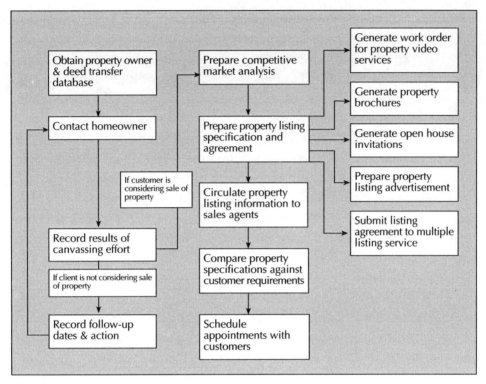

Figure A: Data Flow Diagram

This flow chart shows the process for soliciting and distributing residential property listings.

2.3 Request For Information and Proposal

Once you have completed the requirements definition, work with your consultant to draft a detailed request for proposal. This document will be the "blueprint" of the *System's* required functions. In addition, the RFP should take into account the reasonable growth of your business, and each vendor should indicate how such growth will be supported by the proposed *System*.

The RFP is critical to crystallizing your thought process in preparing the requirements definition. It also helps you objectively define requirements so you can evaluate each vendor's response in terms of your requirements. Then you can compare "apples to apples" when reviewing each vendor's response to your own requirements. You can also use the RFP to inform the vendors of the ground rules for proposal submission, such as deadlines, format and content. Since your *System* selection will be influenced by the vendor's response to the RFP, it is important that you advise the vendors that the RFP and their responses to it will be attached to and form an integral part of the final agreement with the selected vendor.

Given the RFP's important role in the *System* selection process, you should spend a good deal of time in its preparation. Remember, once the *System* is implemented its conformance to your requirements will be judged against the RFP. There is a saying in the computer industry—"garbage in—garbage out". Although this is probably true of most endeavors, it is particularly important to keep in mind during the RFP drafting process. Appendix C contains a sample RFP.

Once the RFP has been completed, it should be sent to a selected group of vendors which you and your consultant have identified as having solutions for or expertise in your industry. Vendors with potentially suitable *Systems* can also be identified by distributing a Request for Information (RFI), a sample of which is reprinted in Appendix B. The RFI contains only a sub-set of the questions contained in the RFP, so any confidential information can be removed. Another effective way to identify vendors is through your industry association. Usually, vendors who specialize in providing solutions or services to companies in a particular industry promote themselves through industry trade groups, publications and conventions.

Avoid indiscriminate distribution of your RFP. Otherwise you will waste valuable management time reviewing proposals that do not have a high probability of being selected. In addition, the RFP will no doubt contain confidential company information that you should maintain control over. Confidentiality issues are addressed in Section 2 of Chapter Four.

3. DUE DILIGENCE

3.1 System Options

A *System* is comprised of several different components:

☐ **COMPUTER HARDWARE:** Computer Hardware includes the central processing unit (CPU), and any number of peripheral devices.

The CPU includes a processor and memory. This is what is commonly referred to as the "computer." The CPU stores data, processes instructions generated by the software and acts as the "traffic cop" directing the flow of data.

There are three general categories of computers, although the lines of demarcation are quickly fading: microcomputers which include personal computers (used at home and for small business applications); mini and super-mini computers also known as "servers"; and mainframe computers. Mini, super-mini and mainframe computers have more powerful processors, greater data storage capacity and are principally used for business applications. In recent years the trend has been away from mainframe computers to mini, super-mini and microcomputers. The latter are less expensive, allow processing power to be easily increased by simply adding another CPU to the network and support distributed processing. However, mainframe computers have certain advantages over networked computers, such as easier troubleshooting and more reliable security.

Peripheral devices include equipment physically connected to the CPU which perform such functions as displaying, transmitting or printing data. Although there are many types of peripheral devices, the most common are printers, modems, direct access storage devices ("DASD") and monitors.

☐ **SOFTWARE:** Software generally falls into three categories, (a) system, operating or network software, (b) application software and (c) relational database management software (RDBMS).

System and operating software consists of a series of instructions that controls and directs the internal operation of the computer's hardware components. It also schedules time and memory among competing applications software being executed by the CPU. Commonly used system software programs include the Disk Operating System (DOS®), Windows®

(3.1, 95® and NT®)[1] used by micro computers and the UNIX®[2] operating system used predominantly by mini and super-mini computers. Network software is another form of system software. It directs the flow of data among the various *System* components comprising a network (discussed below).

Application software consists of a series of instructions which process information for a specific function. Word processing, inventory management, financial and accounting programs are all examples of application software. In any *System* acquisition, the quality and completeness of the application software will most directly determine how closely the *System* satisfies your requirements. Therefore, you should select your applications software first. Then select the operating system software (some applications run under more than one operating system software), and finally select the hardware. All these selections require a careful evaluation process.

RDBMS software is generally used as the foundation for developing application software employed to retrieve, manage and work with large volumes of data. For example, RDBMS software would be used to develop a real estate brokerage property listing program. Brokers would then be able to conduct searches on any number of data categories, sort the results of the search in a preferred format and narrow or expand the original search parameters. ORACLE®[3], SYBASE®[4] and INFORMIX®[5] are all examples of RDBMS software.

☐ **SOURCE OR OBJECT CODE**: Software can be licensed in either "source" or "object" code format. Object code may also be referred to as "run-time". "Development use" is another variation by which software may be licensed and is commonly found in RDBMS license agreements. A development use license allows the computer programmer to create the data tables, data flow and processing routines necessary to customize RDBMS software to the user's particular requirements. Once the customization is complete, the user receives an object or run-time license to use the RDBMS software.

---

1. Registered trademarks of Microsoft Corporation.
2. Registered trademark of UNIX Systems Laboratories.
3. Registered trademark of Oracle Systems Corporation.
4. Registered trademark of SYBASE Inc.
5. Registered trademark of INFORMIX Corporation.

Source code is the computer program both written and understood by the programmer. Source code consists of instructions directing the software program's operation and, being similar to text material, it can be printed out, read and studied. Therefore, once a programmer has access to source code, he or she will be able to discern its structure and write his or her own version of the software program. Object code is the version of the software program in which the source code is translated (referred to as "compiled") into the machine language. Object code is also called "binary code" because it consists of 0s and 1s, which have little meaning for humans but which the computer understands as commands.

Because object code cannot be readily deciphered by humans, software is generally licensed in object code rather than source code format. Vendors prefer object code licenses to preserve confidentiality of the program's logic, structure and sequence, and to protect the vendor's trade secret and proprietary information. Access to the actual source code would facilitate the rapid development of competing programs, thereby depriving the vendor of a reasonable return on its software development investment. Furthermore, licensing source code may jeopardize the vendor's ability to claim the software as a trade secret.

☐ **NETWORK:** Unless the requirements definition involves only a single user having access to the *System* at any one time, different users will have to be connected to each other. Such connections are made with a network. Networks may consist of wire, cable, laser or radio wave connections. Networks manage and direct the flow of data. Network configurations can be based upon: (a) *central processing approach* in which data is entered through a terminal, stored and processed by the CPU and then sent back to the terminal where the data was entered or (b) a *distributed processing approach* in which data is entered through a terminal and is either processed by the CPU to which the terminal is directly connected or is routed to another CPU responsible for processing and storage of the relevant data, and then routed back to the originating data entry device. In the distributed processing environment, software and data reside on several different CPU and peripheral devices. Therefore, care must be taken to ensure compatibility among the various *System* devices. Diagrams depicting central and distributed computer network configurations are shown as *Figures B* and *C*, respectively.

Networks consist of any number of computers, disk drive arrays, pe-

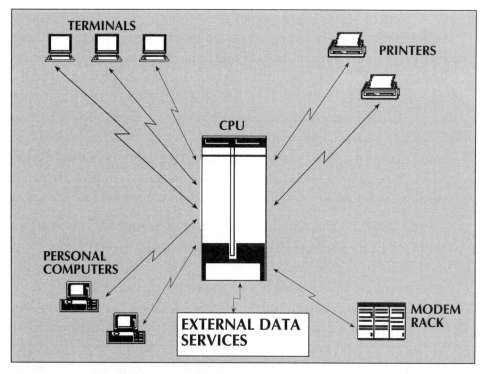

Figure B: Central Processing Diagram

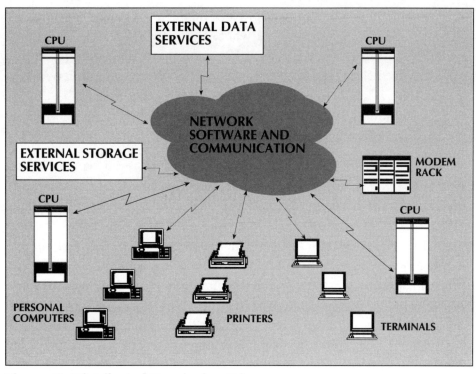

Figure C: Distributed Processing Diagram

ripheral equipment and multiplexors, all of which are managed by network software. Depending on where the network devices are located, networks can be classified as either a Local Area Network (LAN) or a Wide Area Network (WAN). In the LAN environment, all network devices are located in close proximity to each other (usually within the same building); in the WAN environment, network devices can be located anywhere in the world.

Each of the above can be contracted for and acquired separately or as part of an over-all turn-key solution or the provision of a complete *System* (discussed later in Chapter Five). If you choose to acquire each component of the *System* independently, be prepared for a time consuming and complex task. The hardware, software and network must be selected not only on the basis of functionality but, more importantly, compatibility with each other. In addition, once the preferred components are identified, they must be evaluated for performance characteristics. This task is analogous to building a new house and having responsibility for coordinating the work of all the various trades to ensure that everything fits together when completed. Alternatively, you can acquire *System* components through one vendor by contracting for a turn-key solution. Referencing the RFP which identifies all of your requirements, including performance, it becomes the turn-key vendor's responsibility to deliver a fully compatible and complete *System*.

Regardless of which acquisition method you employ, the application software should be your prime area of focus because it is the central component of the *System* that performs the actual business functions. Next you should consider performance, also called through-put capacity. Through-put capacity is the amount of time taken by the *System* to perform specified tasks. Although vendors make claims regarding the performance attributes of their *Systems*, such figures cannot be viewed in a vacuum. Through-put can and almost always is affected by each of the various *System* components including the operating system software, network, and application software. In addition, the through-put capacity of the overall *System* should be evaluated in the context of:

☐ **PEAK PROCESSING:** *Systems* should be sized according to peak usage rather than the average times of usage. Otherwise, response time will be significantly degraded as usage rises. Some consulting companies, such as The Gartner Group, conduct their own tests of equipment and maintain benchmark test results. In addition, new products are frequently benchmarked and compared in the computer and information industry trade press.

☐ **CONTEMPLATED USE:** The manner in which the *System* will be used will affect through-put capacity. For example, you need to consider such factors as the number and expansiveness of database inquires, the number of concurrent users and the number of application programs being executed at the same time and appropriately weigh each factor in the evaluation.

3.2 Evaluation Criteria

After having reviewed the proposals in response to the RFP, selecting the ones which most closely match the requirements definition and are within your budget constraints, you should next evaluate their accuracy. This involves a multi-step process consisting of the following:

☐ **VENDOR PRESENTATION:** Each vendor should be invited to demonstrate the use and operation of their proposed *System*. This opportunity should be used to observe the functionality of the *System* and confirm that it satisfies the requirements definition. Evaluate the user interface to see if it is "user friendly". That is, see how easy or hard it is to learn how to use the *System* and how difficult it is to recover from user error. You should also use this opportunity to ask questions of each vendor to reveal their depth of industry knowledge. The greater the industry knowledge, the better chances are that the vendor will keep the proposed *System* current with changes in your industry.

☐ **REFERENCES:** Ask the vendor to provide you with a general list of all clients and a list of all users of the proposed *System*. This will allow you to decide which clients and users to contact for reference purposes.

☐ **SITE VISITS:** Site visits allow you to see how the proposed *System* operates in actual business environments as opposed to the controlled environment of a vendor demonstration. If possible, try visiting a reference client, without the vendor being present. Try to spend time with the actual day to day users of the proposed *System*. These individuals can best tell you the *System's* strengths and weaknesses. Ascertain the length of time it took to implement the *System* and the completeness and quality of the training program. Did the client/user have to conduct business differently in order to accommodate the proposed *System*? How did the vendor respond when the user experienced an operational problem? How often did they receive *System* updates?

☐ **FINANCIAL CONDITION:** Even if you have found the ideal *System*, it will be of little value and, indeed a liability, if the vendor goes out of business. Therefore, insist that each vendor provide you with audited financial statements for the preceding three years. In addition, obtain an independent credit report which includes a lien and judgment search.

☐ **LITIGATION SEARCH:** Litigation involving a vendor should be included in your evaluation process. If the litigation involves an infringement claim, your uninterrupted use of the proposed *System* could be in jeopardy. Moreover, litigation tends to interfere with attention to company, management and technology development. This can delay implementation, maintenance and *System* updates. Litigation also threatens the viability of the more thinly capitalized vendors. Your attorney will be able to perform a litigation search to reveal any current lawsuits to which a vendor is a party.

☐ **PERSONNEL:** Successful implementation is not only dependent upon the functionality and quality of the chosen *System* but also the individuals assigned by the vendor to provide development, installation, training and maintenance. Ask the vendor to provide you with skills and experience summaries for each person assigned to your project. You should evaluate each person's credentials as though you were considering employing them directly. Once you are satisfied with the project personnel, you should obtain the vendor's commitment not to reassign these individuals to another project until their respective tasks have been completed. This is discussed later in Section 19 of Chapter Six.

☐ **CONCURRENT PROJECTS:** Implementation of a new *System* usually involves the coordination of several disparate requirements. Therefore, a project implementation schedule should be developed between you and the vendor identifying each person's responsibilities. You should also determine what other projects the vendor has started or has otherwise committed to. These other projects may compete for the vendor's resources and management time. With this information, you can then perform your own independent evaluation to verify that the schedule is feasible.

☐ **THIRD PARTIES:** More and more frequently software programs are developed by vendors who use software development tools to enhance functionality, speed up development or simplify maintenance of the *System*. Your evaluation of each vendor's proposal should include the proposed *System's* reliance on software tools provided by entities other than your vendor. If for any reason your vendor's access to such tools is interrupted or cut off, this can seriously hamper enhancement, maintenance or other support for the proposed *System*.

☐ **USER GROUP:** A user group is comprised of companies similar to yours that use the proposed *System*. These companies meet on a regular basis to identify modifications, enhancements and other improvements for the vendor to consider. The vendor may decide to implement some or all of these recommendations and provide the resulting enhancements as part of ongoing maintenance to all of its customers using the *System*. Consequently, the risk of *System* obsolescence is reduced. If a vendor works with a user group, this indicates the *System's* continued commercial viability as well as the vendor's commitment to the proposed *System* and the industry for which it has been developed.

☐ **TRIAL USE:** After having performed all the diligence described in the preceding paragraphs, there is nothing better than actually using the proposed *System* for a trial period. Use of any *System*, even for a trial basis, requires an investment of management, personnel time and resources. Therefore, even if the vendor is willing to allow trial use, be sure to do so only after you have performed the necessary prequalifications before the trial period begins. For example, assuming that the proposed *System* has the functionality you require, it still may not be the right choice if it depends on software tools provided by a third party that is in bankruptcy. (Trial use is discussed further in Section 3 of Chapter Four).

Chances are that no one vendor will be able to score a perfect "10" on these evaluation criteria. Therefore, you will have to prioritize these criteria giving more weight to those factors most important to the operation of your business. Using this approach, you can then limit final negotiations to the two or three vendors who come closest to meeting all the criteria.

4. LEGAL REVIEW

This is the "self-serving" part of the book so it will be kept short.

The acquisition of any *System* should be memorialized in a well negotiated agreement from both a business and legal standpoint. In many instances the selected *System* will form the nerve center of your business. Consequently, the importance of a well-constructed contract should not be underestimated. Just as you would not see a podiatrist for a stomach ailment, you should consult an attorney that specializes in this field of practice for *System* procurement. The remainder of this book includes a wealth of information, including the concepts, nuances and legal implications associated with the *System* procurement process so you can wisely allocate your legal budget.

SOFTWARE

1. INTRODUCTION

Unlike computer hardware where you actually own (i.e., receive title) the physical equipment purchased, title to software remains with the vendor who grants a license for its use. A transfer of title away from the vendor would have serious economic ramifications since it would allow the new owner to sell, distribute, modify or otherwise dispose of the software in any manner he or she wishes. Given the low cost[6] and ease with which software can be duplicated, transfer of title would effectively prevent the vendor from ever recovering the investment it made in developing the software, let alone obtaining a reasonable return. Therefore, by taking advantage of protection afforded under copyright law and incorporating appropriate licensing restrictions, the vendor can control the use and distribution of its software.

Selection of application software involves functional and cost considerations discussed in Chapters Two and Four; the structure and legal framework under which it is licensed, discussed in Chapters Five and Six; and whether it is pre-packaged, customized or custom developed, which is the subject of this Chapter.

---

6. Research and development expenses account for the majority of the vendor's software costs.

2. PRE-PACKAGED SOFTWARE

Software programs that can be used without any modifications fall into the "pre-packaged software" category. Pre-packaged software includes operating and network system software as well as application programs developed for a particular business function or industry group. Common examples of pre-packaged software include word processing, spreadsheet and many accounting and billing programs. Benefits of pre-packaged software include:

☐ **LOWER LICENSE FEES:** Vendors incur substantial costs in developing software. Because many pre-packaged software programs can be licensed on a mass basis, vendors can charge lower license fees and still earn a reasonable return.

☐ **IMMEDIATE AVAILABILITY:** *System* implementation will usually streamline the operation of your business, resulting in lower costs and/or greater revenue. Because software development is a lengthy and time consuming process, pre-packaged software which satisfies the requirements definition can significantly expedite the return on your *System* investment.

☐ **VERIFIABLE CAPABILITY:** Pre-packaged software generally has a large installed population of users. If not, it may be a reason you should explore. Published reviews are often available. Consequently, you have many sources from which the software's capabilities can be verified.

☐ **REGULAR UPDATES:** Due to the large population of users, vendors of pre-packaged software generally produce software enhancements containing improvements and/or corrections. These enhancements are made available on a regular basis, so there is less risk of functional obsolescence.

3. CUSTOMIZED SOFTWARE DEVELOPMENT

Many times the requirements definition cannot be completely satisfied with pre-packaged software, so customization may be necessary. For example, a pre-packaged real estate property listing program may have to be customized to provide data categories appropriate to the types of properties represented by a brokerage company. "Customized software" is the term used for describing pre-packaged software that has been enhanced or otherwise modified to support the user's unique requirements. In many cases most of the benefits of pre-packaged software will still apply to customized software. You should, however, pay special attention to the following:

☐ **INTEGRATION OF UPDATES:** In order to benefit from the use of regular updates to pre-packaged software, you should require the vendor to develop the customized portion in a manner that will not affect the ordinary installation of updates. Keep in mind however that this may not always be possible if the customization effort is extensive.

☐ **SUPPORT:** Vendors do not always provide a warranty for software that has been customized to satisfy the user's unique requirements.[7] Therefore, the vendor will usually claim that it cannot be held accountable if the program, as customized, fails to operate properly. While it is your responsibility to prepare the requirements definition to include all of your needs, the vendor should take responsibility for making sure the customized software satisfies the requirements definition. Although the vendor's warranty and maintenance costs may be higher for non-standard software, it is economically reasonable for the vendor to charge an appropriate fee.

☐ **TAXES:** Later in Section 5 of Chapter Five, we will review the applicability of sales tax to certain *System* procurements. Generally, sales tax is not levied on software services such as programming to customize pre-packaged software. In order to avoid paying sales tax on these services, be sure to execute separate agreements for the pre-packaged software license and the customization work.

☐ **CONFIDENTIALITY:** Many times customization involves your confidential or proprietary business methods. In order to maintain your competitive advantage, the vendor should be precluded from relicensing customized elements in the pre-packaged software. Alternatively, you may consider allowing such use by the vendor in return for a royalty.[8]

☐ **USER INVOLVEMENT:** Effective software design requires that it be developed as several independent modules which are then integrated together to form the complete *System*. Waiting until development is complete to review and test the software will cause you to lose valuable time to correct any deficiencies in software design or programming. Therefore,

---

7. Why? Because most vendors train their support staffs to service the vendor's standard products. In a large company it is not generally feasible to train a large support staff in the workings of several pieces of customized software.

8. Be aware that software royalty arrangements are tricky and fraught with pitfalls.

you should meet with the vendor at regular intervals in order to view the work being performed, address any problems or issues that may have arisen and validate that the schedule is still feasible.

4. CUSTOM SOFTWARE DEVELOPMENT

When your requirements are so unique as to require a significant amount of customization, you may be better served by having the vendor develop new software according to your specifications. By way of analogy, it is usually less difficult to build a new house than engage in major renovation.

The same issues discussed in connection with customized software must be addressed in your software development agreement. Because custom software is developed according to your specifications from your requirements definition, you need to draft and negotiate your agreement carefully. Pay special attention to the following issues:

☐ **REQUIREMENTS:** Custom-developed software is only as good as the requirements definition. Poor requirements definition is still one of the major reasons *Systems* fail. The customer will say *I told the vendor all the functions I need the software to perform, but it is just not working.* At the same time the vendor will genuinely believe that it has delivered software satisfying the customer's requirements. Who's right? Both are probably wrong.

Suppose I asked you to build me a house with a living room, dining room, kitchen, four bedrooms and three bathrooms. Clearly, this is not enough information. What are the room dimensions? What fixtures are needed in the bathrooms and kitchen? How many cars does the garage have to accommodate? Where should the windows be placed? Software development requires similar detail in the requirements definition.

☐ **RESPONSIBILITIES:** Software development and its implementation requires the coordination of many different events as well as resources.[9] For example, in order to develop software, it may be necessary to acquire: (a) additional or more powerful computer hardware than is needed for the actual use of the software, (b) a RDBMS or (c) a communications

---

9. With a turn-key agreement, many of these events are coordinated by the vendor. However, your involvement will still be necessary. In fact it may be preferable for you to take responsibility for some items such as selecting the telecommunications provider.

network and related software.[10] Also the development effort may have to be located at your office. This may be necessary in order for the development team to have direct access to your staff. As such, you will have to provide office space, facilities and support. The responsibility for each resource as well as allocation of the associated cost should be negotiated and properly documented in your agreement.

☐ **VENDOR PERSONNEL:** Successful software development requires technical competence as well as a working knowledge of the customer's business. Consequently, vendor personnel will usually devote a significant amount of time with your staff in order to understand your business and its operations. Your investment in educating the vendor's personnel should be protected by limiting the vendor's ability to re-assign such personnel until the development is complete and the software has been accepted.

☐ **REVENUE SHARING:** Software represents a valuable asset due to the significant cost of development and the potential revenue to be derived from subsequent licensing to other parties. If your custom software is useful to a large market (i.e., has a high potential sales volume) you can benefit by negotiating a lower development fee or a royalty arrangement.

☐ **TITLE AND CONFIDENTIALITY:** Software can provide you with competitive advantages that outweigh any financial gain you may get by letting the vendor license the software to other entities. In such a case, your agreement should clearly grant you sole and exclusive ownership rights. In addition, have the vendor undertake an obligation of confidentiality with respect to the software in general and the underlying business processes incorporated into it. As long as the business knowledge and information gained in developing the software is not generally known outside of your company, the vendor will not be able to use such information to develop similar software. Keep in mind however, that the benefits of ownership and confidentiality come with a price. If the vendor cannot subsidize its development cost by having the right to license other entities, you will pay more for the customization.

---

[*] 10. Although you will probably have to acquire these items in order to use the software for its intended purposes, performance capabilities required for software development may be greater than that needed for actual use. Therefore, the cost is likewise greater. In particular, RDBMS vendors charge license fees which vary significantly depending on whether the RDBMS software is being used for development or operational use. In addition, by the time development is complete, new more powerful and less costly versions of such items may be available.

CHAPTER

4

PRELIMINARY CONSIDERATIONS

1. INTRODUCTION

Several agreements may precede actual execution of the *System* procurement agreement. The most common of these—non-disclosure, trial use and beta test agreements—will be considered in this Chapter. Sample agreements are reprinted at the end of the Chapter.[11]

2. CONFIDENTIALITY

The RFP will include information describing your business operation, your requirements and the objectives expected to be accomplished by the *System*. All of this information is confidential. Likewise, each response to your RFP will include confidential information describing the proposed *System's* functionality, technical design, pricing and contract conditions. Therefore, it is in both parties' interest to respect each other's confidential information as such information is disclosed in the negotiation process and to use this information only for the purposes identified in the RFP.

Prior to delivery of the RFP, the parties should execute a confidentiality agreement. Selected key provisions usually found in these agreements are discussed below. A sample Mutual Confidentiality Agreement is reprinted

---

11. A disk containing an electronic copy of the agreements reprinted in this book can be ordered by completing the order form at the end of this book.

at the end of this Chapter with certain sections in bold print to identify preferred wording.

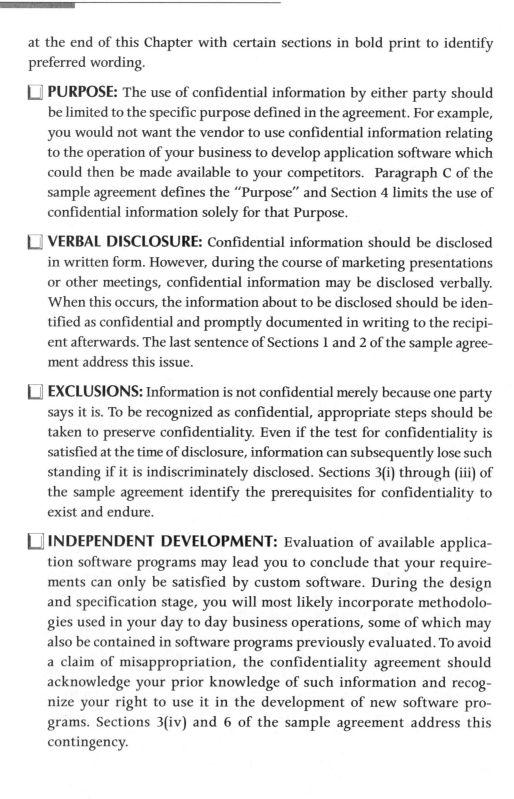

PURPOSE: The use of confidential information by either party should be limited to the specific purpose defined in the agreement. For example, you would not want the vendor to use confidential information relating to the operation of your business to develop application software which could then be made available to your competitors. Paragraph C of the sample agreement defines the "Purpose" and Section 4 limits the use of confidential information solely for that Purpose.

VERBAL DISCLOSURE: Confidential information should be disclosed in written form. However, during the course of marketing presentations or other meetings, confidential information may be disclosed verbally. When this occurs, the information about to be disclosed should be identified as confidential and promptly documented in writing to the recipient afterwards. The last sentence of Sections 1 and 2 of the sample agreement address this issue.

EXCLUSIONS: Information is not confidential merely because one party says it is. To be recognized as confidential, appropriate steps should be taken to preserve confidentiality. Even if the test for confidentiality is satisfied at the time of disclosure, information can subsequently lose such standing if it is indiscriminately disclosed. Sections 3(i) through (iii) of the sample agreement identify the prerequisites for confidentiality to exist and endure.

INDEPENDENT DEVELOPMENT: Evaluation of available application software programs may lead you to conclude that your requirements can only be satisfied by custom software. During the design and specification stage, you will most likely incorporate methodologies used in your day to day business operations, some of which may also be contained in software programs previously evaluated. To avoid a claim of misappropriation, the confidentiality agreement should acknowledge your prior knowledge of such information and recognize your right to use it in the development of new software programs. Sections 3(iv) and 6 of the sample agreement address this contingency.

◻ **PROCEDURES:** Confidentiality agreements usually require the receiving party to use "the highest degree of care" to safeguard the confidentiality of information received from the other party. The obligation imposed by such language, as well as the extent of compliance, is difficult to measure. Since it is in each party's best commercial interest to use effective means to protect their own confidential information, requiring the other party's information to be protected in a similar manner provides both a more effective and measurable standard. The first sentence of Section 4 and the last sentence of Section 5 of the sample agreement define confidentiality procedures.

3. TRIAL USE

Installation and training associated with *System* implementation usually require a significant investment of management time and attention. However, when you have identified software that appears to best satisfy your requirements, using the *System* on a trial basis is an ideal way to ensure you have made the right choice. Many vendors will agree to free use for a trial period. From the vendor's viewpoint, if the software can perform as represented during the marketing discussions, trial use will most likely result in a sale.

If the software is performing in a satisfactory manner, it is unlikely that you would return it. Therefore, you should negotiate the license agreement before the trial period begins. If you wait to negotiate the license agreement until after the trial use period has commenced or expired, you will lose negotiating leverage.

The license agreement should contain many of the same terms and conditions as the trial use agreement. Ideally, it should be attached to the trial use agreement as a schedule which becomes effective in the event you decide to license the software.[12] Selected key provisions usually found in a software trial use agreement are discussed below. A sample agreement is reprinted at the end of this Chapter with certain sections in bold print to identify preferred wording.

---

12. Chapter Six provides a detailed analysis of the clauses usually contained in procurement agreements.

☐ **CONFIDENTIALITY:** You may be required to provide the vendor with confidential or proprietary information relating to your business as a condition of trial use. Therefore, the vendor should be required to maintain the confidentiality of such information and to use it only for purposes contemplated by the trial use. Section 3.1 of the sample agreement addresses this issue.

Vendors invest a significant amount of time and money in developing software. Consequently any entity to whom the software or related information is disclosed will be required to maintain its confidentiality. Section 3.2 of the sample agreement contains wording for the vendor's protection. However, as discussed earlier in Section 2 of this Chapter, your efforts to preserve confidentiality of the vendor's information should be no more rigorous than those which you normally take to protect your own confidential material.

☐ **PAYMENT:** Vendors provide only a license to use the software during the trial period at no fee. Additional services performed by the vendor will usually carry a charge. You should nevertheless attempt to have installation and training performed at no charge or, at least, at the vendor's cost.

☐ **RETURN:** Trial use agreements generally provide that if the software is not returned promptly after the trial use period expires, you have agreed to license the software by default. The enforceability of such a clause varies from state to state. However, to preserve your rights, the vendor should be required to give written notice requesting return of the software. The third sentence of Section 4.1 of the sample agreement outlines the return obligation in this manner.

☐**WARRANTY AND LIABILITY:** Since vendors do not receive payment for a trial license, they are unwilling to assume warranty obligations or other liability. Therefore, Section 6.1 of the sample agreement absolves the vendor from any warranty obligation if the software is problem ridden.[13] Section 7.1 of the sample agreement continues this theme by likewise absolving the vendor from liability. Such exclusions are customary in trial use agreements. However, the limitation of liability should be

---

☐* 13. Although warranty obligations are generally excluded during trial use, in practice, vendors endeavor to correct all problems. Failure to do so may cause you to reject the software.

reciprocal and three exceptions should be carved out when: (a) there is a breach of the confidentiality obligation; (b) the vendor has infringed the proprietary rights of a third party in developing the software or (c) the vendor has acted in a manner which has caused personal or bodily injury.

☐ **HARDWARE AND OPERATING ENVIRONMENT:** Software programs provided for trial use will generally require a specific hardware, operating system, RDBMS and/or network operating environment. Unless the vendor is willing to furnish the necessary environment at no charge, any benefit from the trial use may turn out to be illusory if you ultimately reject the software.

Although the vendor may be assuming additional expense, chances are that it already has the necessary environment and can readily provide it to you at a nominal charge. Section 8.1 of the sample agreement contains sample wording for this purpose. Alternatively, the vendor may be able to arrange for a trial use of the hardware and operating environment because once you decide to license the software you will probably have to acquire the other components as well.

4. BETA TESTING

Computer hardware and software is designed, manufactured or developed by the vendor in a laboratory environment. Therefore it needs to be tested in a real production environment prior to commercial release. It is quite common for such testing to be performed by an unrelated third party, usually a prospective customer. In this way, the vendor benefits by receiving objective feedback as to the *System's* strengths, weaknesses, performance and overall effectiveness. In addition, the vendor may benefit from ideas for functional enhancements. A customer that agrees to perform beta testing benefits by: (a) using the *System* before its competitors; (b) receiving a higher level of support and training from the vendor; (c) possibly convincing the vendor to incorporate specific capabilities desired by the customer in the *System's* initial release and/or (d) receiving price concessions when the *System* is released for general availability.

If you have the opportunity and decide to perform beta testing, you will need to execute a beta test agreement in order to clearly define your obligations and entitlements. In fact, the vendor will insist on a beta test agreement in order to preserve its proprietary rights and maintain confidentiality of the *System* prior to its release. Selected key provisions are discussed below. A sample software beta test agreement is reprinted at the end of this Chapter with certain sections in bold print to identify preferred wording.

☐ **TERM:** Beta test agreements are limited in duration to the time required to evaluate the *System*. In order to recover your investment of time and resources in performing the beta test, the agreement should grant you an option to license the *System* upon its commercial release. In addition, the license agreement and fees payable to the vendor should be negotiated and attached to the beta test agreement as a schedule.

☐ **FEE:** In the event you decide to acquire the *System*, fees payable to the vendor should be significantly discounted from those which would be charged after commercial release. This will serve to compensate you for performing the beta test.

☐ **VENDOR RESPONSIBILITIES:** As a beta tester, one of the benefits you should receive is a higher level of support from the vendor. This generally results in your staff being trained more quickly on the *System*. Trained users are in the vendor's interest since using the *System* in actual production will disclose any deficiencies. The beta test agreement should therefore require the vendor to assign an individual to be responsible for supporting your use as well as committing a minimum number of hours per week to resolve problems or issues that arise. Assuming the vendor is motivated to complete the *System* for commercial availability, it can hardly complain when you request support. Section 4(a) of the sample agreement recites the vendor's support and training obligation.

☐ **CUSTOMER RESPONSIBILITIES:** Section 4(b) of the sample agreement describes the typical user responsibilities. However, in performing these responsibilities you should be reimbursed for any costs or other expenses incurred in diagnosing or correcting a problem. Section 4(b) addresses the vendor's reimbursement obligation.

☐ **CONFIDENTIALITY:** Since vendors invest a significant amount of time and money in *System* development, any person to whom the *System* is disclosed will be required to maintain its confidentiality. This is particularly true prior to commercial release. Section 5(a) of the sample agreement recites wording appropriate for the vendor's protection. Once again, be sure to limit your obligation to those efforts which you normally take to protect your own confidential material.

As part of the beta test, you will be required to provide the vendor with written reports describing the *System's* performance. In so doing, it may be necessary to disclose confidential or proprietary information relating to your business. Therefore, the vendor should be required to maintain the confidentiality of such information and to use it only for purposes relating to the beta test. Section 5(b) of the sample agreement recites wording for this purpose.

☐ **WARRANTY AND LIABILITY:** The purpose of beta testing is to discover defects or deficiencies. This is why Sections 7 and 8 of the sample agreement absolve the vendor from any warranty obligation or liability if the *System* is problem ridden. These exclusions are customary in beta test agreements. However, the limitation of liability should be reciprocal and three exceptions should carved out when: (a) there is a breach of the confidentiality obligation; (b) the vendor has infringed the proprietary rights of a third party in developing the *System* or (c) the vendor has acted in a manner which has caused you to suffer personal or bodily injury.

MUTUAL CONFIDENTIALITY AGREEMENT

AGREEMENT dated this 28th day of August, 1996 by and between ABC Systems, Inc. with offices at 50 Main Street, White Plains, NY 11477 (hereinafter referred to as ("ABC") and Professional Trading Company, Ltd. with offices at 100 Park Avenue, New York, NY 10017 (hereinafter referred to as ("PTC").

A.   WHEREAS, PTC operates a securities brokerage company and as such possesses certain confidential information relating thereto ("PTC Information") as hereinafter defined;

B.   WHEREAS, ABC is the owner of, and markets a computer software program known as "STOCK" designed to provide automated trading of securities in the over the counter market (the "ABC Information") as hereinafter defined;

C.   WHEREAS, PTC has prepared a Request For Proposal dated August 1, 1996 ("RFP") and the **Parties desire ABC to tender a proposal in response to PTC's RFP proposing therein licensing STOCK to PTC ("Purpose")** and;

D.   WHEREAS, PTC and ABC desire that the other maintain the confidentiality of the PTC Information and the ABC Information.

NOW, THEREFORE, the parties agree as follows:

1.   As used herein, "PTC Information" shall include all information and data furnished by PTC to ABC, whether in oral, written, graphic or machine-readable form, including without limitation, specifications, user, operations or systems manuals, diagrams, graphs, models, sketches, technical data, research, business or financial information, plans, strategies, forecasts, forecast assumptions, business practices, marketing information and material, customer names, proprietary ideas, concepts, know-how, methodologies and all other information related to PTC's business. PTC Information shall also include confidential information received by PTC from a third party. **In order for any information provided verbally by PTC to ABC to come within the definition of PTC Information, it shall be identified as confidential at the time of disclosure and within five (5) business days after verbal disclosure thereof by PTC, such information shall be documented in writing specifying that PTC considers such information confidential.**

2.   As used herein, "ABC Information" shall include all information and data furnished by ABC to PTC, whether in oral, written, graphic or machine-readable form, in connection with STOCK version 3, including, without limitation, object code, source code, source listings, computer programs, specifications, user, operations or systems manuals, diagrams, graphs, technical data, research, business or financial information, plans, strategies, forecasts, forecast assumptions, business practices, procedures, marketing information, trade secrets and other proprietary ideas, concepts, know-how, methodologies and information related to STOCK or ABC. **In order for any information provided verbally by ABC to PTC to come within the definition of ABC Information, it shall be identified as confidential at the time of disclosure and within five (5) business days after verbal disclosure thereof by ABC, such information shall be documented in writing specifying that ABC considers such information confidential.**

3.   As used herein, "Confidential Information" shall include the PTC Information and the ABC Information, individually and collectively. Notwithstanding anything to the contrary contained in this Agreement, **Confidential Information shall not include information: (a) in the public domain (other than as a result of a breach of this Agreement); (b) generally known and disclosed to PTC or ABC by persons or entities engaged in a comparable business (other than as a result of a breach of this Agreement or any other agreement to which such persons or entities are parties); (c) in PTC or ABC's possession prior to its receipt from the other pursuant to this Agreement or (d) independently developed by PTC or ABC.**

4.   PTC and ABC agree to **use procedures no less rigorous than those used to protect and preserve the confidentiality of their own proprietary information** to maintain the confidentiality of the Confidential Information of the other and shall not, directly or indirectly, (a) transfer or disclose any Confidential Information to a third party (other than to their respective employees); (b) **use any Confidential Information other than as contemplated under this Agreement solely in connection with the Purpose** or (c) take any other action with respect to the Confidential Information inconsistent with the confidential and proprietary nature of such information. PTC and ABC further agree to return all Confidential Information (and all copies thereof) to the other at the conclusion of its review and evaluation thereof, or immediately upon a party's written request therefor.

5. PTC and ABC shall be permitted to disclose the Confidential Information to their respective employees having a need for access thereto in connection with their employment and who have executed confidentiality agreements containing provisions similar to those contained in this Agreement and specifying that other parties are third party beneficiaries thereof entitled to enforce the provisions thereof as though a party thereto. **PTC and ABC shall each take steps, no less rigorous than those it takes to protect its own proprietary information, to prevent their respective employees from acting in a manner inconsistent with the terms of this Agreement.**

6. **ABC acknowledges and agrees that PTC is engaged in the business of securities trading, and as such currently possesses knowledge and information relating to the functionality and capabilities required for computer systems in support thereof. Therefore, nothing contained in this Agreement shall prevent PTC from, on its own or through third parties, designing, developing or acquiring computer systems similar to STOCK so long as PTC does not make use of any ABC Information in connection therewith.**

7. ABC represents and warrants to PTC that it has, and will continue to have, the right to disclose to PTC the ABC Information without the consent of any third party.

8. PTC and ABC acknowledge and agree that the other may suffer irreparable injury not compensable by money damages and therefore may not have an adequate remedy at law in the event of an unauthorized use or disclosure of the Confidential Information in breach of the provisions of this Agreement. Accordingly, PTC or ABC may be entitled to injunctive relief to prevent or curtail any such breach, threatened or actual, by the other. The foregoing shall be in addition and without prejudice to such other rights as PTC or ABC may have at law or in equity.

9. Nothing in this Agreement shall constitute a waiver of any trade secret, patent, trademark, copyright or other right either party may have in the PTC Information or the ABC Information. A copyright notice on any material embodying the PTC Information or the ABC Information shall not in and of itself be deemed to constitute or evidence a publication or the public disclosure of confidential information.

10. (a) This Agreement shall be governed by and construed in accordance with the laws of the State of New York .

(b) The provisions of this Agreement are severable and the unenforceability of any provision of this Agreement shall not affect the enforceability of any other provision hereof. In addition, in the event that any provision of this Agreement (or any portion thereof) is determined by a court to be unenforceable as drafted by virtue of the scope, duration, extent or character of any obligation contained therein, the parties acknowledge that it is their intention that such provision (or portion thereof) shall be construed in a manner designed to effectuate the purposes of such provision to the maximum extent enforceable under applicable law.

11. This Agreement in no way constitutes an agreement by the parties to exchange or make available any particular Confidential Information or other information, and the extent of such exchange or availability shall be as agreed upon by the parties from time to time.

IN WITNESS WHEREOF, the parties have caused this Agreement to be executed and do each hereby warrant and represent that their respective signatory whose signature appears below has been and is on the date of this Agreement duly authorized by all necessary and appropriate corporate action to execute this Agreement.

ABC Systems, Inc.

By: _____

Name: _____

Title: _____

Professional Trading Company, Inc.

By: _____

Name: _____

Title: _____

TRIAL USE AGREEMENT

1. DEFINITIONS

As used in this document the following terms shall have the meanings set forth below:

(1.1) "Agreement" shall mean this agreement, any attached exhibits or schedules and any amendments to this Agreement which are in writing and signed by both parties.

(1.2) "Customer" shall mean Professional Trading Company, Ltd. with its principal place of business at 100 Park Avenue, New York NY 10017.

(1.3) "Documentation" shall mean, to the extent then available, ABC's standard technical and user operations manuals for the SOFTWARE which it makes available to other customers of the SOFTWARE at no charge.

(1.4) "SOFTWARE" shall mean the computer software program in object code format and Documentation as identified in **Schedule "A"** to this Agreement.

(1.5) "ABC" shall mean ABC Systems, Inc., 50 Main Street, White Plains, NY 11477.

(1.6) "Use" shall mean to load, execute and display the SOFTWARE.

(1.7) "Trial Use Term" shall mean the period commencing on the date hereof and continuing for a period of ninety (90) days after installation of the SOFTWARE, unless sooner terminated in accordance with Section 9.

2. LICENSE

(2.1) ABC hereby grants the Customer a personal, nontransferable and non-exclusive license for a period of the Trial Use Term to Use one (1) copy of the SOFTWARE.

(2.2) Customer shall Use the SOFTWARE only for processing its own data.

(2.3) All SOFTWARE and modifications made to the SOFTWARE shall remain the property of ABC.

(2.4) Customer shall not reverse engineer, decompile or disassemble the SOFTWARE.

3. DISCLOSURE

(3.1) As used herein, "CUSTOMER Information" shall include all information and data furnished by CUSTOMER to ABC, whether in oral, written, graphic or machine-readable form, including without limitation, specifications, user, operations or systems manuals, diagrams, graphs, models, sketches, technical data, research, business or financial information, plans, strategies, forecasts, forecast assumptions, business practices, marketing information and material, customer names, proprietary ideas, concepts, know-how, methodologies and all other information related to CUSTOMER's business. CUSTOMER Information shall also include confidential information received by CUSTOMER from a third party. In order for any information provided verbally by CUSTOMER to ABC to come within the definition of CUSTOMER Information, it shall be identified as confidential at the time of disclosure and within five (5) business days after verbal disclosure thereof by CUSTOMER, such information shall be documented in writing specifying that CUSTOMER considers such information confidential.

(3.2) As used herein, "ABC Information" shall include all information and data furnished by ABC to CUSTOMER, whether in oral, written, graphic or machine-readable form, in connection with the SOFTWARE, including, without limitation, object code, source code, source listings, computer programs, specifications, user, operations or systems manuals, diagrams, graphs, technical data, research, business or financial information, plans, strategies, forecasts, forecast assumptions, business practices, procedures, marketing information, trade secrets and other proprietary ideas, concepts, know-how, methodologies and information related to the SOFTWARE or ABC. **In order for any information provided verbally by ABC to CUSTOMER to come within the definition of ABC Information, it shall be identified as confidential at the time of disclosure and within five (5) business days after verbal disclosure thereof by ABC, such information shall be documented in writing specifying that ABC considers such information confidential.**

(3.3) As used herein, "Confidential Information" shall include the CUSTOMER Information and the ABC Information, individually and collectively. Notwithstanding anything to the contrary contained in this Agreement, **Confidential Information**

shall not include information (a) in the public domain (other than as a result of a breach of this Agreement); (b) generally known and disclosed to CUSTOMER or ABC by persons or entities engaged in a comparable business (other than as a result of a breach of this Agreement or any other agreement to which such persons or entities are parties); (c) in CUSTOMER or ABC's possession prior to its receipt from the other pursuant to this Agreement or (d) independently developed by CUSTOMER or ABC.

(3.4) CUSTOMER and ABC agree to **use procedures no less rigorous than those used to protect and preserve the confidentiality of their own proprietary information to** maintain the confidentiality of the Confidential Information of the other and shall not, directly or indirectly, (a) transfer or disclose any Confidential Information to a third party (other than to their respective employees); (b) **use any Confidential Information other than as contemplated under this Agreement** or (c) take any other action with respect to the Confidential Information inconsistent with the confidential and proprietary nature of such information. CUSTOMER and ABC further agree to return all Confidential Information (and all copies thereof) to the other upon termination of this Agreement.

(3.5) CUSTOMER and ABC shall be permitted to disclose the Confidential Information to their respective **employees having a need for access thereto in connection with their employment and who have executed confidentiality agreements containing provisions similar to those contained in this Agreement** and specifying that other parties are third party beneficiaries thereof entitled to enforce the provisions thereof as though a party thereto. **CUSTOMER and ABC shall each take steps, no less rigorous than those it takes to protect and preserve its own proprietary information, to prevent their respective employees from acting in a manner inconsistent with the terms of this Agreement.**

(3.6) **ABC acknowledges and agrees that CUSTOMER is engaged in the business of securities trading, and as such currently possesses knowledge and information relating to the functionality and capabilities required for computer systems in support thereof. Therefore, nothing contained in this Agreement shall prevent CUSTOMER from, on its own or through third parties, designing, developing or acquiring computer systems similar to the SOFTWARE so long as CUSTOMER does not make use of any ABC Information in connection therewith.**

(3.7)   The SOFTWARE, its logos, product names and other support materials, if any, are either patented, copyrighted, trademarked, or otherwise proprietary to ABC . Customer agrees never to remove any such notices and product identification. A copyright notice on the SOFTWARE shall not be deemed in and of itself to constitute or evidence a publication or public disclosure.

4.   PAYMENTS

(4.1)   The Customer shall pay for any work performed by ABC to modify the SOFTWARE. ABC shall perform such work in accordance with ABC's Consulting Services Agreement. In the event that Customer fails to return the SOFTWARE **within thirty (30) days after ABC has requested return thereof in writing (such request not to be made prior to termination of this Agreement)**, Customer will be deemed to have accepted a permanent license to the SOFTWARE in accordance with the terms and conditions of the Software License Agreement attached hereto as Schedule "B".

(4.2)   Customer shall have an option to acquire a permanent license to the SOFTWARE upon written notice to ABC given within forty five (45) days subsequent to termination of the Trial Use Term. The permanent license shall be subject to the terms and conditions of the Software License Agreement attached hereto as Schedule "B". Customer shall pay ABC a license fee in the amount of seventy five thousand dollars ($75,000), payable as described in the Software License Agreement.

5.   PATENT AND COPYRIGHT INDEMNIFICATION

(5.1)   ABC agrees to defend and/or handle at its own expense, any claim or action against Customer for actual or alleged infringement of any intellectual or industrial property right, including without limitation, trademarks, service marks, patents, copyrights, misappropriation of trade secrets or any similar property rights, based upon the SOFTWARE or Customer's use thereof. ABC further agrees to indemnify and hold Customer harmless from and against any and all liabilities, costs, losses, damages and expenses (including reasonable attorney's fees) associated with such claim or action. Customer shall reasonably cooperate with ABC in the defense of such claim or action to the extent that such cooperation is given at such times and in a manner that does not negatively affect Customer's business in Customer's sole discretion and further, ABC reimburses Customer's expenses and pays Customer Customer's hourly billing rate for all such assistance.

(5.2) ABC shall have the sole right to conduct the defense of any such claim or action and all negotiations for its settlement or compromise. Notwithstanding the foregoing, in the event that ABC shall fail to appoint an attorney within ten (10) calendar days after the claim having first been made or action commenced or the attorney appointed by ABC is, in Customer's reasonable judgment not suitably qualified to represent Customer, Customer shall have the right to select and appoint an alternative attorney and the reasonable cost and expense thereof shall be paid by ABC.

6. NO WARRANTY

(6.1) ABC MAKES NO WARRANTY, EXPRESS OR IMPLIED, INCLUDING WITHOUT LIMITATION, THE IMPLIED WARRANTIES OF MERCHANTABILITY OR FITNESS FOR A PARTICULAR PURPOSE WITH RESPECT TO THE SOFTWARE. CUSTOMER AGREES TO TAKE AND/OR USE THE SOFTWARE AS IS.

7. NO LIABILITY

(7.1) EXCEPT FOR A BREACH OF ARTICLES 2, 3, 4 OR 5, NEITHER PARTY SHALL HAVE LIABILITY TO THE OTHER. THE FOREGOING LIMITATION OF LIABILITY SHALL NOT APPLY TO CLAIMS FOR PERSONAL INJURY OR DAMAGE TO REAL OR PERSONAL PROPERTY CAUSED BY WILLFUL OR NEGLIGENT ACTS OF ABC, ITS EMPLOYEES OR CONTRACTORS.

8. INSTALLATION & TRAINING

(8.1) For the duration of the Trial Use Term, ABC shall furnish [and install] at no charge to the Customer, the SOFTWARE, all computer hardware, operating system software, networks and/or relational database management systems necessary for the proper operation of the SOFTWARE.

(8.2) ABC shall provide ten (10) hours of training to Customer in the use, operation and maintenance of the SOFTWARE [at no charge to the Customer]. Training will be conducted at Customer's offices in New York. ABC shall assume and be responsible for the payment of all transportation, room and board expenses of its employees in furnishing such training.

9. TERMINATION

(9.1) This Agreement shall terminate upon the earlier of (i) expiration of the Trial Use Term or (ii) immediately if the Customer or ABC: (a) shall fail to comply with any term or condition of this Agreement and such failure shall continue for a period in excess of thirty (30) days after receipt of notice advising of such failure or (b) shall become insolvent or a party bankrupt to a bankruptcy or receivership proceeding or any similar action. In the event that termination results from a breach by or bankruptcy **of the Customer**, Customer shall upon such termination return to ABC the SOFTWARE together with all copies and modifications in any form.

10. GENERAL

(10.1) No modification of this Agreement shall be valid or binding on either party unless acknowledged in writing and signed by the duly authorized officer of each party. All notices or other communications given under this Agreement shall be in writing, sent to the address hereinbefore set forth as principal place of business or such other addresses as ABC or the Customer may designate in writing.

(10.2) Both parties understand and agree that violation of Section 3 of this Agreement may cause damage to the other party in an amount which is impossible or extremely difficult to ascertain. Accordingly, without limitation to any other remedy available at law, the injured party shall be entitled to seek injunctive relief restraining the other party from continuing to violate the terms and provisions of said Section.

(10.3) Neither party shall be liable to the other for any delay or failure to perform its obligations under this Agreement if such delay or failure arises from any cause beyond the reasonable control of such party, including but not limited to labor disputes, strikes, other labor or industrial disturbances, acts of God, floods, lightning, shortages of materials, utility or communication failures, earthquakes, casualty, war, riots, actions, restrictions, regulations or orders of any government, agency or subdivision thereof.

(10.4) The parties acknowledge that each has read all the terms of this Agreement, is authorized to enter into it, agrees to be bound by its terms and conditions and that it is the complete and exclusive statement of the agreement between the parties which supersedes all prior communications and agreements between the parties relating to the subject matter of this Agreement.

(10.5) If any provision of this Agreement shall be deemed invalid and/or inoperative, under any applicable statute or rule of law, it is to that extent to be deemed modified so as to provide the most similar enforceable economic effect and shall have no effect as to any other provision contained in this Agreement.

(10.6) Any forbearance or delay on the part of either party in enforcing any provision of this Agreement or any of its rights hereunder shall not be construed as a waiver of such provision or of a right to enforce same.

(10.7) The provisions of Articles 3-7, 9 and 10 shall survive termination of this Agreement or any portion thereof.

(10.8) Any claim or dispute relating to this Agreement shall be governed by the laws of the State of New York.

IN WITNESS WHEREOF, the parties have caused this Agreement to be executed and do each hereby warrant and represent that their respective signatory whose signature appears below has been and is on the date of this Agreement duly authorized by all necessary and appropriate corporate action to execute this Agreement.

Professional Trading Company, Ltd.

By: _____

Name: _____

Title: _____

Date: _____

ABC SYSTEMS, INC.

By: _____

Name: _____

Title: _____

Date: _____

BETA TEST AGREEMENT
FOR SOFTWARE TESTING

BETA Test Agreement between ABC Systems, Inc., 50 Main Street, White Plains, NY 11477 ("ABC") and World Wide Realty Company, Ltd. with its principal place of business at 270 Park Avenue, New York NY 10017 ("Customer").

WHEREAS, ABC has designed and developed a proprietary computer software program including documentation therefor known as **REBLE** as more particularly identified in Schedule "A" (hereinafter referred to as the "SOFTWARE"); and

WHEREAS, both parties desire that Customer use, evaluate and conduct tests and report to ABC on and with respect to the SOFTWARE.

NOW, THEREFORE, the parties hereto agree as follows:

1. License

ABC hereby grants to Customer, subject to the terms and conditions stated herein, a temporary, personal, non-transferable and nonexclusive license to use the SOFTWARE **without charge** for the term specified in Paragraph 2.

2. Term

The license granted herein shall be effective from the date of Customer's receipt of the SOFTWARE and shall remain in force until: (a) ABC determines that the objectives of the beta test have been satisfied; (b) Customer discontinues the use of such SOFTWARE; (c) until the SOFTWARE is authorized for general release by ABC as a standard ABC product; (d) until ABC terminates this Agreement as provided herein or (e) one hundred twenty (120) days after ABC installs the SOFTWARE, whichever occurs earlier.

3. SOFTWARE Use

The license granted herein includes the right to copy the SOFTWARE for the purpose of evaluating the SOFTWARE as defined in Section 4(b) for archival or emergency restart purposes. Except as provided herein, no right to reproduce or copy the SOFTWARE in whole or in part is granted. ABC's copyright and/or trade secret rights will continue to exist in all copies the SOFTWARE. Customer shall not remove any proprietary or statutory copyright notices included with the SOFTWARE and shall reproduce all such notices on all copies made by the Customer in any form.

4. Responsibilities

(a) During the Term, ABC shall perform or provide the following **without charge to the Customer**:

1. Deliver and install a beta version of the SOFTWARE for the Customer.

2. **Assign Robin Moore as ABC's systems engineer to support Customer's activities during beta testing.**

3. Deliver a product manual, user's guide and such other documentation necessary for the use of the SOFTWARE.

4. Provide a minimum of ten (10) person hours of support assistance (as requested by the Customer) on a weekly basis for the resolution of issues that arise during beta testing. ABC will use best efforts to: (i) fix reported errors and (ii) provide Customer with support and consultation concerning the SOFTWARE.

5. ABC shall provide ten (10) hours of training to Customer in the use and operation of the SOFTWARE. Training will be conducted at Customer's offices. ABC shall assume and be responsible for the payment of all transportation, room and board expenses of its employees in furnishing such training.

(b) During the Term, Customer shall perform or provide the following:

1. Appoint Alex Peterson as the project leader who will provide overall coordination for testing and reporting during the beta test.

2. Inform ABC of all errors, difficulties or other problems with the SOFTWARE and reasonably cooperate with ABC, **at ABC' s expense, in the identification, investigation and resolution of same.**

3. Provide a written report describing Customer's evaluation of the SOFTWARE upon termination of beta testing.

5. Non-Disclosure

(a) The SOFTWARE and all related information received by the Customer from ABC, whether written or oral, have been developed by ABC at great expenditures of time, resources and money. Therefore, Customer shall use the **same degree of care as it uses for its own confidential information** to preserve and safeguard the confidentiality of the SOFTWARE and all related information where such information is provided to Customer in writing or **if disclosed orally, confirmation of the oral disclosure is furnished to Customer within thirty (30) days thereafter**. The SOFTWARE shall not be duplicated and/or disclosed to others, in whole or in part, without ABC's prior written consent. CUSTOMER shall not disclose or otherwise make known to any party any of the terms of this Agreement, or that it is undertaking or has undertaken the beta test or the results and evaluations thereof, unless otherwise agreed to in writing by ABC. All CUSTOMER personnel who receive or use the SOFTWARE or data shall, before their usage, be informed of Customer's obligations hereunder.

(b) ABC shall not disclose to any third party or use for any purpose other than Customer's beta use of the SOFTWARE Customer's confidential information concerning the Customer's business, trade secrets, methods or processes without the prior written consent of the Customer. ABC acknowledges that Customer confidential information may be contained in reports describing the beta test reports and agrees that the foregoing strictures of confidentiality shall apply to all such information contained therein. All ABC personnel shall be informed of ABC's obligations hereunder.

(c) Neither party shall incur any obligation hereunder with respect to those portions of the SOFTWARE or other information claimed confidential which: (i) at the time of disclosure is part of the public domain other than through a breach of this Agreement; (ii) at the time of disclosure, is already known to the nondisclosing party; (iii) subsequent to the time of disclosure, becomes part of the public domain through no fault of the nondisclosing party or (iv) is independently developed by the nondisclosing party without a breach of this Agreement.

(d) ABC acknowledges and agrees that CUSTOMER is engaged in the business of real estate brokerage, and as such currently possesses knowledge and information relating to the functionality and capabilities required for computer systems in support thereof. Therefore, nothing contained in this Agreement shall prevent CUSTOMER from, on its own or through third parties, designing, developing or acquiring computer systems similar to the SOFTWARE so long as CUSTOMER does not make use of any ABC confidential information in connection therewith.

6. Patent and Copyright Indemnification

(a) ABC agrees to defend and/or handle at its own expense, any claim or action against Customer for actual or alleged infringement of any intellectual or industrial property right, including without limitation, trademarks, service marks, patents, copyrights, misappropriation of trade secrets or any similar property rights, based upon the SOFTWARE or Customer's use thereof. ABC further agrees to indemnify and hold Customer harmless from and against any and all liabilities, costs, losses, damages and expenses (including reasonable attorney's fees) associated with such claim or action. Customer shall reasonably cooperate with ABC in the defense of such claim or action to the extent that such cooperation is given at such times and in a manner that does not negatively affect Customer's business in Customer's sole discretion and further, ABC reimburses Customer's expenses and pays Customer Customer's hourly billing rate for all such assistance.

(b) ABC shall have the sole right to conduct the defense of any such claim or action and all negotiations for its settlement or compromise. Notwithstanding the foregoing, in the event that ABC shall fail to appoint an attorney within ten (10) calendar days after the claim having first been made or action commenced or the attorney appointed by ABC is, in Customer's reasonable judgment not suitably qualified to represent Customer, Customer shall have the right to select and appoint an alternative attorney and the reasonable cost and expense thereof shall be paid by ABC.

7. No Warranty

IT IS UNDERSTOOD AND AGREED BY THE CUSTOMER THAT THE SOFTWARE HAS NOT BEEN TESTED AND MAY INCLUDE SOME DEFECTS, AND THAT ABC DISCLAIMS ALL WARRANTIES OF MERCHANTABILITY AND FITNESS FOR A PARTICULAR PURPOSE AND THAT THE SOFTWARE IS LICENSED **AS IS**. THE CUSTOMER SHALL HAVE THE SOLE RESPONSIBILITY FOR ADEQUATE PROTECTION OF ITS DATA USED IN CONNECTION WITH THE SOFTWARE.

8. Limited Liability

EXCEPT FOR A BREACH OF SECTIONS 5 OR 6 OF THIS AGREEMENT, NEITHER PARTY SHALL HAVE ANY LIABILITY FOR ANY DAMAGES INCLUDING, BUT NOT LIMITED TO, DIRECT, SPECIAL, INDIRECT, CONSEQUENTIAL DAMAGES. THE FOREGOING LIMITATION OF LIABILITY SHALL NOT APPLY TO CLAIMS FOR PERSONAL INJURY OR DAMAGE TO REAL OR PERSONAL PROPERTY CAUSED BY WILLFUL OR NEGLIGENT ACTS OF ABC, ITS EMPLOYEES OR CONTRACTORS.

9. Issuance of Program.

(a) It is understood that ABC will not be obligated to make the SOFTWARE available as a standard ABC product.

10. Post Beta Test License Fee

If, upon termination of this Agreement by reason that the SOFTWARE is authorized for general release as a standard ABC product and Customer elects to continue the use of the SOFTWARE, Customer shall have an option to acquire a permanent license to the SOFTWARE upon written notice to ABC given within one (1) year subsequent to termination of the this Agreement. The permanent license shall be subject to the terms and conditions of the Software License Agreement attached hereto as Schedule "C". Customer shall pay ABC a license fee in the amount of ten thousand dollars ($10,000), payable as described in the Software License Agreement.

11. Termination

The license granted hereby shall terminate at the end the Term. If Customer fails to comply with any of its obligations hereunder, ABC shall have the right, at any time, to terminate this Agreement and take immediate possession of the SOFTWARE and all copies wherever located. Within five (5) days after termination of this Agreement, Customer (a) will return to ABC the SOFTWARE in the form provided by ABC and all copies in whole or in part made by Customer, or (b) upon request by ABC destroy the SOFTWARE and all copies, and certify in writing that they have been destroyed. **Customer shall have the right to terminate this Agreement at any time upon written notice to ABC.** Notwithstanding the termination of this Agreement, the provisions of Sections 5 and 6 and the obligations thereunder shall survive.

12. Proprietary Rights

The SOFTWARE and all copies thereof are the sole and exclusive property of ABC, and title thereto remains in ABC.

13. Applicable Law

This Agreement shall be governed by the laws of the State of New York.

14. General

This Agreement supersedes all prior agreements concerning the subject matter herein and may not be changed or terminated except by a written communication signed by the party against who the same is sought to be enforced. If any of the provisions of this Agreement are invalid under any applicable statue or rule of law, such provisions or portions thereof are to that extent deemed to be omitted. The waiver or failure of either party to exercise in any respect any right provided for herein shall not be deemed a waiver of any further right hereunder.

IN WITNESS WHEREOF, the parties have caused this Agreement to be executed and do each hereby warrant and represent that their respective signatory whose signature appears below has been and is on the date of this Agreement duly authorized by all necessary and appropriate corporate action to execute this Agreement.

ABC Systems, Inc.   World Wide Realty Company, Ltd.

_____   _____

By: _____   By: _____

Title: _____   Title: _____

Date: _____   Date: _____

C H A P T E R

5

STRUCTURE

1. INTRODUCTION

The structure of the *System* procurement process is important to its overall success. Whether your company has previous data processing experience or expertise will affect your choice of implementation strategies. This Chapter examines turn-key and outsourcing *System* implementation strategies (including service bureau and facilities management) as well as *System* leasing, tax and source code escrow considerations.

2. TURN-KEY SOLUTIONS

Chapter Two summarized the process you must undertake to select a *System* that supports your requirements. As discussed in that Chapter, you cannot make your choice in a vacuum. You must ask the following questions: Does the computer hardware have the necessary storage capacity and processing power to efficiently execute the desired application software? Does it support the operating system required by the application software? Can the application software support multiple users? If so, how many? Which network operating system is it compatible with? The selection process is further complicated by the rapid pace at which technology is changing. As the various elements comprising the *System* are individually upgraded in the future, will the vendor continue to maintain compatibility with previous versions so that you can take advantage of the enhanced capabilities?

If elements of the *System* are acquired through several different vendors it is unrealistic to expect that any one vendor will guarantee performance or compatibility for the entire *System*. Even if one vendor were to provide such an assurance, you should find out whether it is given just to get the business for now, or the whether the vendor has a plan and adequate resources to support the commitment in the future. However, vendors that provide a "turn-key" solution assume responsibility for providing a complete *System* to support your requirements.

Turn-key vendors generally fall into two categories, original equipment manufacturers (OEM) and system integrators.

☐ **OEM:** As the manufacturer[14] of computer hardware, the OEM often offers application software packages which it has either developed or has the right to license. Hardware, operating system software and application software are then bundled together and offered for installation as one complete *System*. The OEM will also ensure the required network and training are provided.

☐ **SYSTEM INTEGRATOR:** System integrators are generally not involved in the manufacturing or development process associated with the various *System* components. These companies have expertise in selecting compatible components that will comprise the *System*, integrating them to support your requirements, coordinating installation and providing overall training.

When evaluating turn-key solutions, you should keep in mind significant distinctions between the system integrator and the OEM. System integrators do not sell all of the various components comprising the *System* in the regular course of their business. For each client, the system integrator selects the components based on performance, functionality, price, upgrade potential and overall inter-compatibility. This affords the benefit of selecting "best of breed" since the system integrator (unlike the OEM) is not limited to only those *System* components that it sells. This independence that gives the system integrator an advantage also reveals a weakness. Because it has no recurring experience with the actual components being implemented, the system integrator may not be able to provide the level of after-sale support (in terms of warranty, maintenance and enhancements) normally provided by the OEM.

---

14. An entity that assembles all the components of computer hardware is also referred to as an OEM. OEM has also been used to refer to software development or licensing companies. When the software company provides a turn-key solution, computer hardware, operating system software, network and training are bundled together and implemented as one *System*.

Although turn-key solutions reduce the risks associated with *System* selection and implementation, they are not a panacea. Even if you select a turn-key vendor, evaluation criteria discussed in Chapter Two should still form an integral part of your selection process.

3. OUTSOURCING

Instead of purchasing or leasing a *System*, you can arrange for the vendor to provide computer data processing services through a service bureau or time sharing arrangement. In another variant of outsourcing, companies that have an in-house data processing (DP) department can transfer total control of their DP department to the outsourcing vendor[15]. The vendor then assumes responsibility for providing *System* services, including maintenance and support, for the customer.

3.1 Service Bureau

In many ways the use of a service bureau is analogous to the purchase of pre-packaged software, except that the *System* is managed and controlled by the service bureau. In the service bureau arrangement, access to the service bureau's computer facilities is provided in return for a per transaction fee. Service bureaus furnish standard processing services which consist of shared hardware and network resources providing access to standardized software programs. Service bureaus can provide computer data processing services in batch processing, as on-line interactive or in a hybrid manner.

Batch processing requires the customer to send accumulated data to the service bureau for processing. Upon completion, reports embodying the processed data are returned to the customer in printed or electronic format. On-line interactive processing allows the customer to have a direct electronic connection to the service bureau computer so that data can be entered directly and in real time. The data is then immediately processed with the results made available to the customer in real time. On-line interactive processing is the more prevalent use of service bureau facilities.

During the 1960s and 1970s, service bureaus were the only avenue by which computer data processing was available to most businesses. The cost

---

15. In fact, the outsourcing vendor usually purchases the customer's existing *Systems* and hires its DP employees.

of large mainframe computers and the support staff necessary to maintain such *Systems* made in-house acquisition inefficient. In contrast, the 1980s saw a trend away from service bureaus towards in-house ownership. The rationale for switching from a service bureau to an in-house *System* was to capitalize the benefits of a fixed cost asset. As a firm grew, its service bureau charges grew with each transaction. It was therefore believed that an in-house system, being a fixed asset, would deliver lower costs as the firm's transactions increased.

Today however, service bureaus are still prevalent. Although transaction costs initially decreased, in-house systems can result in escalating costs. The need for frequent updates, the rising costs of running a data center and an application development shop, in terms of qualified programmers, support personnel and management time, may erase the benefit flowing from the in-house *System* acquisition. In addition, although the cost of computer hardware has dramatically decreased, software costs in general, and application software costs in particular, still represent a significant investment.

The service bureau arrangement allows a firm to pay for only as much data processing support as it uses, thus providing a way to manage and forecast costs. The service bureau option may also afford certain tax benefits. Why? Because computer acquisitions must be depreciated over three to five years, while service bureau fees are deductible as a current business expense. Additional benefits of service bureau arrangements include the service bureau vendor's ability to: (a) acquire computer equipment and software at significantly reduced prices and (b) leverage the computer acquisition and its operations personnel over several client firms resulting in lower transaction costs passed onto the user. However, the most significant benefit resulting from service bureau processing is that you are left to do what you do best which is manage and run your own core business while the service bureau does what it does best which is manage the computer data processing requirements.

As with any *System* procurement, whether the service bureau arrangement adequately supports your business needs depends upon how completely your requirements are defined. In addition, the issues discussed in the following sections should be taken into account, negotiated upon and properly reflected in the service bureau agreement. A sample service bureau user agreement is reprinted at the end of this Chapter with certain sections in bold print to identify preferred wording.

☐ **SERVICES:** You must clearly define the services to be furnished by the service bureau vendor as well as the time periods during which they will be made available. Because application software is the critical component of the overall *System,* the definition of services should reference the specific software and include its user, operations and training manuals as schedules to the agreement. Sections 1.2, 1.3 and Schedules A and B of the sample agreement contain typical wording for services. You will note that Schedule B of the sample agreement makes reference to the customer's detailed functional requirements as amending the vendor's user and operations manuals.

☐ **EQUIPMENT:** It is generally your responsibility to acquire the equipment necessary to access the service bureau[16]. However, service bureau vendors frequently have volume discount agreements with equipment vendors, so they may be able to sell, rent or lease you the required equipment at a good price.

☐ **SECURITY:** The principal reason allowing the service bureau's per transaction data processing cost to be less than if you were to implement an in-house *System* also poses a security risk. Because the service bureau provides the same or similar services to many different customers, it is critical that the vendor implement appropriate security measures to prevent unauthorized access to your data records. Although identification numbers and passwords are suitable security methods, as part of the due diligence process you should visit the vendor's facilities and see first hand how security is implemented and ensured. Section 4 of the sample agreement outlines the vendor's data security obligations.

Another component of security is the frequency of data back-ups and the location where such back-ups are stored. With on-line interactive service bureau facilities, data will probably be updated frequently. At a minimum back-ups should be made once a week. A copy of each back-up should be provided to you and an off-site data storage facility approved by you. Since you own the data, you should have unrestricted access to retrieve it without the vendor's consent. Section 4 of the sample agreement outlines the vendor's obligations and your rights with respect to data back-up.

---

16. Although some service bureau providers will supply you with and maintain the necessary equipment.

☐ **DISASTER RECOVERY:** If access to the service bureau's facilities is interrupted, the vendor should be obligated to provide back-up processing facilities within a defined period of time. This is especially important when the service bureau is providing on-line interactive capabilities, because there is a frequent need for data updates and access thereto. It has become common for service bureau vendors to arrange for disaster recovery through companies that provide such facilities as their main line of business. Section 4 of the sample agreement contains typical wording for disaster recovery.

☐ **LIABILITY:** Service bureau vendors generally limit their liability for data processing errors to reprocessing the data at no charge and/or waiving the applicable transaction fee. Although it is difficult to get the vendor to agree to assume a greater amount of liability, the vendor may agree to additional liability when the frequency of errors during any calendar month exceeds a predefined threshold. The last sentence of Section 7 of the sample agreement contains wording for limits on liability.

☐ **OWNERSHIP:** Although the computer equipment and software is owned by the vendor, the data processed by the service bureau is your property. Because the data is stored on and retrieved through magnetic tape or other electronic media, the agreement should recognize your ownership of the physical movable media which contains your information. The vendor should be obligated to provide a machine readable disk or tape containing a complete archive of your data upon termination of the agreement. Without such a clause, you may be forced to re-enter all your data anew. Section 10 of the sample agreement outlines your ownership rights and the vendor's obligations with respect to data.

☐ **TERM:** The term of the service bureau arrangement is one of the most important clauses you negotiate. You will quickly become dependent on the service bureau's facilities and converting to a new *System* is time consuming and expensive. Consequently, you must ensure that your access to the service bureau continues for an appropriate length of time. You need to consider: (a) potential changes in your business volumes (e.g., whether the service bureau can accommodate increased volumes or whether decreased volumes makes the per transaction charge onerous) and (b) the useful life of the *System* provided by the service bureau and whether it is subject to rapid obsolescence (e.g., find out if the vendor provides assurances regarding *System* updates).

In order to preserve access to the service bureau's facilities, the agreement should give you the option of extending the term for successive and defined periods. As long as the vendor can reasonably increase its fees, it should have no objection to giving you this option. Section 11.1 of the sample agreement contains typical wording for defining the term of the agreement.

WIND-DOWN PERIOD: During conversion to a new *System*, the entire *System* selection process must be repeated and your data converted to a format compatible with the new *System*. Yet, operation of your business must continue uninterrupted. Therefore, the agreement should allow for a wind-down period during which time a new vendor can be selected and conversion to the new *System* proceed in an orderly fashion. Section 11.2 of the sample agreement contains typical wording for the wind-down period.

IN-HOUSE IMPLEMENTATION: Depending upon how your business grows and how your requirements change over time, you may want to negotiate an option to acquire the computer hardware and license the software provided by the service bureau for an in-house *System*. In-house implementation offers significant advantages because your personnel will not have to be trained in the operation of a new *System*. Data need not be converted and management time need not be wasted evaluating new *Systems*. In order for the option to be meaningful, the terms and conditions of the acquisition should be clearly defined. Preferably the actual hardware and software license agreements should be attached as schedules to the service bureau agreement. In addition, because computer hardware can quickly become obsolete, the agreement should allow you the flexibility to acquire all, some or none of the equipment. Furthermore, you should also have the option of simply acquiring only a license to the software programs. Section 11.3 of the sample agreement contains typical wording for in-house implementation.

TERMINATION: The service bureau arrangement imposes a variety of material obligations on the vendor. The vendor's failure to perform any one of these obligations can have damaging consequences to your business. Consequently, you should have the right to terminate the agreement in the event the vendor is unable to cure a failure within a defined cure period. Conversely, payment of fees is the only material obligation on your part. Because your business is dependent on availability of the service bureau's facilities, a balancing of the equities favors termination by the vendor only in the event you have failed to pay the required fees within the prescribed time frame and applicable cure period. The second sentence of Section 12.1 of the sample agreement contains typical wording for termination.

☐ **DISPUTE RESOLUTION**[17]**:** From time to time the level of compliance with the agreement's terms and conditions may come into question. If the vendor disallows access to the service bureau's facilities until the issues are resolved, the ramifications to your business could be disastrous. Consider the detrimental effect of not having payroll, invoicing or other management information records accessible for distribution. Therefore, it is critical that the vendor continues to provide services while a resolution is being negotiated. Section 14.10 of the sample agreement contains typical wording for dispute resolution.

3.2 Facilities Management

Many businesses do not have the necessary personnel required to manage the day to day operation of their *Systems*. When the *System* is comprised of custom software programs, the lack of qualified and knowledgeable personnel further exacerbates this problem.

Facilities management entails contracting with a vendor that specializes in providing primary support for acquiring, maintaining, enhancing and supporting in all respects the day to day *System* operation. As opposed to the service bureau arrangement, where many users can be given access to the vendor's *System*, the facilities management vendor supports and maintains the *System* for the exclusive use of one customer.

Many of the advantages and concerns associated with the service bureau arrangement are applicable to facilities management as well. There are some issues unique to facilities management which you should be aware of. These are discussed below.

☐ **PAY SCALE:** Qualified support personnel necessary to operate and support the *System* usually have generous compensation and benefit packages. Contracting with a facilities management vendor allows you maintain the current pay scale and benefit programs for your employees while still receiving the necessary specialized services.

---

[*] 17. Dispute resolution is discussed in more detail in Chapter Seven. It is important to raise the issue in this Section due to the almost total dependence users of service bureau facilities have on the service bureau.

☐ **NEW SYSTEM TRANSITION:** A facilities management arrangement can prove invaluable when a new in-house *System* is implemented. In such cases, all components of the *System* are acquired by you and the vendor provides the qualified personnel necessary for operations to continue until your own staff are adequately trained.

☐ **OWNERSHIP:** When application software is owned or licensed by the customer and provided to the facilities management vendor, important ownership issues arise. Although you may own the software or a license for its use, the software may be modified or otherwise enhanced by the facilities management vendor during the term of the agreement. In addition, the vendor may incorporate its own proprietary programs within the software. Upon termination of the agreement who owns these modifications? Obviously, they are critical to the ongoing operation of your business and therefore ownership is preferred. This may not be possible however, especially when the vendor's own proprietary programs have been incorporated. A fair compromise would be to allow your continued use of the software, as modified, pursuant to a non-exclusive license for the modifications made by the vendor.

4. SYSTEM LEASE

Over the years, the cost of computer hardware and its processing power have had an inverse relationship. As processing power has steadily increased, prices have decreased. On the other hand, application software has assumed a more prominent role in the procurement process and it is quite common for the software to represent a majority of the *System's* overall cost. The complex nature of today's *Systems* have also contributed to the increased cost. Consequently, total procurement costs can be quite significant and therefore lease financing should be considered.

Leasing can be arranged directly with the vendor of the *System* component(s) or through a third party leasing company. In either case, the transaction can be structured as a capital lease or an operating lease. A capital lease should be considered whenever the anticipated useful life of the *System* is greater than the lease term and you intend to exercise the purchase option at lease termination. An operating lease is appropriate in cases where the technology underlying the *System* or your requirements is changing rapidly and the *System* will either become obsolete or insufficient to support your needs. Because the lessor of an operating lease is betting that it can lease the *System* to another party at the end of the lease, your monthly payments will generally be less than under a capital lease. In addition, you will not be locked into a technology platform for an extended period of time. Beyond the obvious benefit to cash flow by spreading the acquisition costs over a period of up to five years, operating leases provide "off balance sheet financing" inasmuch as the total amount of all lease payments need not be carried as a balance sheet liability.

Aside from the contractual issues associated with a direct *System* purchase or licensing (discussed later in Chapter Six), the following provisions usually contained in lease agreements require careful review and negotiation.

☐ **FAIR MARKET VALUE:** Capital leases generally provide that the lessee has an option to purchase the leased equipment[18] at either a specified price or the equipment's fair market value at the end of the lease term. A specified exercise price for the purchase option is subject to negotiation just as any other price term. However, the exercise price should be evaluated in combination with the monthly lease payment and the cost of money. A higher exercise price may be more attractive from an economic standpoint because it will reduce the monthly lease payment and, in times of high interest rates, may result in a present value less than the face amount of the exercise price. If you expect that the *System* will depreciate in value at an accelerated pace, a purchase option at fair market value may result in a lower price paid at lease termination. The rapid pace at which technology changes in today's environment may result in a very low fair market value and if the *System* is still adequately supporting your requirements, its low market value only serves to reduce your acquisition costs.

Lease agreements may provide that fair market value is subject to mutual agreement between the lessor and lessee. In the event agreement cannot be reached, the matter is submitted to arbitration with the lessee responsible for the arbitration costs. Although I am an advocate of alternative means to resolve disputes, including arbitration, it is not fair for the lessee to absorb the entire cost. The lease agreement should require both parties to share the cost of arbitration equally.

---

18. Although the term "equipment" generally connotes hardware, in the context of a lease agreement "equipment" is a defined term that can include any component of the *System* including software.

☐ **INSTALLATION DATE:** Lease agreements generally provide that the installation date for **each** item of equipment is both the date installed by the vendor and satisfactory completion of the vendor's diagnostic tests. The installation date is commonly used by the lessor as the date upon which the lease and/or lease payments commence. However, in cases where the *System* is comprised of several different components, the installation date for any individual item of equipment should not necessarily trigger obligations of payment under the lease agreement as only after all *System* components have been properly installed and accepted will you be able to derive any economic benefit from them.

☐ **TERMINATION OPTION:** The pace at which technology has been accelerating may make incurring fees to terminate a lease financially attractive. A new *System* may process a greater number of transactions within the same or less time thereby reducing transaction costs and/or increasing revenues. In addition, the three to twelve month warranty that comes with a new *System* results in direct savings of maintenance costs which alone could offset an early termination fee. Finally, consider that as *Systems* get older, maintenance is more difficult and costly to obtain.

The termination option should be clearly provided for in the lease agreement. Not unreasonably, the lessor will typically expect to be paid for the remaining payments due under the lease, discounted to their net present value plus administration costs.

☐ **TAXES:** Lease agreements generally contain a provision making the lessee responsible for indemnifying the lessor against any tax liabilities incurred as a result of the lease transaction. Although such a clause is appropriate to protect the lessor against sales and use taxes, it could create a liability you never anticipated. As the entity that actually purchases the equipment, the lessor may be entitled to certain tax credits. The tax credit is generally taken into consideration by the leasing company in calculating the lease payments. Relying on the tax indemnity clause of the lease agreement, the lessor may demand indemnification in the event the tax credit is disallowed. Application of the tax clause in this manner should be specifically excluded in the lease agreement. The leasing company should be fully familiar with the applicable tax rules and regulations under which it can qualify for the tax credit and should therefore confirm that the contemplated lease will qualify.

☐ **NET LEASE:** The parties to a lease agreement are the user (the lessee) and the leasing company (the lessor). Although the equipment manufacturer may also be the lessor, it is much more likely that the lessor will be a third party leasing company. Even assuming that the lease is executed by the manufacturer, it is common for the manufacturer to sell and assign the lease agreement to a leasing company. Therefore, in the majority of cases the lessee does not have a direct contractual relationship with the equipment manufacturer. This bifurcated contractual relationship must be kept in mind because most lease agreements are structured as a "net lease" which means that the lessee is responsible for all expenses, costs and liabilities associated with using and maintaining the leased equipment. In addition, net leases contain what is commonly referred to as a "hell or high water" clause which obligates the lessee to pay all amounts due under the lease regardless of any defect or other inability to use the leased equipment. Such a clause may seem unconscionable. However, it has been routinely enforced by the courts. Therefore, to avoid having to make the monthly lease payments when the leased equipment is not functioning properly, the lease agreement should specifically grant you the right to suspend payments until the defects are corrected. If this is not possible, the agreement between the equipment vendor and the leasing company **must** grant you direct recourse against the equipment vendor[19]. The following clause should be considered for this purpose:

Lessor hereby agrees to assign to Lessee during the term of this Agreement all of the rights which Lessor may have against the equipment manufacturer or vendor or both for any breach of warranty, fraud, title, misrepresentation, proprietary rights indemnity or defect in design or manufacture of the Equipment. Such assignment is for the purpose of allowing Lessee at Lessee's cost and expense, to make and prosecute any such claim and to receive and use any money and other adjustments obtained thereunder for repair or replacement of any applicable item of Equipment. Lessor hereby agrees to execute any documents reasonably necessary to enable prosecution of any such claim.

---

19. Although Section 2-1-209 of the Uniform Commercial Code grants the lessee under a finance lease the benefits of the warranties and promises made by the supplier to the lessor under the supply contract, an affirmative obligation should be expressly contained in the agreement to avoid issues concerning applicability of the statute to your transaction.

Clearly, for the foregoing clause to have any benefit, agreements for the procurement of equipment must be carefully reviewed and negotiated to ensure that the lessee has viable remedies which can be enforced against the equipment vendor or manufacturer. This is the subject of Chapter Six.

☐ **SOFTWARE LEASE:** As mentioned earlier, the lessee usually has no direct contractual relationship with the equipment vendor. This can pose several problems to the unwary when software is included in the lease. Software license agreements generally limit use to the licensee which, in a lease transaction, is the leasing company. Another aspect of this problem is how to enforce the purchase option given that the license is between the vendor and the leasing company. In order to avoid problems that can result from the nature of the lease transaction, you should ensure that the software vendor specifically consents to your use and right to exercise any applicable purchase option upon lease termination.

☐ **EQUIPMENT RETURN:** Unless the purchase option is exercised at the end of the lease term, the lessee is required to return all equipment to the Lessor. Lease agreements generally provide that the equipment is to be returned to **any** location in the United States as designated by the lessor. This is an unreasonable burden to place on the lessee and therefore, the lease agreement should specifically identify the return location.

An additional problem can also be created if the lease agreement requires the lessee to store the equipment until the lessor authorizes shipment. If the equipment is kept in the computer room pending shipment, it can interfere with installation of the new *System*. If the equipment is stored off-site, storage and insurance expenses can be significant. Therefore, the lease agreement should allow return shipment at any time upon reasonable notice to the lessor.

5. TAX CONSIDERATIONS

5.1 Sales Tax

Sales tax regulations differ from state to state depending on the *System* component as well as the use to which the *System* is put. Investing some time to structure the transaction properly in view of sales tax regulations can reduce your tax liability, as discussed below.

☐ **SOFTWARE:** Whether software is subject to sales tax is a function of whether the state views software as tangible or intangible property. Pre-packaged software that is already developed and can be purchased "off-the-shelf" is generally viewed as a tangible product subject to sales tax. Software that must be developed or customized is generally considered an intangible service and therefore sales tax exempt[20].

The purchase of software may not always fall squarely in the custom or pre-packaged classifications. In many cases pre-packaged software will have to be customized to support unique requirements. Whether sales tax is applicable in this case depends on the extent of modifications and applicable state regulations. States apply different standards in determining the extent of modifications necessary to transform the licensing of pre-packaged software into a customized services transaction. A safe course of action when licensing software requiring customization is to separate the transaction into two agreements; a license agreement for the pre-packaged component, and a software development agreement for the customized work. The software development agreement can also include the installation and training services to be performed by the vendor. If the modifications are insufficient to make the entire transaction a services transaction, you can at least separate out the software development and services. Keep in mind that the amount allocated to software development and services must bear a reasonable relationship to the work performed.

☐ **MAINTENANCE :** Services performed in connection with software may also be subject to taxation. Again, it is important to structure the agreements in a manner which minimizes the incidence of taxation. For example, in some states if software maintenance is not optional or if the maintenance fees are not stated separately in the agreement, sales tax will be assessed on such services.

☐ **HARDWARE:** Computer hardware is generally subject to sales tax. However, when the hardware is used in a manufacturing process, some states provide an exemption. The exemption may also be applicable to related software. In order to qualify, the hardware must be used as an integral

---

[*] 20. You should nevertheless check with your attorney or tax advisor for a tax opinion in connection with the *System* purchase. Several states have enacted regulations which would impose a sales tax on the rendition of services as well.

part of the manufacturing process to actually alter or transform tangible personal property for resale. Use of hardware for prototyping or other preparatory work in the manufacturing process will not qualify. For example, hardware used to control the assembly line process of a factory would be eligible for the exemption.

5.2 Use Tax

In order to avoid the loss of sales tax revenue, certain states impose a use tax on computer equipment or software used in their state but purchased in a different state. The use tax is based on the value of the property which many times is the sales price. As with sales tax, whether and to what extent your *System* procurement will be subject to a use tax should be reviewed with your attorney or tax advisor.

6. ESCROW CONSIDERATIONS

As discussed earlier in this book, software is generally licensed in object code format because source code reveals the program's logic, structure and sequence. Access to source code would facilitate the development of competing programs, thereby defeating a reasonable return to the vendor. In addition, source code licensing may jeopardize the vendor's ability to claim the software as a trade secret.

A vendor's reticence to make source code available is also motivated by a desire to protect users against themselves. By having access to source code, the program's instructions can be modified. Unless a person is well skilled and knowledgeable in the program, modifications may unintentionally result in serious program errors.

The vendor's confidentiality concerns must be weighed against the customer's need for ongoing maintenance and enhancement support in case the vendor is unwilling or unable to provide these services. These competing interests have generally been balanced through the use of escrow agreements. Escrow agreements require the vendor to deposit source code and technical documentation for the software with an independent third party who is instructed to release the deposit to the user upon the occurrence of a pre-defined event, such as bankruptcy of the vendor.

Selected key provisions usually found in an escrow agreement are discussed below. A sample escrow agreement is reprinted at the end of this Chapter with certain sections in bold print to identify preferred wording.

☐ **ESCROW AGENT:** Do not leave selection of the escrow agent up to the vendor. You should be certain that the proposed escrow agent has the ability to protect the deposit material. Should an event occur that gives you access rights, the escrow agent must be capable of performing its obligations under the agreement. There are many companies that serve as escrow agents in the normal course of their business and have the necessary climate and security controls to ensure preservation of the deposit material. In some cases the vendor's law firm acts as escrow agent. Because of possible conflict issues which may arise, and the fact that most law firms do not have the necessary infrastructure to support an escrow arrangement, you are better served by using an escrow agent that specializes in software deposits. In the event that a substitute escrow agent has to be selected, you should still be entitled to consent to the new agent. Section 2 of the sample agreement contains typical wording for the selection of an escrow agency.

☐ **DEPOSIT MATERIAL:** In order for the escrow deposit to have any value, the deposit must contain the complete source listing of the software program together with complete documentation (discussed below) for the current and two most recent versions. In addition, source code and documentation for all modifications to the software should routinely be deposited in escrow. Sections 3(a), 5(a), 5(c) and 5(d) of the sample agreement contain typical wording for the escrow deposit.

☐ **AUDIT:** How can you be sure that the deposit material represents a complete version of the software program's source code? In addition, how do you know if the source code, and the medium on which it is stored, are in satisfactory condition? To answer these questions, you should have the right to inspect the deposit material at any time, and to require the vendor to compile an executable version of the software program so that it can be tested for condition and completeness. Section 3(b) of the sample agreement contains typical wording for an escrow audit.

☐ **CONFIDENTIALITY:** Vendors generally take the position that the software program's source code contains their confidential information. Consequently, the confidentiality obligations under the escrow agreement are usually drafted solely for the vendor's benefit. As discussed earlier, customized and custom software often reflect and contain confidential information which is proprietary to the customer. Therefore, the confidentiality obligations imposed on the escrow agent should be for your benefit as well. Section 4 of the sample agreement contains typical wording for confidentiality.

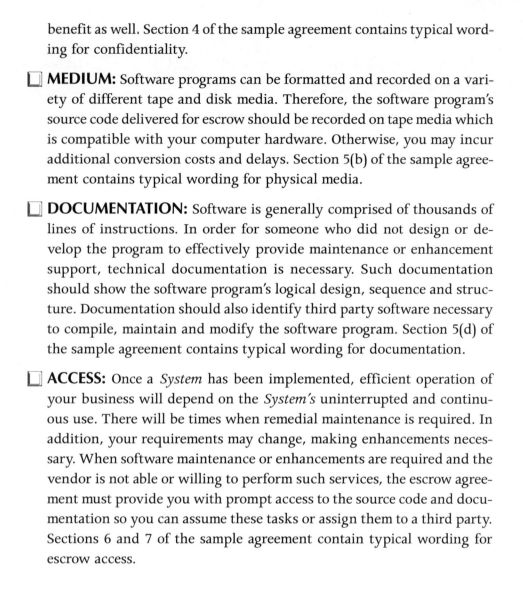 **MEDIUM:** Software programs can be formatted and recorded on a variety of different tape and disk media. Therefore, the software program's source code delivered for escrow should be recorded on tape media which is compatible with your computer hardware. Otherwise, you may incur additional conversion costs and delays. Section 5(b) of the sample agreement contains typical wording for physical media.

DOCUMENTATION: Software is generally comprised of thousands of lines of instructions. In order for someone who did not design or develop the program to effectively provide maintenance or enhancement support, technical documentation is necessary. Such documentation should show the software program's logical design, sequence and structure. Documentation should also identify third party software necessary to compile, maintain and modify the software program. Section 5(d) of the sample agreement contains typical wording for documentation.

ACCESS: Once a *System* has been implemented, efficient operation of your business will depend on the *System's* uninterrupted and continuous use. There will be times when remedial maintenance is required. In addition, your requirements may change, making enhancements necessary. When software maintenance or enhancements are required and the vendor is not able or willing to perform such services, the escrow agreement must provide you with prompt access to the source code and documentation so you can assume these tasks or assign them to a third party. Sections 6 and 7 of the sample agreement contain typical wording for escrow access.

SERVICE BUREAU USER AGREEMENT

Agreement made this 28th day of August, 1996 by and between ABC Systems, Inc. ("ABC"), 50 Main Street, White Plains, New York 11477 and Professional Trading Company, Ltd. ("Customer"), 100 Park Avenue, New York, NY 10017.

Customer desires to engage ABC to provide data processing and other services **(more particularly described in Schedule "A" attached hereto hereinafter referred to as "Services")** in order to furnish to Customer an on-line trading system, on a non-exclusive basis, **consisting of the application programs set forth in Schedule "B" attached hereto.**

In consideration of the following terms and conditions, the parties agree as follows:

1. <u>SERVICES</u>

    1.1. Customer hereby engages ABC and ABC agrees to make the Services available to Customer. By an amendment to Schedule "A", Customer and ABC may agree that ABC will perform additional services which shall be included within the term "Services" under this Agreement.

    1.2. The Services shall be accessible from remote terminal devices, the specifications of which are described in Schedule "C", attached hereto.

    1.3 The Services shall be made available during the hours of 8:00 a.m. to 5:00 p.m. (east coast time) on each business day in New York City, except days observed as holidays by the New York Stock Exchange, American Stock Exchange and the National Association of Securities Dealers.

2. <u>CHARGES</u>

    2.1 Customer agrees to pay ABC for Services provided under this Agreement at the rates set forth in Schedule "D", attached hereto.

    2.2. The charges specified in Schedule "D" do not include and the Customer shall pay for: (a) terminals, modems, printers and other equipment necessary for Customer to access and use the Services from Customer's office and (b) installation and maintenance of communication lines between Customer and ABC.

2.3 Customer shall pay any sales taxes imposed as a result of the provision of Services to the Customer.

2.4 The Customer shall pay all reasonable travel and accommodation expenses incurred by ABC in performing its obligations hereunder. Expenses which: (a) individually are in excess of two hundred fifty dollars ($250) or (b) during any calendar month, would cause total expenses incurred in such month to exceed five hundred dollars ($500) shall not be incurred without Customer's prior written consent.

2.5 Invoices shall be payable within thirty (30) days from Customer's receipt of the invoice therefor.

3. DATA AND COMMUNICATION SERVICES

Customer shall pay for, provide, install and maintain in good operating condition terminals, modems, printers, all other required equipment and communication lines to ABC necessary for Customer to access and use the Services from its office.

4. SECURITY & ACCESS TO SERVICES

ABC shall exercise full control and security over all data and other information furnished by Customer to ABC as such data may be modified or added to as a result of the provision of Services (the "Customer's Data"). Security provisions shall include: (a) maintaining a back-up copy of Customer's Data at a location other than ABC's place of business agreed to by Customer and to which Customer shall have free unrestricted access, without ABC's consent being required, during normal business hours (the "Back-Up Facility"). Back-ups shall be made on a weekly basis with one copy thereof provided to Customer and one copy provided to the Back-Up Facility; (b) ABC shall provide Customer with a log of Customer's Data on a weekly basis after execution of each back-up and (c) requiring access to the Services and Customer's Data by unique identification number(s) and password(s) which ABC shall maintain as confidential. ABC shall change the identification number(s) and password(s) every thirty (30) days or upon a request by Customer.

5. IMPROVEMENTS

Provided that Customer's access to and use of the Services is not adversely affected and in order to continuously improve the quality of Service to the Customer, if ABC is able to establish more efficient procedures for the provision of Services, ABC shall have the right, subject to Customer's prior written consent, to substitute such more efficient procedures.

6. BACK-UP PROCESSING ARRANGEMENTS

At no additional charge to Customer, ABC shall provide backup processing facilities covering equipment, data, operating systems, and application software which will allow for continuation of Services within two (2) hours after the occurrence of an event which prevents ABC from furnishing the Services in the manner regularly provided.

7. LIMITATION OF LIABILITY

If there is any error in or loss of data resulting from use of the Services caused by defects in the Services or in software or hardware provided by ABC ("Error"), provided that Customer supplies reasonable proof of claim to ABC within sixty (60) days of any such Error, Customer's remedy shall be to receive a credit for the charges billed by ABC to Customer in processing the data associated with the Error and to re-process the transactions resulting in the Error at no charge to Customer. **In the event that the number of Errors during any calendar month exceed ten (10), ABC shall pay Customer a re-processing fee of one hundred dollars ($100) for each and every Error occurring during such month.**

8. RESPONSIBILITY FOR ACCURACY OF DATA

Customer shall be responsible for the accuracy of data which Customer transmits to ABC. Moreover, except as otherwise set forth to the contrary in this Agreement, it is Customer's responsibility to maintain appropriate backup files and programs and to include appropriate error detection procedures.

9. DISCLOSURE

(9.1) As used herein, "CUSTOMER Information" shall include all information and data furnished by CUSTOMER to ABC, whether in oral, written, graphic or machine-readable form, including without limitation, specifications, user, operations or systems manuals, diagrams, graphs, models, sketches, technical data, research, business or financial information, plans, strategies, forecasts, forecast assumptions, business practices, marketing information and material, customer names, proprietary ideas, concepts, know-how, methodologies and all other information related to CUSTOMER's business. CUSTOMER Information shall also include confidential information received by CUSTOMER from a third party. In order for any information provided verbally by CUSTOMER to ABC to come within the definition of CUSTOMER Information, it shall be identified as confidential at the time of disclosure and within five (5) business days after verbal disclosure thereof by CUSTOMER, such information shall be documented in writing specifying that CUSTOMER considers such information confidential.

(9.2) As used herein, "ABC Information" shall include all information and data furnished by ABC to CUSTOMER, whether in oral, written, graphic or machine-readable form, in connection with the SERVICES, including, without limitation, object code, source code, source listings, computer programs, specifications, user, operations or systems manuals, diagrams, graphs, technical data, research, business or financial information, plans, strategies, forecasts, forecast assumptions, business practices, procedures, marketing information, trade secrets and other proprietary ideas, concepts, know-how, methodologies and information related to the SERVICES or ABC. **In order for any information provided verbally by ABC to CUSTOMER to come within the definition of ABC Information, it shall be identified as confidential at the time of disclosure and within five (5) business days after verbal disclosure thereof by ABC, such information shall be documented in writing specifying that ABC considers such information confidential.**

(9.3) As used herein, "Confidential Information" shall include the CUSTOMER Information and the ABC Information, individually and collectively. Notwithstanding anything to the contrary contained in this Agreement, **Confidential Information shall not include information: (a) in the public domain (other than as a result of a breach of this Agreement); (b) generally known and disclosed to CUSTOMER or ABC by persons or entities engaged in a comparable business (other than as a result of a breach of this Agreement or any other agreement to which such persons or entities are parties); (c) in CUSTOMER or ABC's possession prior to its receipt from the other pursuant to this Agreement or (d) independently developed by CUSTOMER or ABC.**

(9.4) CUSTOMER and ABC agree to **use procedures no less rigorous than those used to protect and preserve the confidentiality of their own proprietary information to** maintain the confidentiality of the Confidential Information of the other and shall not, directly or indirectly, (a) transfer or disclose any Confidential Information to a third party (other than to their respective employees); (b) **use any Confidential Information other than as contemplated under this Agreement** or (c) take any other action with respect to the Confidential Information inconsistent with the confidential and proprietary nature of such information. CUSTOMER and ABC further agree to return all Confidential Information (and all copies thereof) to the other upon termination of this Agreement.

(9.5) CUSTOMER and ABC shall be permitted to disclose the Confidential Information to their respective employees **having a need for access thereto in connection with their employment and who have executed confidentiality agreements containing provisions similar to those contained in this Agreement and specifying that other parties are third party beneficiaries thereof entitled to enforce the provisions thereof as though a party thereto. CUSTOMER and ABC shall each take steps, no less rigorous than those it takes to protect and preserve its own proprietary information, to prevent their respective employees from acting in a manner inconsistent with the terms of this Agreement.**

(9.6) ABC acknowledges and agrees that CUSTOMER is engaged in the business of securities trading, and as such currently possesses knowledge and information relating to the functionality and capabilities required for computer systems in support thereof. Therefore, nothing contained in this Agreement shall prevent CUSTOMER from, on its own or through third parties, designing, developing or acquiring computer systems similar to the SERVICES so long as CUSTOMER does not make use of any ABC Information in connection therewith.

10. OWNERSHIP

It is agreed that the Customer's Data, and all movable media upon which Customer's Data is stored, Customer Information including all specifications and other requirements given by Customer to ABC is and shall continue to remain the property of the Customer. Within five (5) business days after termination of this Agreement (irrespective of the cause of termination), ABC agrees to provide a machine readable disk or tape (at the Customer's option) on which the Customer's Data is stored.

11. <u>TERM</u>

11.1 This Agreement shall have a term commencing upon execution hereof and continue for a period of five (5) years from the **date that Customer can first make live production use** of the Services. **Customer shall have the option of renewing this Agreement for successive periods of twelve (12) months each upon notice to ABC delivered at least sixty (60) days prior to expiration of the then current term. Subsequent to the initial five (5) year term and for each twelve (12) month period thereafter, ABC may increase the fees payable by Customer by an amount equal to the lesser of seven percent (7%) per annum or the increase in the CPI for the immediately preceding calendar year.**

11.2 Upon termination of this Agreement (irrespective of the cause of termination), at Customer's option, ABC shall continue to provide the Services for a period of up to one hundred eighty (180) days and shall reasonably cooperate with Customer, all at Customer's cost and expense, in order that Customer may procure alternative data processing services to support its requirements. If requested by ABC, Customer shall pay for the provision of Services during such period in advance.

11.3 Customer shall at any time during the term of this Agreement and for a period of up to one year after the termination hereof (irrespective of the cause of termination) have the option to purchase from ABC any of the following: a non-exclusive license for the operating, network and application software comprising the Services or the necessary hardware upon which such software executes. In the event Customer exercises the option granted by this Section 11.3, the purchase of the hardware and software licenses shall be in accordance with the terms and conditions of the Hardware Purchase and Sale and Software License Agreements attached hereto as Schedule "E".

12. TERMINATION

12.1 Subject to Section 11.2, Customer or ABC may terminate this Agreement effective upon a material breach hereof by the other party which continues in excess of fifteen (15) days after receipt of written notice specifying in detail the breach claimed. **Customer shall not be deemed in material breach of this Agreement unless Customer has failed, without cause, to comply with its obligations as set forth in Article 2 hereof for a period in excess of sixty (60) days.**

12.2 Upon termination of this Agreement in accordance with all applicable provisions, all of Customer's Data shall be furnished to Customer by ABC in machine readable format on diskette or tape at Customer's option.

13. TRAINING

ABC shall provide thirty (30) hours of training to Customer in the use of the Services. Training will be conducted in not less two or greater than three (3) hour sessions at Customer's offices in New York. ABC shall assume and be responsible for the payment of all transportation, room and board expenses of its employees in furnishing such Services. ABC shall provide ten (10) copies of the user manual suitable for Customer's personnel to become knowledgeable in the use and operation of the Services.

14. GENERAL

14.1 ABC warrants that, upon execution hereof and continuing during the term of this Agreement, it has the unqualified right, without requiring the consent of any third party, to enter into this Agreement and provide the Services to Customer.

14.2 No modifications of this Agreement shall be valid or binding on either party unless acknowledged in writing and signed by the duly authorized officer of each party. All notices or other communications given under this Agreement shall be in writing, sent to the address hereinbefore set forth as principal place of business or such other addresses as ABC or the Customer may designate in writing by certified mail (return receipt requested) or personal delivery. Notice shall be deemed given upon receipt.

14.3 Both parties understand and agree that violation of Section 9 of this Agreement may cause damage to the other party in an amount which is impossible or extremely difficult to ascertain. Accordingly, without limitation to any other remedy available at law, the injured party may be entitled to seek injunctive relief restraining the other party from continuing to violate the terms and provisions of said Section.

14.4 The parties acknowledge that each has read all the terms of this Agreement, agrees to be bound by its terms and conditions and that it is the complete and exclusive statement of the agreement between the parties which supersedes all prior communications and agreements between the parties relating to the subject matter of this Agreement.

14.5 If any provision of this Agreement shall be deemed invalid and/or inoperative, under any applicable statute or rule of law, it is to that extent to be deemed modified so as to provide the most similar enforceable economic effect and shall have no effect as to any other provision contained in this Agreement.

14.6 Each of the Customer and ABC shall designate a responsible individual with authority as Project Coordinator to serve as project leader. The Customer's Project Coordinator shall provide or coordinate the provision of information about the Customer, its practice, external and internal procedures and such other information as ABC may reasonably require in order to fulfill its obligations under this Agreement.

14.7 Any forbearance or delay on the part of either party in enforcing any provision of this Agreement or any of its rights hereunder shall not be construed as a waiver of such provision or of a right to enforce same.

14.8 The provisions of Articles and/or Sections 4, 7, 9, 10, 11.2, 11.3, 12 and 14 shall survive termination of this Agreement or any portion thereof.

14.9 (a) The parties shall use all reasonable efforts to amicably resolve any dispute or controversy arising directly out of this Agreement by referring such dispute or controversy to a senior management executive of each party who was not directly involved in the procurement and day to day management of the Services. The management executive selected by each party shall have the authority to bind its company to the terms of any settlement agreed to. If the parties, after good faith efforts, fail to resolve the dispute or controversy, the matter shall be referred to and settled by arbitration in accordance with the rules of XYZ Dispute Resolution Services.

(b) In connection with any breach or threatened breach by either party of the confidential information obligations of this Agreement, the non-breaching party may, at any time seek by application to the United States District Court for the Southern District of New York or the Supreme Court of the State of New York for the County of New York any such temporary or provisional relief or remedy ("provisional remedy") provided for by the laws of the United States of America or the laws of the State of New York as would be available in an action based upon such dispute or controversy in the absence of this Section 14.9. No such application to either said Court for a provisional remedy, nor any act or conduct by either party in furtherance of or in opposition to such application, shall constitute a relinquishment or waiver of any right to have the underlying dispute or controversy with respect to which such application is made settled by arbitration.

(c) **In any arbitration proceeding, each party shall select one arbitrator who has technical software systems knowledge of real time trading systems.** The two arbitrators so selected shall appoint a third **so qualified arbitrator**. A majority decision of the arbitrators shall be binding. Each party shall bear its own costs associated with such arbitration. **The arbitration proceeding shall be kept confidential.**

14.10 Pending resolution of any dispute or controversy as provided in Section 14.9, each of the parties shall continue to perform its obligations under this Agreement and a failure to perform its obligations by either party pending the resolution process shall be deemed a separate breach of this Agreement.

14.11 Any dispute arising under this Agreement shall be governed by the laws of the State of New York.

IN WITNESS WHEREOF, the parties have caused this Agreement to be executed and do each hereby warrant and represent that their respective signatory whose signature appears below has been and is on the date of this Agreement duly authorized by all necessary and appropriate corporate action to execute this Agreement.

PROFESSIONAL TRADING
COMPANY, LTD.   ABC SYSTEMS, INC.

By: _____   By: _____

Name: _____   Name: _____

Title: _____   Title: _____

Date: _____   Date: _____

SCHEDULE A TO SERVICE
BUREAU USER AGREEMENT
BETWEEN ABC SYSTEMS, INC. ("ABC")
AND PROFESSIONAL TRADING COMPANY, LTD. ("CUSTOMER")
DATED AUGUST 28, 1996

The Services shall include access to the application programs identified in Schedule "B" to this Agreement by up to ten (10) Alpha Computer terminals and five (5) Excelsior Laser printers. ABC shall execute the software programs comprising the Services on Superior Computer equipment, model SC-1000 and shall ensure that the processing time for each Execution (as defined in Schedule "F" of this Agreement) does not exceed one (1) second from the time all information is entered to complete Execution of the respective trade.

SCHEDULE B TO SERVICE
BUREAU USER AGREEMENT
BETWEEN ABC SYSTEMS, INC. ("ABC")
AND PROFESSIONAL TRADING COMPANY, LTD. ("CUSTOMER")
DATED AUGUST 28, 1996

The Application Program to be made available to Customer as part of the Services is version 3 ABC's "STOCK" trading program which is more particularly described in the STOCK program user manual dated April 4, 1996, as amended by Customer's detailed functional requirements dated June 15, 1996 containing 134 pages, each page of which is initialed by the parties hereto and attached hereto as Schedule "F".

SCHEDULE C TO SERVICE
BUREAU USER AGREEMENT
BETWEEN ABC SYSTEMS, INC. ("ABC")
AND PROFESSIONAL TRADING COMPANY, LTD. ("CUSTOMER")
DATED AUGUST 28, 1996

Equipment used by Customer to access the Services shall be in conformity with the following specifications:

IBM or compatible personal computers with minimum 486 processor speed, 8 MB RAM, 700 MB storage, 28.8 BPS byschronous error deleting and correction modem.

SCHEDULE D TO SERVICE
BUREAU USER AGREEMENT
BETWEEN ABC SYSTEMS, INC.("ABC")
AND PROFESSIONAL TRADING COMPANY, LTD. ("CUSTOMER")
DATED AUGUST 28, 1996

(1) Commencing with the first month (or portion thereof) that Services are available to Customer and for each month thereafter during the term of this Agreement, Customer shall pay ABC the greater of:

$20,000 per month (pro-rated if Services commence or terminate on other than the first or last day of the month, respectively)

or

$7.00 per Execution

(2) As used herein, the term "Execution" shall mean each matching of an instruction to buy or sell a security with a corresponding instruction to sell or buy a security.

SCHEDULE E TO SERVICE
BUREAU USER AGREEMENT
BETWEEN ABC SYSTEMS, INC. ("ABC")
AND PROFESSIONAL TRADING COMPANY, LTD. ("CUSTOMER")
DATED AUGUST 28, 1996

This Schedule would contain the agreements referred to in Section 11.3 of the Agreement, an analysis of which is contained in Chapter 6 of this Book.

ESCROW AGREEMENT

Agreement made as of the 28th day of August, 1996, between ABC Systems, Inc. having its principal office at 50 Main Street, White Plains, NY 11477 ("ABC"); Professional Trading Company, Ltd. having its principal office at 100 Park Avenue, New York, NY 10017 ("PTC") and XYZ Data Security, Inc. having its principal place of business at 35 Madison Avenue, New York, NY 10118 ("Escrow Agent").

WITNESSETH:

WHEREAS, ABC is in the business of licensing computer software technology;

WHEREAS, PTC and ABC have entered a Master Software License Agreement, dated August 28, 1996, (the "License Agreement") pursuant to which ABC granted PTC a perpetual, non-exclusive, not-transferable license to software as identified in the License Agreement ("SOFTWARE").

NOW, THEREFORE, in consideration of the mutual promises and subject to the terms and conditions set forth herein, the parties hereto agree as follows:

1. **License Agreement**   Except as otherwise contemplated by this Agreement, this Agreement is made pursuant to and subject to the terms of the License Agreement, which is deemed incorporated herein by this reference and shall constitute part of this Agreement as if fully set forth herein. All capitalized terms not otherwise defined herein shall have the definitions set forth in the License Agreement.

2. **Escrow Agent** The parties have designated:

> XYZ Data Security, Inc.
> 35 Madison Avenue
> New York, NY 10118
> (212) 555-7770

as the Escrow Agent and ABC has consented to said designation. **Any successor escrow agent must be mutually acceptable to the parties.** ABC agrees to pay Escrow Agent as set forth in the Escrow Agent's Service Agreement.

3. **Deposits**

(a)   On the date of this Agreement, ABC shall deposit with the Escrow Agent and the Escrow Agent shall accept from ABC the Source Code and Documentation (as defined in Section 5(d) (collectively "Source Code") for the SOFTWARE as it exists in its most current version as of the date hereof and the two most recent prior versions thereof. Thereafter, ABC shall promptly supplement the Source Code deposited hereunder with all updates, corrections, enhancements, changes and revisions thereto made by ABC so that the Source Code constitutes the most current version of the SOFTWARE licensed to PTC (collectively and individually "Deposit").

(b)   The Escrow Agent will issue to ABC a receipt for the Deposit upon delivery. PTC shall have the right, from time to time: (i) to have ABC review, compile and test the Source Code in its current version in PTC's presence; and/or (ii) to verify, audit and inspect the Deposit to confirm compliance with this Agreement. PTC shall pay ABC its then current time and material consulting rates for ABC's services performed under this Section.

(c)   The DEPOSIT shall remain the exclusive property of ABC and the Escrow Agent shall not use the DEPOSIT except as specifically provided for in this Agreement.

4. **Confidentiality**

(a) Escrow Agent acknowledges and understands that the DEPOSIT is to be kept strictly confidential and is trade secret and highly sensitive. Escrow Agent further acknowledges and agrees that unauthorized disclosure of the DEPOSIT may subject ABC, its affiliated companies, employees, customers and/or suppliers, **and PTC**, its parent, subsidiaries, affiliated companies, employees, customers and/or suppliers to substantial harm. Escrow Agent agrees to treat the DEPOSIT as trade secret and proprietary, to hold same in trust and confidence for ABC **and PTC** and provide security provisions, at a minimum, to the extent that Escrow Agent would provide security for its own similar information.

(b) Escrow Agent will establish appropriate safeguards by agreement, instruction and otherwise, to enable Escrow Agent, its employees, representatives, agents and suppliers to comply with the obligations set forth herein. **At the request of ABC and/or PTC,** Escrow Agent agrees to give ABC access to Escrow Agent's facilities and security records, during Escrow Agent's normal business hours, for the purpose of ABC's conducting such audit of Escrow Agent's operations as it deems necessary to ensure that Escrow Agent has established reasonable and adequate safeguards for protecting the DEPOSIT as required hereunder.

(c) Escrow Agent shall afford ABC **and PTC,** with all reasonable assistance as is necessary for the conduct of such audit. In the event ABC **or PTC** determines Escrow Agent has not established adequate and reasonable measures for compliance with Escrow Agent's obligations hereunder, Escrow Agent shall be notified and Escrow Agent will immediately take corrective action as is appropriate and necessary under the circumstances.

5. **Representations, Warranties and Covenants**

ABC hereby represents, warrants and covenants to PTC that:

(a) The Source Code for the most recent version of the SOFTWARE and the two (2) most recent prior versions shall be kept on Deposit with the Escrow Agent as part of the Deposit material.

(b) The Source Code delivered to the Escrow Agent pursuant hereto is and shall be contained on the same medium and in the same format as the SOFTWARE delivered and licensed to PTC and shall consist of source code comprising the SOFTWARE as defined in the License Agreement.

(c) ABC will promptly supplement the Deposit with all updates, revisions, corrections, enhancements or other changes made by ABC so that the Source Code constitutes a machine-readable program and documentation for the most current and prior two (2) versions of the SOFTWARE licensed to PTC.

(d) The Deposit delivered to Escrow Agent now consists, and at all times during the term of this Agreement will consist, of a full source of the language statement of the program or programs comprising of the SOFTWARE and Documentation in sufficient detail to allow a reasonably skilled programmer to understand, the logic, sequence and structure of the SOFTWARE so that the SOFTWARE may be maintained and enhanced. All third party software necessary to compile, maintain and modify the SOFTWARE shall be sufficiently disclosed in the Documentation. Documentation shall include by way of example the following: master file maintenance, trading operations functions, trader functions, workstation functions, batch processing, system operations and operator's guide. Documentation shall be provided in written form as well as electronic format for use in connection with the "Microsoft Word" word processing program version 6.0. The documentation referred to in this Section 5(d) shall be defined as "Documentation" for purposes of this Agreement.

6. **Access Events** PTC, its successors and permitted assigns, shall receive one copy of the DEPOSIT to be used in accordance with the License Agreement upon the occurrence of any one of the following "Access Events" during the term of the License Agreement: ABC shall: (i) take corporate action in furtherance of winding-up, liquidating or dissolving itself; (ii) become insolvent or be unable to pay its debts as they become due; (iii) make an assignment for the general benefit of creditors; (iv) file a voluntary petition in bankruptcy or be adjudicated as bankrupt; (v) have an involuntary petition filed in bankruptcy under any law relating to bankruptcy, insolvency or reorganization or relief of debtors or seeking an entry of an order for relief or the appointment of a receiver, trustee or other similar official for it or any substantial part of its property or affairs and such appointment is made and not terminated or discharged within sixty (60) days or (vi) fail to discharge any of its maintenance or other support or enhancement obligations with respect to any SOFTWARE in accordance with the warranties or other standards for such maintenance and other services set forth in any license, maintenance or other program services agreement from time to time in effect between ABC and PTC, within the time periods set forth in such agreements.

7. **Access to DEPOSIT** Upon the occurrence of an Access Event, PTC shall give the Escrow Agent written notice thereof and the Escrow Agent shall

immediately send notice thereof to ABC by personal delivery, or by certified or registered mail or by overnight courier service, postage prepaid, return receipt requested in all cases (the "Escrow Agent Notice"). If ABC desires to dispute the occurrence of such Access Event, ABC shall, within five (5) business days after receipt of the Escrow Agent Notice, deliver to the Escrow Agent a sworn statement of an executive officer of ABC (the "Affidavit") stating that no Access Event has occurred. If the Escrow Agent does not receive the Affidavit within fifteen (15) business days after having sent the Escrow Agent Notice, PTC shall be given access to the DEPOSIT in accordance with this Agreement. Disputes with respect to the occurrence of an Access Event shall be resolved in the same manner as described in Section 14 of the License Agreement.

8. **Obligations of PTC** It is expressly understood and agreed that if the DEPOSIT is delivered or disclosed to PTC by Escrow Agent pursuant to this Agreement, the following provisions shall apply and such delivery or disclosure shall be subject to these provisions.

(a) PTC shall have the right and shall use the DEPOSIT solely to support (including maintenance and enhancement within the rights granted to PTC under the License Agreement) the SOFTWARE licensed to PTC.

(b) PTC shall not copy (except up to two copies for back-up and archival purposes), disclose (subject to the exceptions set forth in the License Agreement), sell, distribute, sub-license or deliver the DEPOSIT to any third party without prior written consent of ABC.

9. **Limitation on Escrow Agent's Responsibility and Liability**

(a) The Escrow Agent shall not be obligated or required to examine or inspect the Deposit or any updates, corrections, enhancements, changes and revisions thereto. The Escrow Agent's obligation for safekeeping shall be limited to providing the same degree of care for the Deposit as it maintains for its valuable documents and those of its customers lodged in the same location with appropriate atmospheric and other safeguards. However, the parties agree and acknowledge that the Escrow Agent shall not be responsible for any loss or damage to any Deposit due to changes in such atmospheric conditions (including, but not limited to, failure of the air conditioning system), unless such changes are proximately caused by the negligence or malfeasance of the Escrow Agent.

(b) The Escrow Agent shall be protected in acting upon any written notice, request, waiver, consent, receipt or other paper or document furnished to it by authorized representatives of PTC and ABC.

(c) In no event shall the Escrow Agent be liable for any act or failure to act under the provisions of this Escrow Agreement except where its acts are the result of its negligence or malfeasance. The Escrow Agent shall have no duties except those which are expressly set forth herein and it shall not be bound by any notice of a claim or demand with respect thereto or any waiver, modification, amendment, termination or rescission of this Escrow Agreement, unless in writing executed by ABC and PTC and if its duties herein are adversely affected, unless it shall have given its prior written consent thereto.

10. **Assignment** No party hereto shall assign this Agreement or any rights or obligations hereunder without the prior written consent of the other party.

11. **Notices** Any notice or other communication hereunder shall be in accordance with the notice provisions set forth in the License Agreement.

12. **Governing Law** This Agreement shall be interpreted in accordance with the laws of the State of New York.

13. **Modification, Amendment, Supplement or Waiver** No modification, amendment, supplement to or waiver of this Agreement or any of its provision shall be binding upon the parties hereto unless made in writing and duly signed by the parties to this Agreement. A failure or delay of either party to this Agreement or to enforce at any time any of the provisions of this Agreement or to require at any time performance of any of the provisions hereof shall in no way be construed to be a waiver of such provisions of this Agreement. A waiver by either party of any of the terms and conditions of this Agreement in any one instance shall not be deemed a waiver of such terms or conditions in the future or of any subsequent breach thereof.

14. **Entirety of Agreement** This Agreement constitutes the entire agreement between the parties with respect to escrow of the SOFTWARE.

15. <u>Severability</u> In the event any one or more of the provisions of this Agreement shall for any reason be held to be invalid, illegal or unenforceable, the remaining provisions of this Agreement shall be unimpaired and the invalid, illegal or unenforceable provision(s) shall be replaced by a mutually acceptable provision(s), which being valid, legal and enforceable, comes closest to the intention of the parties underlying the invalid, illegal or unenforceable provision(s).

16. <u>Headings</u> The headings of this Agreement are for purposes of reference only and shall not in any way limit or otherwise affect the meaning or interpretation of any of the terms hereof.

IN WITNESS WHEREOF, the parties have caused this Agreement to be executed and do each hereby warrant and represent that their respective signatory whose signature appears below has been and is on the date of this Agreement duly authorized by all necessary and appropriate corporate action to execute this Agreement.

Professional Trading Company, Ltd.   ABC Systems, Inc.

_____   _____

Signature   Signature

_____   _____

Name   Name

_____   _____

Title   Title

_____   _____

Date   Date

XYZ Data Security, Inc.

_____   _____

Signature   Name

_____   _____

Title   Date

AGREEMENT CLAUSES and ANALYSIS.

1. INTRODUCTION

System procurement agreements define the vendor's obligations with respect to functionality, delivery, maintenance and support. Similarly, confidentiality and payment obligations as well as your rights to use, modify and otherwise implement the *System* will be expressly specified in the agreement.

In this Chapter the various clauses that comprise the salient rights and obligations expressed in *System* procurement agreements will be analyzed in the context of: (a) software license, (b) software development, (c) hardware and (d) software maintenance agreements[21]. The deliberate focus on software reflects its pivotal role in the *System* procurement process. Recommended wording follows the discussion of each clause and the complete form of agreement is reprinted in Appendix A.

---

21. The clauses reviewed in this Chapter assume that individual agreements are executed for each component of the *System* as opposed to a turn-key solution. However, the analysis is generally applicable to both types of agreements.

2. DELIVERABLES

The Deliverables clause identifies what the vendor has committed to furnish. This section of the agreement should clearly describe what is being procured in sufficient detail or you may find yourself paying additional fees for material or services you thought were included in the original price.

2.1 Pre-Packaged Software and Hardware

Computer hardware and pre-packaged software deliverables are straightforward and simple to define. Pre-packaged software can be defined by reference to the user manual for the software version being licensed, a copy of which should be attached as a schedule to the agreement. Likewise, computer hardware can be readily described by features and model numbers. In addition when the vendor has submitted a proposal in response to your RFP, the deliverable should be further identified by reference to this document.[22]

The following clause defines the pre-packaged software deliverable.

On or before the dates set forth in Schedule "C"[23] attached to this Agreement and made a part hereof, ABC shall deliver to Customer the Software comprised of version 4 of ABC's "STOCK" program product in object code format[24] as described by the Documentation[25] which is attached to this Agreement as Schedule "A" and made a part hereof. The SOFTWARE shall have all of the functions, features, performance, compatibility and enhancement characteristics described in Customer's RFP. In the event of an inconsistency between the Documentation and the RFP, the RFP shall prevail.

The last sentence of the preceding clause underscores the importance of independently defining required functionality in an RFP so that the vendor can deliver a *System* that meets your requirements. Although a user's guide or a functional specification may accurately describe the *System*, you still need to refer to your RFP and make sure that it takes precedence.

---

22. This approach is applicable to, and recommended for, the procurement of customized and custom software as well.

23. Schedule references throughout the sample clauses in this Chapter are in random order.

24. As discussed earlier in Chapter Three, software and in particular pre-packaged software, is generally licensed in object code format.

25. Documentation is discussed in Section 4 of this Chapter. Throughout the sample clauses contained in this Chapter, words with either full or complete capitalization have been defined elsewhere in the full agreements located in Appendix A.

2.2 Custom Software Development

Custom software poses greater difficulty in defining deliverables because the software does not yet exist. For this type of procurement, the requirements definition you develop is essential to the preparation of a system design and functional specification. In the same way that architectural plans define a house yet to be built, the functional specification and system design will delineate the functions and capabilities of the software program. Consequently, the requirements definition should be referenced in and attached as a schedule to the agreement.

The following clause defines the custom software deliverable:

On or before the dates set forth in Schedule "C" attached to this Agreement and made a part hereof, ABC shall deliver to Customer:

(a) the Functional Specification to be attached to this Agreement as Schedule "A" and made a part hereof upon its Acceptance;

(b) the System Design Specification to be attached to this Agreement as Schedule "B" and made a part hereof upon its Acceptance;

(c) software programs, in source code format[26], to be developed by ABC consistent with the System Design Specification and which have the capabilities described in the Functional Specification. However, to avoid doubt, the Software shall have all of the functions, features, performance, compatibility and enhancement characteristics described in Customer's RFP. In the event of an inconsistency between the Functional Specification and the RFP, the RFP shall prevail; and

(d) Documentation in addition to the System Design and Functional Specifications, as identified in Section 6 of this Agreement.

2.3 Customized Software Development

Defining the customized software deliverable presents many of the same issues related to custom software. In addition, customized software procurement requires consideration of sales tax consequences. You will recall that it is advisable to execute a license agreement for the pre-packaged

---

26. Because custom software is specifically developed for your purposes you should receive the program's source code in order to facilitate modifications and enhancements which may be necessary to suit your requirements.

software and a separate agreement for the required customization in order to limit the incidence of sales tax.[27]

The license agreement should contain the following deliverable clause:

On or before the dates set forth in Schedule "C" attached to this Agreement and made a part hereof, ABC shall deliver to Customer the: (a) Software comprised of version 4 of ABC's "STOCK" program product in object code format as more particularly described in Schedule "A" attached to this Agreement and made a part hereof and (b) Documentation.

The customized software development services agreement should contain the following deliverable clause:

On or before the dates set forth in Schedule "C" attached to this Agreement and made a part hereof, ABC shall deliver to Customer:

(a) the Functional Specification to be attached to this Agreement as Schedule "A" and made a part hereof upon its Acceptance;

(b) the System Design Specification to be attached to this Agreement as Schedule "B" and made a part hereof upon its Acceptance;

(c) software programs, in source code format, to be developed by ABC consistent with the System Design Specification which have the capabilities described in the Functional Specification and integrated with the Standard Software[28] so as to form a part thereof. The Standard Software as modified by the Functional and System Design Specifications shall be referred to as the "SOFTWARE". The SOFTWARE shall have all of the functions, features, performance, compatibility and enhancement characteristics described in the RFP. In the event of an inconsistency between the Standard Software documentation, Functional Specification, and the RFP, the RFP shall prevail; and

(d) Documentation in addition to the System Design and Functional Specification, as identified in Section 4.2 of this Agreement.

---

27. Included as one of the sample agreements in Appendix A is a simplified software license agreement to be used in connection with customized software procurement. Because some of the vendor's deliverable obligations cannot be validated for compliance until the customized software development work is completed, their acceptance should be deferred until the work defined in the agreement for customized software development services is completed.

28. The "Standard Software" referred to in this clause is the pre-packaged software licensed under the license agreement.

2.4 Third Party Software

Earlier in Chapter Two we discussed the possibility that proper operation of the vendor's application software (prepackaged, customized or custom) may require software programs licensed by other entities. A RDBMS is the third party software most often required. Regardless of whether you are negotiating an individual license agreement for the vendor's software or a turn-key solution, the vendor should be made responsible for delivering the necessary third party software, its relevant documentation and license for its use.

The following clause can be used to define the third party software deliverable when the license fee for such software is included in the total fees payable to the vendor:

On or before the dates set forth in Schedule "C" attached to this Agreement and made a part hereof, ABC shall deliver to Customer:

(a) version 7 of the DATABUILDER program product as more particularly described by version 7 of the "DATABUILDER User's Guide" attached to this Agreement as Schedule "K" and made a part hereof (the "DATABUILDER Software");

(b) version 7 of the DATABUILDER user, operations, maintenance and training guides; and

(c) a perpetual, nonexclusive and fully paid license to use the DATABUILDER Software in connection with the SOFTWARE.

3. SOFTWARE LICENSE

3.1 Common Licensing Provisions

In Chapter Two, we reviewed the rationale behind the general practice of licensing software. Software development is a lengthy and capital intensive endeavor. The low cost and ease of duplication presents vendors with both an opportunity for, and a risk to, recovering their investment. By maintaining title, vendors can control the use, duplication, modification and distribution through appropriately circumscribed licensing provisions. Common restrictions found in licensing agreements include limitations on the: (a) maximum number of concurrent users that can access the software and/or (b) type and/or number of CPU's upon which the software can be executed. Such clauses however, have the practical effect of requiring you to purchase additional licenses as your business grows.

The following clause is typical of standard licensing provisions commonly found in pre-packaged, customized or custom software agreements:[29]

(a)   ABC hereby grants the Customer a personal, nontransferable, non-exclusive, paid-up and irrevocable license[30] for up to seven (7) concurrent users to access and use one (1) copy of the SOFTWARE and Documentation. The license granted herein allows the Customer to use the SOFTWARE in object code format.

(b)   The license granted hereby is limited to Customer's use of the SOFTWARE in its normal business operation, as presently conducted, on the Hardware comprised of the single CPU identified in Schedule "C" attached to this Agreement and made a part hereof.

(c)   In the event that the designated CPU is malfunctioning, Customer may execute the SOFTWARE on a different CPU during the period of such malfunction.

(d)   Upon thirty (30) days prior written notice, Customer may transfer the SOFTWARE to another CPU of equal processing power or to a CPU of greater processing power upon payment of an additional license fee calculated in accordance with Schedule "K" attached to this Agreement and made a part hereof. Such notice shall specify the date of the transfer and thereafter the Hardware shall be the CPU designated in such notice.

(e)   Customer shall be entitled to make up to two (2) copies of the SOFTWARE for back-up or archival purposes. Customer shall keep a record of each copy made, where such copy is located and in whose custody it is in.

(f)   Customer shall not reverse engineer, decompile, disassemble, re-engineer or otherwise attempt to discover the source code or the structural framework of the SOFTWARE.

Knowing the practical ramifications of the foregoing provision will allow

---

29. The licensing provision is the most important clause negotiated. Therefore, we have departed from the usual practice of providing a recommended clause. Instead, licensing language usually found in vendor agreements is reproduced in order to highlight areas of concern and suggest alternative negotiating strategies.

30. In cases where customized or custom software is developed, direct ownership of the programs to be developed should be negotiated with the vendor. You may wish to refer back to the discussion in Sections 3 and 4 of Chapter Two. Clearly, if ownership vests in you, licensing considerations become moot.

you to negotiate a licensing clause appropriate to your contemplated use. Each is discussed below.

☐ **LIMITED USERS:** Paragraph (a) limits the number of people who can use the software at the same time to seven[31]. When negotiating the licensing clause it is obviously preferable to have no limitation on the maximum number of concurrent users. In particular, where the licensing clause limits execution of the software to a particular CPU, an argument can be made that a user limitation is superfluous. Each CPU has its respective maximum processing capacity as well as the maximum number of terminal devices it can support. If too many users are accessing the software, hardware capacity will be exceeded and software performance will be significantly degraded.

When the vendor nevertheless insists on such a limitation, you should consider the total number of users expected to use the software (concurrently and sequentially) and increase it by a percentage representing future growth of your business. This approach to establishing the maximum number of users will delay the imposition of additional license fees until the economic conditions of your business warrant them.

☐ **NORMAL BUSINESS OPERATION:** Paragraph (b) limits use of the software to supporting your "normal business operation as presently conducted". When source code is licensed, a restriction of this nature may be appropriate. Access to source code allows you to modify the software to the point where it can support different requirements from those that were originally contemplated. The fact that software programs frequently use a RDBMS makes modifications even easier to accomplish. For example, a time scheduling software program could be modified to perform client billing as well. When the vendor markets time scheduling and client billing as two separate programs and receives a license fee for each, it suffers an economic loss from this type of modification.

Justification for the limitation is more difficult when only an object code license is granted. Since you are not able to enhance or otherwise modify the software program, why should you be prevented from using it as creatively as possible? Besides, the vendor would seem to be adequately

---

☐* 31. The number of users was arbitrarily selected for purposes of this discussion.

protected if the licensing provision is limited to a particular CPU (discussed in next section).

Regardless of whether a source or object code license is conferred, a limitation on use can, and usually does, create problems of interpretation. What is meant by "normal business operation as presently conducted?". Courts generally interpret such ambiguous limitations narrowly and usually against the vendor. Unfortunately, the presence of this language gives the vendor leverage unless you are willing to test its enforceability in court.

From the vendor's perspective, the use limitation does protect a legitimate concern, which is to prevent your use of the software to process another firm's data. However, this concern should be addressed specifically by the following sentence:

Customer shall have the right to use the SOFTWARE only to process its own data. In no event shall Customer process the data of any other entity.

☐ **DESIGNATED CPU:** Generally, the price of computer hardware has a direct relationship to its processing power. As processing power increases, so does price. Similarly, many software vendors, in particular RDBMS and operating system software vendors, impose a higher license fee based on the hardware's processing power.

A pricing strategy tied to processing power can result in an equitable distribution of license fees and also allows the vendor to reach a broader segment of the market. For example, assume the vendor charged a license fee of fifty thousand dollars regardless of the hardware platform. Customer A, processing ten thousand transactions per day, would pay the same license fee as Customer B, processing five hundred daily transactions. It is likely that Customer B would not be able to justify the license fee resulting in lost revenue to the vendor. In addition, such a pricing strategy discriminates against customers with fewer transactions. A tiered pricing strategy pegged to hardware processing power allows the vendor to accomplish both goals of market penetration and fair pricing.

When the license agreement contains a CPU limitation, care must be exercised to ensure your continued use of the software is not interrupted if the designated CPU becomes inoperable or is replaced with equal or greater processing power. Paragraphs (c) and (d) of the licensing provision reproduced above provide the necessary wording for this purpose.

☐ **COPIES:** Duplication of software is a fairly simple process and unless appropriately controlled can result in lost revenue to the vendor. Uncontrolled duplication will also prejudice the vendor's ability to claim the software as a trade secret.

Uninterrupted use of the software by the customer must be weighed against the vendor's desire to control duplication. Therefore, the license clause should allow you to make a limited number of copies so that the software can be restored if the main copy is damaged, destroyed or is otherwise inaccessible. Paragraph (e) of the licensing provision reproduced above allows the customer to make up to two copies of the software, striking a fair compromise and giving each party the necessary protection desired.

☐ **REVERSE ENGINEERING:** As discussed earlier, object code cannot be understood by humans and therefore, software is generally licensed in object code format to preserve the trade secret and confidential nature of its structure, sequence, architecture and algorithms. Reverse engineering is the process by which the software's object code is dissected and converted to a form which is readily understandable to humans in order to uncover the process by which it was developed. Because reverse engineering can frustrate the vendor's legitimate efforts to maintain confidentiality, the restriction contained in paragraph (e) of the licensing provision reproduced above is appropriate for the vendor's protection and commonly found in the licensing clause.

3.2 Site and Corporate Licenses

When business plans envision continued deployment of the *System* throughout your organization, the licensing provision reproduced in the preceding section will result in the payment of additional license fees. As a hedge against such fees, you should consider investing in a corporate or site license. A corporate license allows you to execute the software on any CPU located anywhere in your organization. Site licenses are limited to CPUs located at a defined location.

Because corporate or site licenses carry better margins for the vendor, you can usually negotiate away restrictions limiting use with greater ease. The following clause is typical of a corporate-wide license.

Customer may use the SOFTWARE to support Customer's current and future data processing requirements on any and all of Customer's central pro-

cessing units, whether owned, leased, rented or otherwise under the control of the Customer, provided that such central processing units are located within the United States.[32]

3.3 Shrink-Wrap Licenses

Pre-packaged software which can be mass marketed is usually sold through mail order and retail stores. Consequently it is not practical to negotiate the terms and conditions of each license and require each user to sign the agreement. Therefore, vendors seek to narrowly define the scope of use to which the software may be put and at the same time limit liability and warranty obligations by resorting to "shrink-wrap" or "self-executing" licenses.

A shrink-wrap license agreement is printed on paper placed on the outside of the software package and covered with clear plastic wrap, so that the agreement may be read by the user prior to opening the package. The agreement typically provides that opening the plastic wrap and/or using the software constitutes acceptance of the terms and conditions of the license agreement.

The enforceability of shrink-wrap licenses is questionable[33]. Courts that have ruled on the subject have reached similar results based on various legal theories. Some courts have decided that the "take it or leave it" nature of shrink-wrap licenses is a akin to a contract of adhesion and therefore against public policy. Other courts have denied enforcement of shrink-wrap licenses on the basis that there cannot be an "acceptance" of the agreement's terms by the mere opening of the software package[34]. We have not devoted much discussion to shrink-wrap licenses because such agreements by their nature are non-negotiable.

---

32. It is common for vendors to control export of computer hardware and software outside the United States in order to comply with applicable United States Department of Commerce regulations. In addition, export to a country that has weak or non-existent laws protecting intellectual property can cause the vendor serious economic harm.

33. This may change if the proposed amendments to the Uniform Commercial Code are adopted. Specifically, the American Law Institute has suggested a provision, Section 2-2203, which would make standard form shrink-wrap licenses enforceable in certain cases.

34. In a recent case decided by the United States District Court for the Western District of Wisconsin, the Court held that a contract was formed at the time the software was purchased and that the terms of a shrink-wrap license agreement subsequently discovered by the user could not be enforced against the user. *ProCD, Inc. v. Zeidenberg* (W.D. Wis. 1996).

4. DOCUMENTATION

4.1 Examples

After devoting a considerable amount of time, money and resources, you now have the "Rolls Royce" of *Systems*. However, when you don't know how to drive and an operator's manual is not provided, your new and expensive car is unlikely to fulfill your requirements. Likewise, comprehensive documentation will, to a large degree, determine the extent to which the *System* implementation is successful and used effectively and efficiently by your personnel.

Documentation can be used to refer to a variety of different materials useful to the design, development, operation, maintenance and modification of the *System*. Documentation can include:

☐ **FUNCTIONAL SPECIFICATION:** Software design and development begins with a detailed description of the business functions expected to be performed. Therefore, this document must be carefully prepared to ensure all of your requirements are properly supported. Completion of the functional specification will be facilitated if a comprehensive requirements definition is prepared.

☐ **SYSTEM DESIGN SPECIFICATIONS:** The logical operation of how data will be processed by the *System* is identified in a system design specification. This document should describe: (a) each process affecting data entry, manipulation, comparison, storage and retrieval;[35] (b) record, file, report, and screen formats; (c) programming language and standards; (d) RDBMS requirements and integration; (e) computer hardware and operating system environment; (f) *System* performance, including response time requirements; (g) interfaces to all required third party *Systems* and information services and (h) *System* diagnostic procedures including error detection.

☐ **USER MANUAL:** Clear and concise directions describing how the *System* is to be used is a basic and fundamental prerequisite to its adoption and effective and efficient use.

☐* 35. Flow charts depicting each process, as well as a written description should be provided by the vendor.

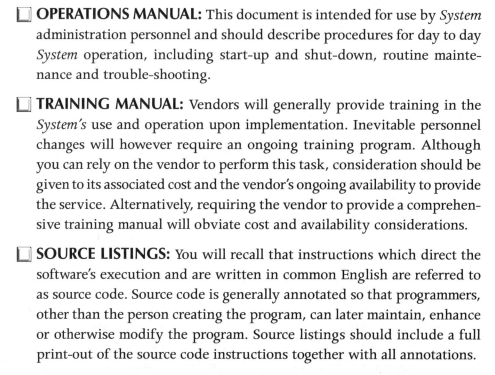

☐ **OPERATIONS MANUAL:** This document is intended for use by *System* administration personnel and should describe procedures for day to day *System* operation, including start-up and shut-down, routine maintenance and trouble-shooting.

☐ **TRAINING MANUAL:** Vendors will generally provide training in the *System's* use and operation upon implementation. Inevitable personnel changes will however require an ongoing training program. Although you can rely on the vendor to perform this task, consideration should be given to its associated cost and the vendor's ongoing availability to provide the service. Alternatively, requiring the vendor to provide a comprehensive training manual will obviate cost and availability considerations.

☐ **SOURCE LISTINGS:** You will recall that instructions which direct the software's execution and are written in common English are referred to as source code. Source code is generally annotated so that programmers, other than the person creating the program, can later maintain, enhance or otherwise modify the program. Source listings should include a full print-out of the source code instructions together with all annotations.

The composition of the procured *System* will to a large extent determine which of the above described materials should be included as part of the vendor's deliverables. Regardless of the type of documentation provided, you should request a copy in printed format as well computer readable disk or tape.

4.2 Pre-Packaged Software and Hardware

User, operations and training documentation usually exists and can be readily identified as a deliverable when pre-packaged software or hardware is procured. However, a functional specification should nevertheless be developed by the vendor with the customer's assistance. The functional specification is generally comprised of the requirements definition, the RFP and the existing user manual. The functional specification helps flesh out the *System's* required capabilities by forcing a function by function review by both parties.[36] In addition, the system design specification and source listings should be delivered to the escrow agent in accordance with the escrow agreement, discussed earlier in Section 6 of Chapter Five.

The following clause contains suitable wording describing the vendor's

---

36. If you agree to simply reference existing documentation, make sure to review its content, sequence and structure to ensure that it is complete and easily understandable.

documentation obligation when pre-packaged software and computer hardware are procured together:

ABC shall provide Customer with the following Documentation:

(a) user, operations and training manuals for the SOFTWARE;

(b) user, operations and training manuals for version 3.5 of the XTX operating system software;

(c) user, operations and training manuals for Superior Computer model SC 500; and

(d) functional specification entitled "Functional Requirements For Professional Trading Company, Ltd." dated May 23, 1996 containing 274 pages, the first page of which is initialed by the parties hereto.[37]

4.3 Custom Software Development

Pre-packaged software and, to a lesser extent customized software, offers the advantage of regular program updates. The economics of custom software render updates costly and less certain,[38] posing a risk as your business grows and new requirements evolve. Functional specifications and, more to the point, system design specifications will give you the flexibility to decide how, and by whom, updates are developed. Therefore, comprehensive documentation is particularly important when custom software is procured.

All too often documentation takes a back seat to software development. Because documentation is usually one of the last tasks scheduled in the development process, it is usually completed in a haphazard manner. Unfortunately, you do not realize the consequences of inadequate documentation until the time you need it most. To avoid this pitfall, standards for the type, structure, content and quality of documentation to be produced by the vendor should be specified in the agreement.

---

37. If the functional specification cannot be prepared prior to execution of the agreement, acceptance provisions similar to those suggested for acceptance of custom software documentation (discussed in Section 12 of this Chapter) should be incorporated in the agreement's acceptance clause.

38. Custom software is developed for your particular requirements and therefore may not be suitable for other companies. Besides, as discussed earlier in Chapter Three, competitive advantages may counsel against allowing competitors to similarly benefit. Because the vendor cannot amortize the development cost across multiple customer sites, it has to levy a higher fee for updates in order to recover its development cost and a reasonable profit margin.

Procurement agreements usually call for documentation to be "of the highest quality" or "state of the art". In some cases, an independent source for standards is referenced. However, either approach may not adequately define the documentation standard. "Highest quality" or "state of the art" are subjective terms and require their own definition. Although referencing independent standards are objective and therefore preferable, considerations leading to their formulation may have little or no relevance to the type of software being developed or how and by whom it will be used. It therefore behooves you to prepare documentation standards independently. Enlisting the assistance of a consultant for this purpose is recommended unless you have in-house expertise. If the vendor takes on this responsibility, you should have the right of review and approval.

The following clause contains suitable wording describing the vendor's documentation obligation for custom software:

ABC shall provide Customer with the following Documentation by the dates set forth in Schedule "B" attached to this Agreement and made a part hereof:

(a) ABC shall prepare a Functional Specification describing each business function to be performed by the SOFTWARE. The Functional Specification shall include: (i) all of the business functions identified in Customer's RFP attached to this Agreement as Schedule "F" and made a part hereof and (ii) Customer's current procedures for the purchase and sale of securities in the over the counter market;

(b) ABC shall prepare a System Design Specification for each business function described in the Functional Specification which shall include (by way of example and not limitation): (i) data inputs and outputs, including codes and acronyms; (ii) program descriptions; (iii) file descriptions, formats and layouts; (iv) report descriptions and layouts; (v) screen descriptions and layouts; (vi) interface requirements and descriptions; (vii) processing flow charts; (viii) programming standards; (ix) processing narratives; (x) editing rules; (xi) error detection procedures; (xii) performance and response time requirements; (xiii) hardware and communication requirements and (ivx) RDBMS requirements; and

(c) user, operations and training manuals.

All Documentation shall be produced in accordance and compliance with the standards identified in Schedule "G" attached to this Agreement and made a part hereof.

4.4 Customized Software Development

Documentation requirements for customized software are similar to those for custom software. However for ease of reference, user, operations and training manuals should be produced for the complete software program, as customized. Also, documentation standards may be easier to define by reference to existing documentation for the pre-packaged software, as long as such documentation is satisfactory.

As discussed earlier, separate license and development agreements should be executed. The license agreement should contain paragraph (a) of the clause recommended above for pre-packaged software documentation.[39] The software development agreement should contain the following clause for customized software documentation:

ABC shall provide Customer with the following Documentation by the dates set forth in Schedule "B" attached to this Agreement and made a part hereof:

(a) ABC shall prepare the Functional Specification document which together with version 4 of the "STOCK" software program's user manual (the "User Manual") shall describe each business function to be performed by the SOFTWARE. The Functional Specification shall include: (i) all of the features and functions described in the User Manual; (ii) all of the business functions identified in Customer's RFP and (iii) Customer's current procedures for the purchase and sale of securities in the over the counter market;

(b) ABC shall prepare a System Design Specification document for each business function described in the Functional Specification which shall include (by way of example and not limitation): (i) data inputs and outputs, including codes and acronyms; (ii) program descriptions; (iii) file descriptions, formats and layouts; (iv) report descriptions and layouts; (v) screen descriptions and layouts; (vi) interface requirements and descriptions; (vii) processing flow charts; (viii) programming standards; (ix) processing narratives; (x) editing rules; (xi) error detection procedures; (xii) performance and response time requirements; (xiii) hardware and communication requirements and (ivx) RDBMS requirements; and

---

39. Although it may appear needlessly duplicative to have user, operations and training manuals delivered under both agreements, existing documentation should be delivered under the license agreement in order to identify functions and features that may still be subject to the vendor's standard warranty, maintenance and update obligations. In addition, pre-packaged software documentation will help identify whether an error existed in the pre-packaged software or results from customized modifications.

(c)   user, operations and training manuals for the SOFTWARE.

All Documentation shall be produced in accordance and compliance with the same standards used to produce documentation for the STOCK software program.

5. PRICING AND PAYMENT TERMS

After weeks of negotiating, the vendor has finally acceded to the price you offered. However, the agreement requires payment of a majority of the total procurement price three weeks before the *System* is to be delivered let alone installed and tested. You've made the required payments but delivery of the *System* was late and never passed the acceptance tests. Unfortunately, the vendor filed for protection under the bankruptcy laws shortly thereafter. The foregoing may be an extreme example but it serves to illustrate that price should never be viewed in a vacuum. A pure "bottom line" approach may also cause you to overlook the possibility that an otherwise budget breaking software license fee may be payable in installments as a royalty over a specified period of time.

Pricing and payment terms will vary depending on the items being procured, their respective states of completion, your negotiating abilities and creativity. A common principle that is applicable to all agreements however cautions that payments be tendered only against milestones that have been achieved. Payment milestones for pre-packaged software, hardware, custom and customized software differ only in the number and type of milestones. When custom or customized software is procured, the payment schedule should be weighted more towards the end of the implementation cycle with the final payment held back until the warranty period has expired.

5.1 Pre-Packaged Software and Hardware

The following clause is recommended when pre-packaged software and hardware are procured together:

1. Customer shall pay ABC one hundred fifty thousand United States dollars ($150,000) for the SOFTWARE License Fee and Hardware, payable as follows:

(a) fifteen thousand dollars ($15,000) upon execution of this Agreement;

(b) twenty thousand dollars ($20,000) upon delivery of the Hardware,

Installation of the SOFTWARE and confirmation by Customer that the SOFTWARE's program files listed in Schedule "J" attached to this Agreement and made a part hereof reside on the Hardware's program libraries;

(c) fifteen thousand dollars ($15,000) upon delivery of all Documentation to Customer;

(d) eighty thousand dollars ($80,000) upon Acceptance of the Hardware and SOFTWARE; and

(e) twenty thousand dollars ($20,000) upon the later of: (i) expiration of the warranty period or (ii) all warranty claims having been properly satisfied by ABC.

2. The Customer shall pay any sales or use tax imposed by the New York State and/or New York City government(s) in connection with the SOFTWARE or Hardware.

3. The Customer shall pay all transportation charges associated with shipment and delivery of the Hardware and SOFTWARE to the Installation Site together with the reasonable expenses incurred by ABC in performing its obligations hereunder. Expenses which: (a) individually are in excess of two hundred fifty dollars ($250) or (b) during any calendar month would cause total expenses incurred in such month to exceed five hundred dollars, shall not be incurred without Customer's prior written consent.

4. Invoices shall be payable within thirty (30) days after Customer's receipt of ABC's invoice, so long as the amounts stated therein are not reasonably in dispute.

5.2 Custom Software Development

The following clause is recommended when custom software is procured on a fixed cost basis. Fixed price development limits your risk, however vendors are not always willing to execute such agreements when the deliverables have not been adequately defined in functional and design specifications. Therefore, paragraph 2[40] of the following clause affords both parties the right to terminate

---

40. Paragraph 2 of the recommended clause should not be included when the functional and system design specifications have been agreed to before the agreement is signed. It is up to the vendor to ensure that it has properly estimated the work effort and can deliver the software within the fixed cost.

the agreement in the event that consensus cannot be reached with respect to the specifications and the associated development cost.[41]

1. Subject to paragraph 2 of this Article, Customer shall pay ABC one hundred thousand United States dollars ($100,000) for the SOFTWARE license fee[42], payable as follows:

(a) ten thousand dollars ($10,000) upon execution of this Agreement;

(b) five thousand dollars ($5,000) upon Acceptance of the Functional Specifications;

(c) five thousand dollars ($5,000) upon Acceptance of the System Design Specifications;

(d) ten thousand dollars ($10,000) upon delivery and Installation of the SOFTWARE and confirmation by Customer that the SOFTWARE's program files listed in Schedule "K" attached to this Agreement and made a part hereof reside on the Hardware's program libraries;

(e) twenty thousand dollars ($20,000) upon Acceptance of the SOFTWARE;

(f) fifteen thousand dollars ($15,000) upon Acceptance of the user, operations and training Documentation; and

(g) thirty five thousand dollars ($35,000) upon the later of: (i) expiration of the warranty period or (ii) all warranty claims having been properly satisfied by ABC.

2. In the event that: (a) the Customer does not give its Acceptance of the Functional Specification or the System Design Specification within the time frames specified in Section 7 of this Agreement or (b) Customer and ABC fail to reach agreement with respect to the fixed charge for development of the SOFTWARE within ten (10) business days after the last date by which the System Design Specification can be Accepted, either party may terminate

---

41. Paragraph 2 of the recommended clause allows the vendor to retain a reasonable amount for its efforts in preparing the functional and system design specifications. If possible, this language should not be included in the agreement. If specifications are not accepted, each party shares in the risk and cost inasmuch as both parties will lose their investment of time and resources devoted to its preparation.

42. If you are to receive ownership of the software being developed, the words "license fee" should be deleted.

this Agreement upon ten (10) business days prior written notice. This Agreement shall terminate automatically five (5) business days after the receipt of such notice by the receiving party if an agreement on the Functional Specification, System Design Specification or the fixed charge, as applicable, has not been reached in writing by the expiration of such five (5) day period. In the event that this Agreement is terminated in accordance with this paragraph, within five (5) business days after the effective date of termination, ABC shall refund all monies paid by Customer in accordance with this Section less: (a) three thousand five hundred dollars ($3,500) in the event this Agreement is terminated for failure to reach agreement with respect to the Functional Specification or (b) seven thousand dollars ($7,000) in the event this Agreement is terminated for failure to reach agreement with respect to the System Design Specification or the fixed price for development of the SOFTWARE, which amount(s) vendor shall be entitled to retain for its efforts in connection with preparation of the Specification(s).

3. The Customer shall pay any sales or use tax imposed by the New York State and/or New York City government(s) in connection with the SOFTWARE.

4. The Customer shall reimburse the reasonable expenses incurred by ABC in performing its obligations hereunder. Expenses which: (a) individually are in excess of two hundred fifty dollars ($250) or (b) during any calendar month would cause total expenses incurred in such month to exceed five hundred dollars, shall not be incurred without Customer's prior written consent.

5. Invoices shall be payable within thirty (30) days after Customer's receipt of ABC's invoice, so long as the amounts stated therein are not reasonably in dispute.

5.3 Customized Software Development

Customized software procurement will entail payments under both license and customized software development agreements. Although the customized software deliverable is based on pre-existing software, its value is dependent on modifications and enhancements to be developed by the vendor. Therefore, payment milestones should be weighted more towards the completion of tasks identified in the customized software services agreement.

The following payment schedule clause is recommended for the pre-packaged software deliverable under the license agreement:

1. Customer shall pay ABC twenty five thousand dollars ($25,000)[43] for the Licensed Program[44] License Fee, payable as follows:

(a) five thousand dollars ($5,000) upon execution of this Agreement;

(b) five thousand dollars ($5,000) upon delivery and Installation of the SOFTWARE (as defined in the Agreement for Customized Software Services between the parties of even date herewith, the "Development Agreement") and confirmation by Customer that the SOFTWARE's program files listed in Schedule "K" attached to the Development Agreement reside on the Hardware's program libraries;

(c) seven thousand five hundred dollars ($7,500) upon Acceptance of the SOFTWARE; and

(d) seven thousand five hundred dollars ($7,500) upon the later of: (i) expiration of the warranty period applicable to the SOFTWARE or (ii) all SOFTWARE warranty claims having been properly satisfied by ABC.

2. The Customer shall pay any sales or use tax imposed by the New York State and/or New York City government(s) in connection with the Licensed Program.

[The balance of this clause consists of paragraphs 3, 4 and 5 of the custom software agreement payment clause.]

The following payment schedule clause is recommended for the customized software deliverable under the customized software services agreement:

1. Subject to paragraph 2 of this Section, Customer shall pay ABC seventy five thousand dollars ($75,000) for the SOFTWARE License Fee[45], payable as follows:

(a) five thousand dollars ($5,000) upon execution of this Agreement;

---

43. The license fee attributable to the pre-packaged software component should be kept to a reasonable minimum in order to limit the incidence of sales tax.

44. The term "Licensed Program" is used in this clause to identify the pre-packaged software and differentiate it from the customized software which is referred to as the "SOFTWARE" in the customized software services agreement.

45. If you are to receive ownership of the software being developed, the words "license fee" should be deleted.

(b) five thousand dollars ($5,000) upon Acceptance of the Functional Specification;

(c) five thousand dollars ($5,000) upon Acceptance of the System Design Specification;

(d) ten thousand dollars ($10,000) upon delivery and Installation of the SOFTWARE and confirmation by Customer that the SOFTWARE's program files listed in Schedule "K" attached to this Agreement and made a part hereof reside on the Hardware's program libraries;

(e) twenty thousand dollars ($20,000) upon Acceptance of the SOFTWARE;

(f) ten thousand dollars ($10,000) upon Acceptance of the user, operations and training Documentation; and

(g) twenty thousand dollars ($20,000) upon the later of: (i) expiration of the warranty period or (ii) all warranty claims having been properly satisfied by ABC.

2. In the event that: (a) the Customer does not give its Acceptance of the Functional Specification or the System Design Specification within the time frames specified in Schedule B of this Agreement or (b) Customer and ABC fail to reach agreement with respect to a fixed charge for development of the SOFTWARE within ten (10) business days after the last date by which the System Design Specification can be Accepted, either party may terminate this Agreement and the License Agreement upon ten (10) business days prior written notice. This Agreement and the License Agreement shall terminate automatically five (5) business days after the receipt of such notice by the receiving party if an agreement on the Functional Specification, System Design Specification or fixed charge, as applicable, has not been reached in writing by the expiration of such five (5) day period. In the event that this Agreement and the License Agreement are terminated in accordance with this paragraph, within five (5) business days after the effective date of termination, ABC shall refund all monies paid by Customer to ABC under: (a) the License Agreement and (b) in accordance with this Section less: (i) three thousand five hundred dollars ($3,500) in the event the Agreements are terminated for failure to reach agreement with respect to the Functional Specification or (ii) seven thousand dollars ($7,000) in the event the Agreements are terminated for failure to reach agreement with respect to the System Design Specification or the fixed charge for development of the

SOFTWARE, which amount(s) vendor shall be entitled to retain for its efforts in connection with preparation of the Specification(s).[46]

[The balance of this clause consists of paragraphs 3, 4 and 5 of the custom software agreement payment clause.]

6. PRICE PROTECTION

You have negotiated price to the bone. No other customer will ever be given a lower price. Vendors may make this claim and many times it is genuine. Still, how can you be sure? An effective provision, commonly referred to as a "most favored customer clause", is useful in ensuring that you will benefit from a lower price at which the vendor may sell and/or license the *System* in the future. If the vendor's protestations are indeed real, it should have no objection to the following provision:

ABC warrants that the terms of this Agreement are comparable to or better than the terms offered by ABC to any of its present commercial customers of equal or lesser size for comparable deliverables and/or services. If ABC offers more favorable terms to its commercial customers during the period commencing on the date hereof and expiring one year thereafter, such terms shall also be made available to Customer together with any resulting refund within thirty (30) days from the execution of such agreement.

The one year term during which the provision is effective should afford you sufficient protection without having the effect of penalizing the vendor. It is a fact of life that technological capability and price seem to have an inverse relationship and therefore it is reasonable to expect that the *System* you acquire today may cost less in the future.

7. OWNERSHIP

Earlier in this book, we discussed the general practice of licensing software versus title to computer hardware being granted to the customer upon purchase. Although it is unlikely and cost prohibitive to acquire title to pre-packaged software, title is a reasonable issue for negotiation in connec-

---

46. Paragraph 2 of the recommended clause should not be included where the functional and system design specifications have been agreed to before the agreement is signed. It is up to the vendor to ensure that it has properly estimated the work effort and can deliver the software within the fixed cost.

tion with customized and custom software[47]. Clearly, ownership is the best way to ensure that you benefit exclusively from the time, resources and money invested in software procurement.

Because software is an intangible, any ownership interest must be clearly defined to include copyright as well as the software program's underlying ideas and concepts. Copyright ownership confers the exclusive right to reproduce the software program and extends only to the manner in which the program *is expressed*. Copyright does **not** protect ideas, procedures, concepts or techniques. Therefore, another program can perform all of the same functions and, as long as the manner in which it is *expressed or presented* is the result of independent development, there is no copyright infringement.

This apparent gap in copyright protection limits its effectiveness. Particularly when custom software is developed, your ideas, procedures and concepts should not be used by the vendor to develop a similar software program. Therefore, the following ownership clause grants the customer ownership of the copyright and/or other statutory property rights as well as the ideas, concepts and/or techniques used in developing the software program:

ABC acknowledges that Customer shall have exclusive, unlimited ownership rights to all work performed hereunder, to all materials and/or deliverables prepared for the Customer hereunder and all ideas, concepts, inventions, designs, techniques conceived by Customer or jointly with ABC hereunder, as a combination of components and/or individually, and whether or not this Agreement is satisfactorily completed, all of which shall be deemed work made for hire[48] and made in the course of services rendered and shall belong exclusively to the Customer with the Customer having the right to obtain, hold and render, in its own name patents, copyrights and registrations therefor. In the event that certain other ownership rights do not originally vest in Customer as contemplated hereunder, ABC agrees to irrevocably assign, transfer and convey to the Customer all rights, title and interest therein. ABC and its personnel shall give Customer, and any person designated by Customer, all reasonable assistance and shall execute all necessary documents to assist and/or enable Customer to perfect, preserve, register and/or record its rights in any such work, deliverables or material.

---

47. Please refer to Sections 3 and 4 of Chapter Three.

48 . The words "work for hire" have the specific legal consequence of causing ownership of all software developed and other work performed by the vendor to vest in you.

8. CONFIDENTIALITY

In Chapter Four, we discussed the importance of executing a written confidentiality agreement prior to disclosure of your company's business practices and requirements. You may wish to refer back to that discussion. Because procurement agreements generally contain an "integration clause" stating that all prior understandings and agreements are superseded,[49] confidentiality obligations should be repeated in the procurement agreement as well.

9. SITE PREPARATION

Computer hardware installation and operation usually require a special environment which may consist of raised flooring, power supplies, electric current conditioners, climate control and extensive cabling. The extent to which the site must be prepared is mostly a function of the type of hardware with personal and mainframe computers being at opposite ends of the spectrum.

Site preparation is generally the responsibility of the customer and, if it is not performed properly, can delay installation, cause *System* failures and vitiate warranty coverage. Therefore, detailed site preparation requirements should be attached as a schedule to the hardware procurement agreement. In addition, the vendor should inspect the site with a view towards obtaining its written approval prior to shipment, as expressed in the following site preparation clause:

Customer shall be responsible for preparation of the Installation Site in accordance with the specifications attached to this Agreement as Schedule "M" and made a part hereof. At such time that the Installation Site has been prepared, Customer shall give written notice thereof to ABC and within five (5) business days after receipt of Customer's notice by ABC, ABC shall inspect the Installation Site and either give its approval or disapproval. In the event ABC does not approve the Installation Site, it shall provide detailed reasons therefor within three (3) business days after its inspection in which case Customer shall correct the deficiencies identified by ABC and the inspection process shall be repeated.

---

49. Integration clauses are discussed in Section 19 of this Chapter.

10. DELIVERY

Delivery timeframes for the various deliverables comprising the *System* must be effectively coordinated so that they occur at their prescribed times. Delay in the delivery of any item will disrupt the entire implementation schedule and cause working capital to be tied up and/or finance charges to be incurred for the other items delivered on schedule.

Unfortunately, it is common for delivery schedules to slip. Therefore you should allow for possible delays in your planning process. Although the agreement should afford the vendor reasonable grace periods, additional resources or personnel should be devoted by the vendor to minimize delays and, beyond the applicable grace period, afford you the remedy of termination and/or liquidated damages if such delay occurs,[50] as the following clause provides: [51]

> *The SOFTWARE shall be developed, delivered and implemented in accordance with Schedule "B" attached to this Agreement and made a part hereof. ABC understands that that Customer has contracted for the licensing and/or purchase and delivery of other items of software and/or hardware comprising a major computer system to be implemented for Customer and therefore it is vital that the dates stated in Schedule "B" be met otherwise Customer will incur substantial additional expense and injury. In the event that ABC fails to perform in accordance with the dates stated in Schedule "B", ABC shall assign additional qualified staff to the development, delivery and implementation, as applicable, of the SOFTWARE. Without limiting any of its rights under this Agreement and at law, ABC shall pay Customer one thousand dollars ($1,000), as liquidated damages, for each business day after the fourth business day that it fails to complete a task, milestone or other delivery required to be made or performed in accordance with this Agreement and/or terminate this Agreement in accordance with Section 15.*

---

50. Liquidated damages is discussed in Section 16 of this Chapter; termination is discussed in Section 18.

51. Although referring to and intended for custom and customized software, this clause can also be used in conjunction with the installation provision discussed in Section 11 of this Chapter.

11. INSTALLATION

Installation can be performed by either the vendor or the customer. However, improper installation may result in the vendor disclaiming its warranty obligation. Therefore, for more complex *Systems*, it is recommended that installation be performed by the vendor.

In most agreements, installation can trigger a payment obligation and/or commencement of the warranty period. However, installation alone does not necessarily mean the *System* is error free and can be used productively. Although it may be appropriate for the vendor to require a partial payment upon installation, in no event should the warranty commence until the *System* has been accepted (which is the topic of Section 12).

11.1 Computer Hardware

Installation of computer hardware is usually defined in standard vendor agreements as the date upon which the hardware has successfully operated the vendor's standard installation tests and programs. The vendor's test programs should therefore be reviewed with an eye towards completeness and applicability to your contemplated use. Alternatively, as with acceptance tests, it is to your advantage to independently develop and attach to the agreement the test plans required to demonstrate that installation has occurred, as reflected in the following clause:

1. Installation of the Hardware shall be the responsibility of ABC and shall be completed by the dates specified in the Implementation Schedule attached hereto as Schedule B and made a part hereof. As a condition to Installation, Customer shall prepare the Installation Site in accordance with the site preparation requirements identified in Schedule "F" attached to this Agreement. Installation of the Hardware shall be deemed complete when the Hardware is ready for live production use as evidenced by successful completion of the Installation Tests described in Schedule "G" attached hereto and made a part hereof.

2. If through no fault of the Customer, Installation is not complete by the date specified therefor in the Implementation Schedule, in addition to all other rights and remedies available to the Customer under this Agreement *and at law, ABC shall pay Customer one thousand dollars ($1,000) for each business day after the fourth business day that Installation is not completed.*[52]

11.2 Software

As with hardware, installation tests should be agreed upon and attached as a schedule to the agreement. Software installation tests should demonstrate that each of the data screens within the software can be displayed although data does not necessarily have to be processed at this point, as reflected in the following clause:

1. Installation of the SOFTWARE shall be the responsibility of ABC and shall be completed by the date specified in the Implementation Schedule attached hereto as Schedule F and made a part hereof. As a condition to Installation, Customer shall prepare the Installation Site in accordance with the site preparation requirements identified in Schedule "G" attached hereto and made a part hereof. Installation shall be deemed complete when each of the data screens identified in Schedule "H" can be displayed on the Hardware's terminal devices.

2. If through no fault of the Customer, Installation is not complete by the date specified therefor in the Implementation Schedule, in addition to all other rights and remedies available to the Customer under this Agreement and at law, ABC shall pay Customer one thousand dollars ($1,000) for each business day after the fourth business day that Installation is not completed.

12. ACCEPTANCE

Acceptance is an important milestone in the implementation process, often causing a significant portion of the *System* price to become payable as well as fixing the warranty period's commencement date. Therefore, each major deliverable should be subjected to well defined and comprehensive acceptance test procedures.

---

52. This liquidated damages clause and the one recited in Section 11.2 is suggested in connection with the procurement of hardware and pre-packaged software. For custom and customized software, the liquidated damages clause reproduced in Section 10 of this Chapter is recommended. Custom and customized software generally involve delivery in phases whereas pre-packaged software and hardware can be readily installed.

Although additional work will be required on your part, it behooves you to prepare and perform the test plans by which the various deliverables will be measured. This is because: (a) you know better than anyone else how the *System* will be used and therefore how test plans can replicate each process and (b) particularly with respect to software, the vendor is too close to the program to objectively and vigorously test each function.[53] Assistance from a consultant can expedite preparation of the test plans.

An effective acceptance test strategy will include parallel processing for the duration of the acceptance test and for a limited period of time thereafter. During parallel processing, data is processed using both the then current processing methodology and the new *System*. Results from each are then compared for possible discrepancies and their causes.

12.1 Computer Hardware

Acceptance tests for computer hardware should be designed to demonstrate reliability and, when agreed to by the vendor, performance and compatibility with application software.

☐ **RELIABILITY:** Computer hardware should be capable of operating without interruption for reasonable periods of time. Particularly with respect to on-line processing, hardware availability is critical. Therefore, one aspect of the acceptance test should identify the percentage of time the hardware is not available due to malfunction or required maintenance.[54]

☐ **PERFORMANCE:** Vendors publish performance and response time statistics in connection with the various hardware configurations they sell. However, these statistics may have little value in determining how effectively the hardware executes the application software. Moreover, when the hardware vendor is not furnishing application software, it is unlikely to include performance and response time criteria in the acceptance test because it has no familiarity with the software. A solution to this problem is possible when pre-packaged software is procured and

---

53. This is not meant to in any way impugn the integrity of vendors but rather to make sure that the proper operation of any process is not assumed.

54. Vendors often refer to the hardware's MTBF which is the mean time between failures. MTBF identifies, for a defined period, the total amount of time the hardware is operational divided by the total number of failures. Similar measurements include: the meantime between outages MTBO, mean time to repair MTTR and mean time to service restoral MTSR.

the hardware vendor can obtain a temporary license in order to execute performance and response time tests. [55]

☐ **COMPATIBILITY:** When the RFP has identified compatibility requirements, hardware acceptance tests should not be deemed complete until the application software is installed and shown to properly execute on the hardware.

The following acceptance provision assumes that the vendor has agreed to performance and compatibility criteria. If the test is not successfully completed, the customer would have the right to demand replacement of the hardware or terminate the agreement unless the vendor agrees to provide hardware with greater processing capability at no additional charge:

1. Customer shall prepare and, with the assistance of ABC, execute the Acceptance Test which includes those procedures required to demonstrate that the Hardware is: (a) compatible with and can execute the SOFTWARE[56] yielding response times for each process identified in Schedule "I" no greater than the times set forth alongside each process in said schedule; (b) capable of executing the SOFTWARE on a continuous basis without an Error or hardware related service interruption at least ninety percent (90%) of the time during the acceptance test period of forty five (45) consecutive calendar days; (c) performs in all material respects in accordance with the Documentation and (d) supports Customer's requirements as specified in the RFP. The RFP shall prevail in the event of an inconsistency between the RFP and the standards or documents referred to in this paragraph.

2. If the Hardware is not accepted within sixty (60) calendar days from commencement of the Acceptance Test, Customer may at its option, request a replacement of the Hardware or terminate this Agreement, in which event ABC shall refund all amounts paid by Customer to ABC hereunder and, as liquidated damages for its failure, pay Customer an amount equal to ten percent (10%) of the Hardware purchase price. Notwithstanding the foregoing, unless the Hardware was rejected due to lack of compatibility with the SOFTWARE, and in the event ABC

---

55. However under a turn-key solution agreement, the vendor can be expected to warrant hardware performance and response time in connection with specific application software programs. Turn-key solutions were discussed earlier in Section 2 of Chapter Five.

56. If access to the application software is not available, the vendor's test programs may have to be relied upon.

substitutes hardware acceptable to Customer with greater processing capability at no additional cost, Customer's right to terminate this Agreement shall be suspended for a period of forty five (45) consecutive days during which the Acceptance Test will be repeated in accordance with the criteria set forth in paragraph (1) of this Section.

3. In the event the Hardware is Accepted by Customer, Customer shall execute an Acceptance Certificate, the form of which is attached hereto as Schedule "J".

12.2 Documentation

Ideally, all *System* documentation should be developed and attached to the procurement agreement prior to execution. More often than not, however, functional and system design specifications for custom and customized software are prepared later. Therefore such documentation should be subjected to acceptance procedures as recommended by the following clause:

1. The Documentation developed by ABC pursuant to Section 4 of this Agreement shall be delivered for Customer's Acceptance not later than the dates specified in Schedule B attached hereto. Customer shall have thirty (30) calendar days (the "Review Period") to review each item of Documentation and either accept or reject such Documentation in accordance with this Section.

2. If an item of Documentation is unsatisfactory in any material respect, Customer shall prepare a detailed written description of its objections and deliver them to ABC not later than seven (7) business days after expiration of the Review Period. ABC shall thereupon undertake to modify the Documentation to respond to such objections and shall do so within ten (10) business days of receipt of Customer's objections.

3. If the Documentation continues to be unsatisfactory in any material respect after the revisions made in accordance with paragraph (2) of this Section, Customer may, in its sole discretion and option, grant ABC additional time to modify the Documentation so that it is conforming or terminate this Agreement. In that event ABC shall refund all amounts paid by Customer to ABC hereunder and, as liquidated damages for its failure, pay Customer five thousand dollars ($5,000).

12.3 Software

Since software is the result of a problem-solving process, it is unlikely to be completely error free. In some cases an error condition lies dormant until activated by the execution of a specific set of processes in a particular order. Acceptance test plans should therefore contemplate the manner in which each software function will be used to confirm that it operates properly. In addition, acceptance tests should confirm that the software accurately performs data and system back-up, data verification as well as recovery functions.

For the same reasons given by hardware vendors, software vendors are reticent to provide performance and response time commitments. However, when you are buying custom and customized software the vendor necessarily becomes intimately knowledgeable with respect to the hardware platform upon which the program is developed. Therefore, it is not unreasonable to require performance and response time criteria in the software acceptance test.

The following clause is recommended for pre-packaged, custom and customized software. However, when you are buying customized software, acceptance of the pre-packaged software component (under the separate license agreement) should not be given until the customized work has been accepted.

1. Customer shall prepare Test Plans consistent with the RFP and Functional and System Design Specifications on or before the date which is thirty (30) calendar days prior to the date the SOFTWARE is scheduled for Installation. The Test Plans shall include procedures required to demonstrate that the SOFTWARE operates in all material respects in accordance with the RFP and Functional and System Design Specifications. In the event of an inconsistency between the RFP or Functional or System Design Specifications, the RFP shall prevail. Customer shall prepare the data necessary for performing the Acceptance Test. Customer shall perform the Acceptance Test upon notice from ABC that the SOFTWARE is ready to undergo the Acceptance Test.

2. Within five (5) business days after completion of the Acceptance Test, Customer shall either give its Acceptance of the SOFTWARE or disapprove such results and provide detailed written reasons for such disapproval.

3. If the SOFTWARE or any portion thereof fails to pass the Acceptance Test, ABC will correct all Error(s) not later than fourteen (14) calendar days after receipt of Customer's notice describing the Error(s). Within fourteen (14) calendar days after such corrections have been made, Customer will retest the SOFTWARE. If the SOFTWARE still fails the Acceptance Test after corrections having been made in accordance with this paragraph (3), Customer may in its sole discretion and option, grant ABC additional time to correct the outstanding Error(s) or terminate this Agreement in which event ABC shall refund all amounts paid by Customer to ABC hereunder and, as liquidated damages for its failure, pay Customer ten thousand dollars ($10,000).

4. Acceptance of the SOFTWARE shall be deemed to have occurred upon execution of the an Acceptance Certificate, the form of which is attached hereto as Schedule "J"

13. TRAINING

As with documentation, a comprehensive and structured training program is essential to the efficient and effective use of the *System*. Training can take the form of one or both of the programs described below. Regardless of the training program selected, the agreement should require the vendor to provide a training manual allowing you to decide how ongoing training programs should be structured.

☐ **TRAINING THE TRAINERS:** Under this program, the vendor trains a limited number of staff who will then be responsible for providing initial and ongoing training for all employees. Training the trainers is particularly useful in cases where the population of users is large and/or turnover of staff is frequent.

☐ **USER TRAINING:** The most common form of training is direct user training where the vendor trains all customer personnel in the use and operation of the *System*.

Vendor agreements generally express the training obligation in terms of "person days". For example, "ABC shall provide five (5) person days of training in the use and operation of the System." Terminology of this type is ambiguous and invites disputes. Rather than "person days", training should be expressed in terms of hours. Business must continue during *System* implementation, therefore the maximum and minimum number of hours of training per day should be specified, as well as the number of instructors and their respective competencies.

The following user training clause is recommended for any form of *System* procurement:

> *ABC shall provide thirty (30) hours of training to Customer in the use, operation and maintenance of the System. The training curriculum and ABC's instructors assigned thereto are identified in Schedule "G" attached hereto and made a part hereof. Training will be conducted in not less two or greater than three (3) hour sessions per day at Customer's offices in New York. ABC shall assume and be responsible for the payment of all transportation, room and board expenses of its employees in furnishing such training.*

14. WARRANTY AND MAINTENANCE

This Section will cover the issues which are applicable to both warranty and maintenance obligations of the vendor. A separate software maintenance agreement is included as part of Appendix A.

Vendors frequently make statements with respect to performance, functionality and other *System* features during marketing and sales presentations. Representations can be either verbal or in writing, i.e., brochures, cover letters and even advertising. To the extent relied upon in making your decision, these statements can be considered express warranties. However, as will be discussed in connection with the "integration clause",[57] such statements can be superseded unless specifically included in the warranty and maintenance services clause.

There are at least two axioms which are applicable to negotiation of warranty and maintenance service provisions. First, the vendor will endeavor to define the scope of its warranty as narrowly as possible[58]. The second is the converse of the first, the customer will try to obtain the broadest possible coverage. Somewhere in the middle, the two must meet since neither position is reasonably possible.

Warranty and maintenance provisions often specify that the deliverable will be produced in "good workmanlike manner". In addition, the warranty

---

57. Integration clauses are discussed in Section 19 of this Chapter.
58. Vendor agreements typically disclaim the warranty of merchantability and fitness for a particular purpose as well as any other warranty not specifically contained in the agreement. These disclaimers are generally enforced by the courts to the extent they are conspicuously noted in the agreement.

may be conditioned upon "use under normal operating conditions". The problem with phrases of this type is the lack of an objective standard. Here again, the use of an RFP as well as comprehensive functional and system design documentation is invaluable.

The vendor's response to your RFP caused your consideration of the proposed *System*. Therefore it is appropriate that the RFP be referenced and used to define the breadth of the vendor's warranty and maintenance obligations. Vendors may resist incorporating the RFP for this purpose over concern that it lacks sufficient detail regarding the *System's* use and operation. This is a legitimate concern, but it should not preclude the RFP's use. Rather, the warranty and maintenance services clause should also reference and incorporate the functional and system design specifications (for software procurement) or performance, through-put, compatibility and/or continuous operation requirements (for hardware procurement). Strategically, this puts the burden on the vendor to ensure that the agreement identifies functions, capabilities and/or features required by the RFP but, which the parties have agreed, will not be included in the *System* as implemented. In the event of an inconsistency between the RFP and the functional or system design specifications, the RFP should prevail.

The standard against which warranty and maintenance services are measured is only one of the important issues which should be negotiated and included in the procurement agreement. Others are discussed below:

☐ **COMMENCEMENT:** Commencement of the warranty period should begin only upon *System* acceptance in order to receive the full benefit of warranty services. Similarly, the maintenance services term should begin upon the later of expiration of the warranty period or correction of all error conditions reported during the warranty period.

☐ **WARRANTY TERM:** Warranty length is strictly a function of negotiation with ninety days being the most common. However, where custom or customized software is procured, a longer warranty period is appropriate inasmuch as certain error conditions remain dormant until a particular sequence of processes is executed. The vendor may suggest that error conditions occurring after the warranty period will be corrected under the maintenance services agreement. Although this is true, services under the maintenance agreement are provided for a fee, whereas warranty services are included in the fee paid for *System* procurement.

☐ **RESPONSE TIME:** The time within which the vendor should diagnose and correct an error condition will vary with the type of *System* implemented and should be specified in the warranty and maintenance services clause. For example, every minute that an on-line *System* is down can result in lost revenue and increased costs. At the other end of the spectrum, a personal computer which is one of several within a network, will most likely not impede normal business operations while under repair.

When warranty or maintenance service is contracted for in connection with software that has been licensed with its source code[59] you should have the right to employ a third party or your own qualified employees to correct error conditions which continue beyond specified response time parameters. Furthermore, the vendor should reimburse you for your associated repair costs. Vendors may resist such a provision expressing concern that the error condition may not be properly corrected and/or possibly exacerbated. In cases where the vendor agrees to such a request, expect the vendor to try to condition its consent upon the right to charge you for any additional work, material or expenses it incurs as a result of services improperly performed by a third party or your employees. This is a reasonable position for the vendor to take. However, if the vendor repeatedly fails to perform within the response time parameters, it should be deemed to have assumed the risk and costs associated with work that is improperly performed.

☐ **LOCATION:** The location where warranty or maintenance services are performed will directly affect how quickly you can once again use the *System*. Generally, for more complex *Systems*, work is performed at the customer site. However, when standard service requires work to be performed at the vendor's premises, on-site service can usually be contracted at an additional fee—which may be a wise use of money when you consider that your business data leaves with the *System* when it is shipped to the vendor.

Certain software programs, such as on-line software applications, lend themselves to warranty and maintenance services through telecommunication services. Therefore, the vendor can log-on to the software program remotely,

---

☐ 59. When the vendor has failed to correct error conditions in software licensed in object code format, you should have the right to demand access to the source code deposited in accordance with the escrow agreement.

diagnose the error condition and directly transmit and install the necessary corrections. Although convenient, you should take care to make sure that you know about and consent to the vendor's access.

☐ **UPDATES:** During the warranty and maintenance services term, the vendor will likely develop updates to the software programs. Updates can take the form of: (a) technical enhancements which improve how the software processes data or correct program errors or (b) functional enhancements which add new capabilities or functions. At a minimum, technical enhancements should be licensed or otherwise made available to you during the warranty and maintenance periods at no additional charge. Functional enhancements on the other hand are generally made available for an additional license fee.

☐ **YEAR 2000:** As the new millennium approaches, many computer users will find that their software programs were not designed and developed to accommodate the year 2000 as a valid date. Many software programs currently use two digits instead of four to represent the year, making the assumption that the year is in the 1900's. Therefore, commencing with the year 2000, many of the financial calculations or any other function that is based on a date may result in erroneous information. To avoid the problems associated with date calculations, the vendor should guarantee that the *System* can process date information which includes the year 2000 and beyond.

☐ **VIRUS PROTECTION:** Certain irresponsible people have created computer viruses which can cause your *System* to malfunction. A virus is a software program that can disable or destroy other software programs as well as data. Viruses can be transmitted to your *System* during the process of copying files from an external source such as diskettes, the internet or other service providers of data and/or programs. Unfortunately, unless you have installed a virus checking program, you may be completely unaware that your *System* has been infected until the damage is already done. Many viruses remain dormant until activated by some particular function, others are triggered by date or time. For example, the infamous *Michaelangelo* virus is activated on his birthday.

To guard against the possibility of an infection, you should insist that the vendor check and warrant that the *System* shall be free of all viruses prior to installation.

The following warranty clause is recommended for computer hardware procurements, assuming that the vendor has agreed to performance and compatibility standards:

1. ABC warrants that Customer shall acquire good and clear title to the Hardware being purchased hereunder free and clear of all liens and encumbrances except as set forth in Section 5[60]. ABC also warrants that it has inspected the Hardware for computer viruses and that the Hardware shall be free of all viruses when delivered. ABC further warrants that the Hardware delivered hereunder shall for a period of one hundred eighty (180) calendar days from date of Customer's Acceptance as set forth in Section 7 of this Agreement be: (a) free from defects in material and workmanship; (b) compatible with and can execute the SOFTWARE, yielding response times for each process identified in Schedule "J" attached hereto and made a part hereof no greater than the times set forth alongside each process in said schedule; (c) capable of executing the SOFTWARE on a continuous basis without an Error or hardware related service interruption at least ninety percent (90%) of the time during the warranty period; (d) perform in all respects in accordance with the Documentation; (e) compatible and able to support date calculations for the years 2000 and beyond and (f) support Customer's requirements as defined in the RFP. The RFP shall prevail in the event of any inconsistencies between the RFP and the standards and/or documents referred to in this paragraph. ABC shall continue to provide warranty services to correct any Error notwithstanding expiration of the one hundred eighty (180) warranty period so long as notice of such Error was given to ABC prior thereto. EXCEPT FOR THE FOREGOING WARRANTY, ABC MAKES NO OTHER WARRANTY, EXPRESS OR IMPLIED, INCLUDING WITHOUT LIMITATION, THE IMPLIED WARRANTIES OF MERCHANTABILITY OR FITNESS FOR A PARTICULAR PURPOSE.[61]

2. ABC shall respond to warranty service requests within one (1) hour of Customer's notice and shall have completed all necessary corrections not later than three (3) hours after Customer's notice. In the event that during

---

60. Until the *System* is paid for in full, it is appropriate for the vendor to require a lien in its favor as security for the outstanding balance payable.

61. Warranty and liability disclaimers must be conspicuously noted in the procurement agreement as a prerequisite to its enforcement. Therefore, the disclaimer in the suggested clause is in all capital letters.

any ninety (90) day period, ABC shall fail two (2) times to correct an Error within the time periods aforesaid, Customer shall be entitled, at ABC's cost and expense, to employ its own personnel or a third party contractor of its own choosing to correct Error(s) occurring thereafter if ABC shall again fail to correct an Error within the prescribed time period.

3. In the event that an Error which prevents production use of the Hardware in any material respect as reasonably determined by the Customer is not corrected by ABC within seventy two (72) hours after notice (by telephone) thereof is given by Customer to ABC, without prejudice to any of its other rights and remedies under this Agreement and at law, Customer may terminate this Agreement, in which case ABC shall promptly refund all amounts paid by Customer to ABC hereunder and, as liquidated damages for its failure, pay Customer ten thousand dollars ($10,000).

4. ABC shall perform warranty services at Customer's Installation Site at no additional charge to Customer.

The following warranty clause is recommended for software procurements:

1. ABC warrants that the SOFTWARE, upon Acceptance and for a period of one hundred eighty (180) calendar days thereafter, will operate without an Error. ABC also warrants that it has inspected the SOFTWARE for computer viruses and that the SOFTWARE shall be free of all viruses when delivered. Furthermore, ABC warrants that the SOFTWARE shall be compatible and able to support date calculations for the years 2000 and beyond and have all of the capabilities and functions required by Customer as defined in Customer's RFP. In the event of an inconsistency between the RFP and the Documentation, the RFP shall prevail. EXCEPT FOR THE FORE-GOING, ABC MAKES NO OTHER WARRANTY, EXPRESS OR IM-PLIED, INCLUDING WITHOUT LIMITATION, THE IMPLIED WAR-RANTIES OF MERCHANTABILITY OR FITNESS FOR A PARTICU-LAR PURPOSE.

2. ABC shall respond to service requests within one (1) hour of Customer's notice and shall have completed all necessary corrections not later than three (3) hours after Customer's notice. In the event that, during any ninety (90) day period, ABC shall fail two (2) times to correct any Error within the time periods aforesaid, Customer shall be entitled [to receive access to the

Deposit under the Source Code Agreement and shall further be entitled][62], at ABC's cost and expense, to employ its own personnel or a third party contractor of its own choosing to correct Errors occurring thereafter if ABC shall again fail to correct the Error within the prescribed time period.

3.   In the event that an Error which prevents production use of the SOFTWARE in any material respect as reasonably determined by the Customer is not corrected by ABC within seventy two (72) hours after notice (by telephone) thereof is given by Customer to ABC, Customer may terminate this Agreement in which case ABC shall promptly refund all amounts paid by Customer to ABC hereunder and, as liquidated damages for its failure, pay Customer ten thousand dollars ($10,000).

4. ABC shall perform services at Customer's Installation Site during the warranty period at no additional charge to Customer. Alternatively, with Customer's prior consent, ABC shall be entitled to log-in to Customer's computer system and access the SOFTWARE for the purposes of Error diagnosis, correction and installation.

5. During the term of the warranty period, ABC shall at no additional charge provide Customer with all technical enhancements to the SOFTWARE.

15. INTELLECTUAL PROPERTY RIGHTS INDEMNITY

The competitive nature of the computer industry compels vendors to vigorously investigate and prosecute any instances where their intellectual property rights (IPR's)[63] may have been infringed. Although infringement actions are mainly commenced against vendors, customers are usually named as co-defendants. Therefore, the agreement should contain an indemnity clause which addresses the following issues:

☐ **DEFENSE:** Retaining legal representation to defend against an infringement action is expensive and the facts required for a proper defense are in the vendor's possession. Therefore the vendor should undertake defense efforts immediately after a claim has been asserted or an action commenced.

---

62. The words in brackets should be included when the software is licensed in object code format only.

63. IPR's can and usually are in the form of a trade secret, copyright, patent or trademark.

INDEMNITY: If the claim is successful or a settlement is reached, reasonable royalties for use of the *System* may become payable to the plaintiff. In addition, in the event the *System* is replaced, you will incur conversion, training and other implementation costs. The vendor should take full responsibility for payment and/or reimbursement of all such amounts.

CONTINUED USE: Infringement claims usually include a request for injunctive relief which, if granted by the court, would deny your continued use of the *System* until a decision on the merits of the case is rendered. Such a ruling could have a devastating effect on your business. Therefore, the vendor, at its own cost, should be required to secure an interim license from the plaintiff allowing your continued use. As you are an innocent user of the *System*, the plaintiff will most likely agree to such a request. Besides, depending on the outcome of the action, you may be the plaintiff's future customer.

REPLACEMENT: When continued use of the *System*, either while the action is pending or after its resolution, cannot be arranged, the infringing elements should be replaced, at the vendor's cost, with non-infringing substitutes providing the same capabilities. However, the majority of IPR indemnity clauses drafted by vendors provide that when continued use or replacement cannot be provided at "reasonable cost", the vendor has the right to terminate the agreement and refund the fees paid on a pre-defined depreciated basis. For example, if the *System* is deemed to have a five year useful life and an action is commenced two years after acceptance which ultimately causes the vendor to terminate the agreement, the vendor would only be obligated to refund three fifths of the fees paid for the *System*. The economic justification usually given for such a clause is that the customer had use of the *System* for two years and should therefore pay for such use. However, this fails to take into account the opportunity cost associated with the implementation of a new *System* and therefore should be avoided. Indeed, when a vendor exercises its right to terminate within the first two years after *System* acceptance, liquidated damages should also be payable.

ASSISTANCE: In the course of defending the infringement action, the vendor may seek your assistance in certain aspects of the case. While it behooves you to do so, the vendor should compensate you for time lost in managing your business.

☐ **COUNSEL:** If the vendor fails to retain counsel or engages an attorney who is not reasonably qualified to represent your interest, you should have the right to select and appoint alternative counsel. The vendor should pay all reasonable costs and expenses for legal counsel.

Although the following IPR indemnity clause refers to software, it is recommended for the procurement of any other *System* component. Just substitute the item name where "SOFTWARE" appears.

1. ABC agrees to defend and/or handle at its own expense, any claim or action against Customer for actual or alleged infringement of any intellectual or industrial property right, including without limitation, trademarks, service marks, patents, copyrights, misappropriation of trade secrets or any similar property rights, based upon the SOFTWARE or Customer's use thereof. ABC further agrees to indemnify and hold Customer harmless from and against any and all liabilities, costs, losses, damages and expenses (including reasonable attorney's fees) associated with such claim or action. Customer shall reasonably cooperate with ABC in the defense of such claim or action to the extent that such cooperation is given at such times and in a manner that does not negatively affect Customer's business (in Customer's sole discretion) and further, ABC reimburses Customer's expenses and pays Customer at Customer's hourly billing rate for all such assistance.

2. ABC shall have the sole right to conduct the defense of any such claim or action and all negotiations for its settlement or compromise. Notwithstanding the foregoing, in the event that ABC shall fail to appoint an attorney within ten (10) calendar days after the claim has first been made or action commenced or the attorney appointed by ABC is, in Customer's reasonable judgment, not suitably qualified to represent Customer, Customer shall have the right to select and appoint an alternative attorney and the reasonable cost and expense thereof shall be paid by ABC.

3. If the SOFTWARE becomes or in ABC's reasonable opinion is likely to become the subject of any such claim or action, then, ABC shall use best efforts at its sole expense to either: (a) procure for Customer the right to continue using the SOFTWARE as contemplated hereunder; (b) modify the SOFTWARE and Documentation to render same non-infringing (provided such modification does not adversely affect Customer's use as described in the RFP) or (c) replace same with equally suitable, functionally equivalent, compatible non-infringing SOFTWARE. If none of the foregoing is possible,

ABC shall have the right to terminate this Agreement upon: (i) payment to Customer of all monies paid by Customer for the SOFTWARE License Fee and (ii) if this Agreement is terminated in accordance with this paragraph within the first twenty four (24) months after Acceptance, ABC shall in addition pay Customer an amount equal to fifteen percent (15%) of the SOFTWARE License Fee as liquidated damages.

16. REMEDIES

As with warranties, vendors attempt to narrow the remedies available to a customer in the event of a failed *System* procurement. And, as with warranties, the customer's interest is just the opposite. A dose of practical commercial reality is particularly necessary when negotiating the remedy clause. Let's assume the vendor agrees to assume unlimited liability if it fails to perform. Chances are, unless the vendor has very deep pockets, you have negotiated an empty remedy clause. In addition, the long term business viability of any vendor that agrees to such a clause becomes suspect. Procurement failures occur and such a clause could easily bankrupt a vendor the first time it is invoked. Each party should recognize the inherent risk associated with any commercial transaction and fairly balance these risks through a remedy clause designed to provide compensation for foreseeable losses.

Standard procurement agreements generally contain a remedy clause limiting the vendor's responsibility for *System* failures to either repair or replacement of the defective element. In addition the vendor's overall liability for all causes is limited to a fixed dollar amount, usually equal to the purchase price or license fee. Liability for incidental and consequential damages is specifically excluded.[64] Remedy provisions of this type do not adequately protect the customer. Although the vendor's standard remedy clause can be used as the starting point for discussion purposes, the final clause negotiated should be qualified by the following caveats:

---

64. Damages that could be awarded against a vendor resulting from a failed *System* implementation include: (a) direct damages which represents the additional sum of money the customer would have to pay in order to procure an alternative *System* of equivalent capability and functionality; (b) incidental damages which represents expenses incurred by the customer for evaluation, inspection, transportation, care and custody of the *System* and (c) consequential damages which represents losses which are suffered by the customer which, at the time the agreement was executed, the vendor had reason to know or reasonably foresee.

☐ **TERMINATION:** Limiting remedies to repair and replacement of defective *System* elements does not address the possibility that it may not be possible to repair or replace the defect within a reasonable time, or at all. Therefore, you should have the right to terminate the agreement and seek damages if the defect continues beyond a defined period of time.

☐ **CONFIDENTIALITY:** Limiting remedies to repair and replacement also fails to afford a viable remedy when information is disclosed in contravention of the agreement's confidentiality and non-disclosure obligations. In such a case the only effective remedy is a court order enjoining further disclosures.

☐ **IPR INDEMNITY:** Liability and defense costs for IPR infringement can be substantial, easily using up the entire amount specified as the limit of the vendor's liability. Therefore, amounts payable by the vendor in discharging its obligations under the IPR indemnity clause should not be included in the calculation of, or subject to, liability limits expressed in the agreement.

☐ **INJURY:** Liability limits should only apply to the vendor's failure to perform under the agreement. Recovery for damages and/or injuries to individuals and real or personal property resulting from the commission of willful and/or negligent acts should likewise not be included in the calculation of, or subject to, liability limits expressed in the agreement.

☐ **LIQUIDATED DAMAGES:** When damages are difficult to calculate, the parties can agree to a reasonable amount which they believe is a fair[65] approximation of the financial injury to be suffered by a party upon the other party's failure to perform under the agreement. Particularly since negotiated procurement agreements generally excuse the vendor from consequential and incidental damages, a liquidated damages clause can be very effective in recovering lost profits or time and money expended when an alternative *System* must be procured. Liability limits should therefore be defined with the possibility of liquidated damages in mind.

Vendors are generally reluctant to accept liquidated damage provisions. However, if profits will be negatively affected by a tardy or failed *System*

---

[*] 65. If the amount specified appears distorted to the high side, a court may rule that the amount is intended as a penalty and therefore unenforceable.

implementation, profits will likely be enhanced by an early implementation. Allocating a portion of such profit for payment under a bonus clause
which rewards the vendor for early implementation may make the liquidated damages clause more palatable to the vendor.

Although the following clause refers to software, it is recommended for
procuring any other *System* component. Just substitute the item name where
the word "SOFTWARE" appears.[66]

*1. In all cases involving performance or non-performance of the SOFTWARE,
Customer's primary remedy shall be correction of Errors. For all other
failure(s) by ABC to perform in accordance with this Agreement, including
without limitation, if the SOFTWARE is not Accepted by Customer (due to
no fault of the Customer) or an Error cannot be corrected within the time
periods specified in Section 7 of this Agreement, the Customer shall be entitled to terminate this Agreement in accordance with Section 10 and/or
recover damages as prescribed in paragraph (2) of this Section 11.*

*2. ABC's liability to Customer shall be limited to: (a) the amount of the
SOFTWARE License Fee and all other payments made by Customer under
Section 5 of this Agreement plus (b) the amount of any liquidated damages
payable by ABC pursuant to the various sections of this Agreement. The
foregoing limitation of liability shall not apply to the: (a) payment of costs,
damages and attorney's fees referred to in Section 8 for ABC's indemnity
obligation; (b) claims for personal injury or damage to real or personal property caused by willful or negligent acts of ABC, its employees or contractors
or (c) damages resulting from violation of Section 3 for breach of confidentiality and non-disclosure obligations.*

*3. IN NO EVENT SHALL ABC OR THE CUSTOMER BE LIABLE FOR
INCIDENTAL, SPECIAL OR CONSEQUENTIAL DAMAGES (INCLUD-
ING WITHOUT LIMITATION LOST PROFITS) EVEN IF EITHER
PARTY HAS BEEN ADVISED OF THE POSSIBILITY OF SUCH
DAMAGES.*

When negotiations lead to inclusion of a bonus clause in favor of the
vendor, the following clause is recommended. However, the bonus should

---

66. When customized software is procured, termination of either the software development
agreement or the license agreement should cause a termination of the corresponding agreement.

only be paid after the applicable warranty period has expired to ensure that the *System* is free of defects and fully functional.

Customer shall pay ABC a bonus of two hundred dollars ($200) for each complete business day (exclusive of bank holidays) in New York City that the SOFTWARE has been fully completed and Accepted prior to the date scheduled therefor. The bonus shall only be payable in the event that all Errors have been satisfactorily corrected by the expiration of the warranty period as scheduled in the Implementation Schedule.

17. CHANGE IN SCOPE

As customized or custom software is developed, it is not unusual for the functional and/or system design specifications to be revised periodically. Revisions may be the result of more efficient processing methodologies, a change in business requirements, or changes in the hardware or its operating systems.

The agreement should therefore contemplate the possibility of revisions and provide a mechanism by which they can be incorporated. The following clause outlines the procedure when revisions become necessary as well as the consequent effect on payment and delivery obligations:

1. ABC and the Customer recognize that it may be desirable for the Customer to make changes to the functional and/or system design specifications (a "Revision") during the performance of this Agreement. Customer may request a Revision by giving notice thereof to ABC specifying the nature of the change(s) desired (the "Revision Notice").

2. Within ten (10) calendar days after ABC has received the Revision Notice, it shall provide Customer with a proposal identifying: (a) any addition or reduction in the cost associated with developing the SOFTWARE; (b) the effect, if any, to the Payment Schedule identified in Section 4 of this Agreement; (c) the changes required and to be made to the Documentation; (d) the effect, if any, with respect to the Implementation Schedule and (e) any other change which would be required to any of the other Sections or Schedules of this Agreement (the "Revision Proposal").

3. Upon Customer's written approval of the Revision Proposal, ABC shall, within ten (10) calendar days thereafter, revise the Functional and/or System Design Specifications (the "Revised Specifications") and submit them for Customer's approval. ABC shall not develop or implement any Revision until such time that the Customer has approved the Revised Specifications in writing. Upon Customer's approval of the Revised Specifications, this Agreement shall be deemed amended to reflect the terms and conditions of the Revision Proposal.

18. TERMINATION

Termination of a *System* procurement agreement is an extreme remedy which should only be invoked when it is clear that a party to the agreement will be unable to satisfy its material obligations after a reasonable cure period has been afforded. Termination however, should not necessarily end your right to use the *System*. Moreover, the agreement should specifically address each of the following considerations.

☐ **WIND-DOWN PERIOD:** The time and cost associated with conversion to a new *System* has been referred to earlier. The entire *System* selection process must be repeated and your data will have to be converted to a new format which is compatible with the new *System*. During the transition period, operation of your business must continue uninterrupted. Therefore, the agreement should allow for a wind-down period during which time a vendor can be selected and conversion to the new *System* proceed in an orderly fashion.

☐ **CAUSE OF DEFAULT:** *System* procurement agreements impose a variety of material obligations on the vendor, the failure of any one of which can have damaging consequences to your business. Conversely, there is really only one material obligation on your part, payment of fees. Because your business depends on the *System's* continued availability, a balancing of the equities favors termination by the vendor only in the event that you have failed to pay the fees due within the prescribed time frame and applicable cure period.

☐ **VENDOR DEFAULT:** Termination of the agreement when the vendor has defaulted may not always be a viable remedy if termination results in no longer having access to the *System*. Obviously if termination occurs due to *System* defects and/or failures, this will not be an issue. However, where the *System* is operational but the vendor has failed to perform other material obligations (for example, confidentiality or dedicated project personnel), your continued use of the *System* should be permitted notwithstanding termination.

☐ **OWNERSHIP:** Termination of customized or custom software procurement agreements when the vendor has defaulted should not affect ownership rights to the software, documentation or the related intellectual property. As discussed earlier in Section 7 of this Chapter, ownership should vest in the customer immediately upon creation regardless of whether the agreement is successfully concluded.

Although the following termination clause refers to software, it is recommended for procuring any other *System* component. Just substitute the item name where the word "SOFTWARE" appears.

1. If a party (the "Defaulting Party") is in material breach of or default under this Agreement, and the Defaulting Party does not remedy that breach or default within thirty (30) calendar days after receipt from the other party of written notice of default or breach (provided that if the breach or default is one that cannot be remedied within such thirty (30) day period, this Agreement may be terminated effective immediately upon written notice to the Defaulting Party), the other party shall after the expiry of such thirty (30) calendar day period have the right to terminate this Agreement effective immediately upon written notice to the Defaulting Party.

2. Either party may terminate this Agreement, at any time, by written notice in the event that the other: (a) files a voluntary petition in bankruptcy or under any similar insolvency law; (b) makes an assignment for the benefit of creditors; (c) has filed against it an involuntary petition in bankruptcy or under any similar insolvency law if any such petition is not dismissed within sixty (60) days after filing or (d) a receiver is appointed for, or a levy or attachment is made against, substantially all of its assets, if any such petition is not dismissed or such receiver or levy or attachment is not discharged within sixty (60) days after the filing or appointment.

3. If the Defaulting Party is Customer, the termination of this Agreement by ABC shall (subject to paragraphs (5) and (6) of this Section 11) terminate the License and Customer shall return to ABC all copies of the SOFTWARE in Customer's possession or control.[67]

☐ * 67. When the Customer owns the software, paragraphs 3, 4 and 6 should not be included in the termination clause. If the vendor is concerned with the credit worthiness of the customer, a security agreement in favor of the vendor can serve to protect to vendor's interests, as discussed in Footnote 60.

4. If the Defaulting Party is ABC, the termination of this Agreement by Customer shall not terminate the License and Customer shall, in addition to all of Customer's other rights and remedies, be entitled to retain and use all copies of the SOFTWARE in Customer's possession or control.

5. For the purposes of paragraph (1) of this Section 11, Customer shall be in material breach of or default under this Agreement and ABC shall be entitled to terminate this Agreement only if the breach or default relates to Customer's obligation to pay ABC any amount payable hereunder when due and the breach or default is not remedied within the applicable time period specified therefor. ABC's rights and remedies in respect of any other breach of or default under this Agreement shall be limited to such rights and remedies other than termination of this Agreement and the License, it being acknowledged and agreed by ABC that the License is irrevocable and not terminable except if Customer is in material breach of or default under this Agreement as provided in this paragraph.

6. If this Agreement is terminated by ABC for a material default or breach by the Customer as described in paragraph (5) of this Section 11 , Customer shall be entitled to retain possession of the SOFTWARE and to load, execute and display the SOFTWARE for the period of time, not to exceed six (6) months, required for Customer to wind down its current use of the SOFTWARE or to make a transition to alternate software or facilities.

19. GENERAL PROVISIONS

Procurement agreements generally have a "catch-all" section comprised of a number of independent clauses describing administrative aspects of the agreement. Nine of these clauses are reviewed in the pages that follow. For the sake of brevity, please refer to the article entitled "General" in each of the sample agreements reprinted in Appendix A for the recommended agreement clauses.

☐ **AMENDMENTS:** It is common for agreements to be amended from time to time to reflect changed business terms and conditions. However, each change should be reflected in a written amendment signed by all parties. Otherwise, conduct contrary to express written provisions of the agreement could be interpreted by a court as an amendment to the agreement. Unfortunately, the court's interpretation of the parties' conduct may not necessarily reflect their actual intentions.

☐ **ASSIGNMENT:** Standard vendor agreements usually prevent the customer from assigning the agreement to a third party. Although the vendor has a legitimate interest in prohibiting assignment in certain cases (for example, the credit worthiness of the proposed assignee), a blanket restriction is not appropriate and, in fact, the vendor's right to assign should likewise be circumscribed.

From the customer's point of view, assignment should be allowed where a subsidiary, parent or other affiliated company now in existence or to be formed at some later date may be a user of the *System*. In addition, when the *System* is leased, the leasing company must have the right to assign warranty, indemnity, purchase option and other rights under the *System* procurement agreement (between the vendor and the leasing company) [68].

Assignment by the vendor should likewise be addressed. In particular, with custom or customized software, the customer relies on the vendor's unique skill, knowledge and experience to develop and maintain the software. Assignment by the vendor should therefore be prohibited in order for the customer to realize the benefits of such reliance.

☐ **ESCROW:** The importance of establishing a source code escrow was discussed earlier in Section 6 of Chapter Five. Although a separate source code escrow agreement is executed, the software procurement agreement should likewise make reference to the vendor's deposit obligations in order to preserve your rights to seek damages and/or terminate the procurement agreement in the event the vendor fails to comply with the escrow agreement.

☐ **PROJECT PERSONNEL:** During the course of *System* evaluation, preparation of functional and system design specifications and through your investment of time with the vendor, vendor personnel learn your business, its operation, and requirements. This is a valuable asset which will facilitate the *System's* efficient implementation. To make the most use of this asset, the vendor should agree that it will not re-assign its key personnel until their scheduled tasks have been completed.

---

68. Lease transactions were discussed in Section 4 of Chapter Five.

☐ **NOTICE:** Standard vendor agreements generally allow written notice to be given by regular mail or facsimile transmission with notice deemed given within a few days after notice has been sent. Such a clause can expose you to the possibility of being "deemed" to have received notice without actual receipt. Therefore, the agreement should require that all notices be sent in a form that requires a receipt acknowledgment (for example, certified mail, overnight express mail or delivery by courier) and that notice is deemed given only upon actual receipt.

☐ **INJUNCTIVE RELIEF:** When an agreement is breached, the non-defaulting party's damages can usually be calculated and satisfied by the payment of money. In *System* procurement agreements however, a breach of the confidentiality and non-disclosure provisions may not be compensable through money damages alone. The non-defaulting party may have to seek a court order preventing further violations. Standard vendor agreements usually allow only the vendor to seek injunctive relief and further attempt to secure the customer's prior consent to its imposition. Clearly, the customer has an interest in preserving its confidential information as well. Therefore, both parties should be entitled to seek injunctive relief. However, its availability should not be pre-determined. The party requesting injunctive relief should first have to prove monetary damages alone are not a sufficient remedy.

☐ **NON-WAIVER:** In an ideal world, all *System* procurement agreements would be successfully completed without any problems. However, problems and issues do arise and many are resolved between the parties while implementation continues. In situations where a resolution is not reached, the mere fact that the parties continued to implement the *System* and did not immediately resort to their contractual remedies should not be used by one party to claim a waiver by the other. Such a result would discourage negotiation. Therefore, agreements generally contain a non-waiver clause that preserves a party's remedies even though those remedies were previously available but not invoked.

☐ **FORCE MAJEURE:** A commercial risk which all parties to an agreement must take is that an unforeseen event over which a party has no control can disrupt, delay or prevent successful *System* implementation. When such an event occurs and continues, the agreement should not penalize the affected party but instead should allow a suspension of that portion of the work which cannot continue until the problem is abated. Calling for such a suspension is known as force majeure.

A party claiming force majeure should nevertheless give the other parties notice of the effect anticipated by such delay and the steps being taken to alleviate the consequent problems. Ultimately, there must be a way for the parties to terminate the agreement if the event of force majeure continues beyond a prescribed period of time.

INTEGRATION CLAUSE: Standard vendor agreements generally contain a clause stating that the entire agreement of the parties, including all of the vendor's representations and warranties, are contained in the agreement as executed. The intention is to prevent reliance on any statements made or material provided by the vendor during marketing efforts and not included in the original agreement. Although such a clause is appropriate and serves a useful purpose, you must take care that all material you relied on in selecting the *System* is attached or clearly referred to in the executed agreement or its schedules.

20. CHAPTER SUMMARY

Negotiation of a *System* procurement agreement, like any other agreement, should take into account each parties' reasonable business objectives and constraints. A negotiating posture that seeks to exact the maximum number of concessions from the other party certainly does not foster a spirit of mutual cooperation.

In this Chapter, factors you should consider in negotiating the *System* procurement were reviewed together with an insight into the vendor's motivation, where applicable. Understanding these competing interests will help you negotiate a fair and balanced agreement for all parties.

DISPUTE RESOLUTION

1. INTRODUCTION

A direct by-product of computer technology's explosive growth in the business environment has been an increasing number of disputes between vendors and their customers. Commentators have estimated that approximately 40% of all *Systems* fail in some way. Unfortunately the judicial system does not provide an effective method for rapid and cost effective dispute resolution. The rapid pace at which computer technology becomes obsolete together with the fact that such disputes require technical knowledge for their resolution further exacerbates the deficiencies associated with the judicial system. In this Chapter we will focus on dispute resolution methods which can serve as alternatives to litigation.

2. ALTERNATIVE DISPUTE RESOLUTION

Alternative dispute resolution (ADR) has been referred to as the *Private Court System*. However, this is really a misnomer inasmuch as ADR is much broader. ADR programs stress non-adversarial methods for dispute resolution. Therefore, a more accurate definition of ADR is any method of resolving a dispute that does not require the ultimate decision to be rendered by a judge or jury. ADR programs employ individuals with specialized knowledge in the issues underlying the respective dispute to serve as advisors, mediators and arbitrators (*Neutrals*) who render an opinion as to how the dispute should be resolved. What follows is a discussion of the various forms of ADR that can be used to resolve disputes.

☐ **ARBITRATION:** Arbitration is probably the most widely known form of ADR. In arbitration proceedings the parties submit their dispute to a Neutral for a final binding decision. Arbitration proceedings are not as formal as a trial. The scope of pre-trial discovery[69] is limited and unless otherwise agreed between the parties, the sessions take place in private. In addition, the parties can dictate the extent of issues arbitration will resolve as well as the kind of relief that may be awarded.

☐ **MEDIATION:** Mediation is less formal than arbitration and, unlike arbitration, is non-binding. In mediation, the Neutral will elicit the issues, facts, positions and most importantly, the objectives of the parties and, when appropriate, bring them together to discuss settlement. Mediation programs do not allow for evidentiary hearings and the parties must consent to the settlement. As with arbitration, mediation proceedings are confidential and private.

☐ **ADVISORY OPINION:** In advisory opinion dispute resolution, each party formally presents the issues in dispute to a Neutral who then renders a non-binding opinion. Sometimes the Neutral's opinion will change the perceptions of one or both parties enabling them to reach a resolution. In addition, at the request of both parties, the Neutral in such a case, can act as a mediator, should the advisory opinion not be accepted.

☐ **MINI-TRIAL:** In a mini-trial, the parties present information underlying the dispute to their senior executives in the presence of a Neutral. This program is premised on the belief that once the executives hear the other side's case, they will be able to find mutual grounds on which to settle. Rules of evidence do not apply and pretrial discovery is significantly limited. The senior executives who attend the mini-trial must have authority to settle the dispute and they may not be personally involved in the transaction giving rise to the dispute. If the senior executives cannot agree on a settlement, the Neutral, if requested by the parties, may issue a non-binding opinion as to the likely outcome of the case if it were litigated in court.

---

69. Pre-trial discovery is usually the lengthiest part of traditional litigation proceedings and can continue for several years before the trial even begins.

3. ACCEPTANCE

ADR is an effective alternative to litigation. The experience of Motorola, Inc. demonstrates this point. Since implementation of its plan requiring in-house counsel to seek alternatives to litigation, ADR techniques have reduced Motorola's litigation costs by as much as 75%.

Recent surveys show that Motorola is not unique. One survey has found that since 1990, 406 companies tracked by the Center For Public Resources saved over $150,000,000 in legal fees and expenses. Another survey conducted in 1992 by *Business Week* of 400 senior executives at corporations drawn from the *Business Week Top 1000* found that 97% favored much greater use of ADR resolution methods. In addition, ADR is becoming an integral part of the legal culture in the United States as lawyers become familiar with its processes and benefits. Yet another survey conducted in 1993 by Deloitte & Touche of the legal departments of Fortune 1000 companies and major law firms specializing in litigation yielded the following results:

> *Of the respondents, 72% reported "at least some experience" with ADR. Of this group, 14% were "extensive" users of ADR—participating, on average, in 32 ADR procedures a year. For all users, mediation was employed in 48% of the cases; arbitration 43%.*

> *Time and cost savings were far ahead of all other categories as to why companies preferred ADR over litigation. All users said the cost saving compared to litigation was between 11% and 50%.*

> *In terms of the future, 78% of all ADR users responding to the survey expect to increase reliance on ADR. Of the extensive users, 96% plan to increase ADR use. A total of 83% of company counsels and 75% of law firm attorneys indicated they anticipated more use of ADR in years to come.*

4. BENEFITS[70]

The benefits engendered by using ADR have caused its growing acceptance which this writer believes will continue into the future. For the resolution of disputes involving computer technology, ADR is particularly well suited as discussed below.

---

70. This Section has been adapted from the article entitled *Computer Arbitration: Taking the Byte Out Of Data Processing Disputes*, Cumberland Law Review, 1989, Vol.19 pp. 286-292 and is reprinted here through the courtesy of B. Judson Hennington III, Esq.

☐ **RAPID DISPUTE RESOLUTION:** With extensive back-logs, litigation hardly affords a procedure for speedy dispute resolution. In Chicago, the court docket shows an eight year backlog of civil cases, while in New York, some judges spend only seventeen minutes per case. In the past two years, ten states have had to close their courthouse doors temporarily to civil cases because of the huge criminal related caseloads.

Procedural rules and guidelines which characterize the litigation process, coupled with the highly technical nature of most computer disputes and the judiciary's inability to deal effectively with the litigation explosion, virtually guarantee a long and drawn out claim resolution. The inherently fleeting economic value of *System* technology further exacerbates litigation problems. If a dispute is not resolved quickly, the entire matter may be moot merely because the technology has become outdated. Litigation which threatens to last even a year or two could cut substantially into the useful life of a *System*.

In contrast to litigation, ADR offers an opportunity to quickly resolve computer related disputes. Efficiency is obtained because: (a) discovery is limited; (b) pretrial motions are generally not available; (c) the Neutral will usually be an expert in the parties' field and (d) the Neutral will have a smaller backlog of cases than the typical trial court. A survey conducted in 1990 by the United States Federal Judicial Center, the vast majority of participants believed that ADR reduces the overall cost of litigation and judges stated that ADR reduced their caseload burden.

☐ **PRESERVATION OF GOOD WILL:** Preservation of the user-vendor relationship during resolution of a dispute is essential to both the vendor and its customer. In many instances, the customer is totally dependent on the vendor's knowledge, expertise, and capabilities to provide a mission or business critical *System* in a timely manner. The vendor, on the other hand, will have invested a significant amount of time, money and resources in both developing the *System* and selling it to the customer. This investment is put at risk if an amicable solution is not reached.

Litigation does little, if anything, to preserve or protect this delicate relationship, and the antagonism which typifies a lawsuit renders ongoing project management virtually impossible. ADR programs are focused on constructive dialogue leading to a "win-win" outcome. This focus is made all the more effective by the Neutral's expertise in the subject matter and the informal manner in which he or she can interact with the parties without in any way jeopardizing the parties' other remedies.

☐ **CONFIDENTIALITY:** Private proceedings are important to parties in a *System* related dispute. Such systems often embody the vendor's sensitive, highly confidential, and proprietary information. This information frequently represents a major investment of time and money by the vendor, and in some cases is the vendor's primary corporate asset. Therefore, the vendor has a substantial interest in preserving the confidentiality of this proprietary information. Similarly, the customer's confidential business processes and data will usually be incorporated in the *System*. While the need to preserve such information is not necessarily unique to participants in the computer industry, the highly competitive nature of the business makes protection of such data particularly important.

In addition, procurement failures reflect badly on both the vendor and customer. If a *System* failure becomes public knowledge, such information can severely damage the vendor's reputation in the industry. From the customer's viewpoint, a failed procurement suggests that management is unable to negotiate the demands imposed by changing competitive conditions.

Litigation is ill-suited to protect against the disclosure of proprietary and confidential information. Civil trials are often public, and in many cases proprietary and confidential information will be disclosed in a decision on the merits, if not during discovery or in pretrial motions. While protective orders may be permissible under some circumstances, their availability depends entirely on the discretion of the trial court.

Therefore, when privacy and confidentiality must be maintained, ADR programs are preferable to litigation. Under normal circumstances, there are no discovery concerns. Neither the hearing nor the award is made public. The parties may also choose to impose additional restrictions to maintain confidentiality on themselves and the Neutral in the ADR agreement.

☐ **EXPERTISE:** *System* disputes often involve highly technical issues, and persons unfamiliar with the technology may be incapable of perceiving nuances of the claim which are essential to an appropriate resolution of the dispute.

In litigation, it is extremely unlikely that the jury will possess the expertise necessary to render an appropriate decision. ADR programs on the other hand, permit the parties to select from among prospective Neutrals with *Systems* expertise. As a result, the Neutrals that hear such disputes are better equipped to resolve any technical issues which may arise.

☐ **MINIMIZATION OF COSTS:** ADR is generally less expensive than litigation because of the speed of the process and the minimal discovery involved. Additional cost savings flow from: (a) reducing expenses associated with technology and legal experts required to interpret evidence for the judge or jury and (b) reduction of time expended by company personnel in the defense or prosecution of a claim, all of which can cost a firm millions of dollars in lost research and development, new innovations and revenues in marketing technology. Perhaps the most expensive cost of litigation is the waste of valuable management time. In the *Business Week* survey, 44% of the respondents stated that diversion of management time had a major impact on their business.

5. ADMINISTRATION

Now that you have been convinced of ADR's benefits, how can you use it when necessary? The first step is to make certain that your agreements give you the right to refer disputes for resolution under a selected method of ADR. The sample agreements reproduced in Appendix A contain clauses encompassing various ADR programs. The second step is to select a forum that can identify and refer qualified Neutrals as well as administer the ADR proceeding.

Selecting the right Neutral is critical to the quick and proper resolution of a dispute. The Neutral should have competence in *Systems* development and/or implementation and, if possible, experience in your particular industry group.

Although there are many organizations that administer ADR programs, there is one company that provides such service exclusively to the technology industry—CADRE, Inc.—*Conflict Advisory and Dispute Resolution Enterprise*. I am pleased to announce that I am the founding principal of CADRE[71]. CADRE facilitates non-adversarial means of resolving disputes through mediation and advisory opinion services as well as arbitration and

---

* 71. CADRE's offices are located in New York City.

mini-trial programs for cases in which the non-adversarial procedures fail. In addition, CADRE offers solution structuring, a unique service intended to assist its clients determine the program best suited to their particular needs. For any resolution program selected by the disputing parties, CADRE provides complete case administration.

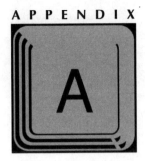

SAMPLE
AGREEMENTS

A disk containing an electronic copy of the agreements reprinted in this book can be ordered by completing the order form at the end of this book.

ABC SYSTEMS, INC.
SOFTWARE LICENSE AGREEMENT

CUSTOMER: Professional Trading Company, Ltd.

ADDRESS: 100 Park Avenue

CITY: New York

STATE: NY ZIP: 10017

CONTACT: John Smith

DATE: September 28, 1996

1. DEFINITIONS

As used in this document the following terms shall have the meanings set forth below:

(1.1) "ABC " shall mean ABC Systems, Inc. 50 Main Street, White Plains, NY 11477.

(1.2) "Acceptance" shall have the meaning stated in Section 6.4 of this Agreement.

(1.3) "Acceptance Test" shall mean the testing process for the SOFTWARE performed in accordance with the Test Plans as specified in Section 6 of this Agreement.

(1.4) "Agreement" shall mean this agreement, any attached exhibits or schedules and any amendments to this Agreement which are in writing and signed by both parties.

(1.5) "Deposit" shall mean the material to be deposited into escrow by ABC in accordance with the Escrow Agreement attached hereto as **Schedule "J"**.

(1.6) "Documentation" shall mean the Functional Specification, user, operations and training manuals for version 4 of the "STOCK" software program, as amended by the Functional Specification.

(1.7) "Functional Specification" shall mean the document entitled "Functional Requirements For Professional Trading Company, Ltd." dated May 23, 1996 containing 274 pages, the first page of which is initialed by the parties hereto.

(1.8) "Error" shall mean an error in the code of the SOFTWARE which pre-vents the SOFTWARE from operating in all material respects in accor-dance with the Documentation and the RFP.

(1.9) "Hardware" shall mean the computer equipment identified in **Schedule "C"** to this Agreement or any replacement of such computer equipment in accordance with Section 3.2 hereof.

(1.10) "Installation" shall have the meaning given it in Section 12.1 of this Agree-ment.

(1.11) "Installation Site" shall mean Customer's address above stated.

(1.12) "License Fee" shall mean the license fee for the SOFTWARE as specified in Section 5.1 of this Agreement.

(1.13) "RFP" shall mean "Customer's Request For Proposal" dated March 1, 1996, a copy of which is attached hereto as **Schedule "F"** and made a part hereof.

(1.14) "SOFTWARE" shall mean version 4 of the Stock computer software pro-gram product in object code format as described by the Documentation. Throughout this Agreement, "SOFTWARE" shall include version 4 of the Stock computer program and the Documentation, individually and/ or collectively, together with all amendments, enhancements and modifi-cations thereto which have been accepted by Customer.

(1.15) "Test Plans" shall mean the procedures and objectives of the Acceptance Test for the SOFTWARE.

(1.16) "Use" shall mean to load, execute and display the SOFTWARE on the Hardware.

2. DELIVERABLES

(2.1) On or before the dates set forth in the Implementation Schedule attached hereto as **Schedule "H"** and made a part hereof, ABC shall deliver to Customer:

(a) SOFTWARE which shall have all of the functions, features, performance, compatibility and enhancement characteristics described in the RFP. In the event of an inconsistency between the Documentation and the RFP, the RFP shall prevail; and

(b) two (2) copies of the Documentation in printed form and one copy in electronic form compatible with Microsoft Word, version 6.0.

3. LICENSE

(3.1) ABC hereby grants the Customer a personal, nontransferable, non-exclusive, paid-up and irrevocable license to Use the SOFTWARE, in object code format, to process its own data. In no event shall Customer have the right to Use the SOFTWARE to process the data of any other entity. One copy of the SOFTWARE may also be Used on a back-up computer during a reasonable, temporary period of inoperability of the Hardware.

(3.2) Upon thirty (30) days prior written notice, Customer may transfer the SOFTWARE to: (a) other Hardware of comparable processing power; or (b) Hardware of greater processing power upon payment of an additional license fee calculated in accordance with **Schedule "D"** attached to this Agreement and made a part hereof. Such notice shall specify the date of the transfer and thereafter the Hardware shall be the hardware designated in such notice.

(3.3) Customer shall be entitled to make up to two (2) copies of the SOFTWARE for back-up or archival purposes. Customer shall keep a record of each copy made, where such copy is located and in whose custody it is in.

(3.4) Customer shall not reverse engineer, decompile, disassemble, re-engineer or otherwise attempt to discover the source code or the structural framework of the SOFTWARE.

(3.5) Customer agrees that the SOFTWARE shall not be exported directly or indirectly, separately or as part of a system. Diversion of Products contrary to U.S. law is prohibited.

4. DISCLOSURE & OWNERSHIP

(4.1) As used herein, "CUSTOMER Information" shall include all information and data furnished by CUSTOMER to ABC, whether in oral, written, graphic or machine-readable form, including without limitation, specifications, user, operations or systems manuals, diagrams, graphs, models, sketches, technical data, research, business or financial information, plans, strategies, forecasts, forecast assumptions, business practices, marketing information and material, customer names, proprietary ideas, concepts, know-how, methodologies and all other information related to CUSTOMER's business. CUSTOMER Information shall also include confidential information received by CUSTOMER from a third party. In order for any information provided verbally by CUSTOMER to ABC to come within the definition of CUSTOMER Information, it shall be identified as confidential at the time of disclosure and within five (5) business days after verbal disclosure thereof by CUSTOMER, such information shall be documented in writing specifying that CUSTOMER considers such information confidential.

(4.2) As used herein, "ABC Information" shall include all information and data furnished by ABC to CUSTOMER, whether in oral, written, graphic or machine-readable form, in connection with the SOFTWARE, including, without limitation, object code, source code, source listings, computer programs, specifications, user, operations or systems manuals, diagrams, graphs, technical data, research, business or financial information, plans, strategies, forecasts, forecast assumptions, business practices, procedures, marketing information, trade secrets and other proprietary ideas, concepts, know-how, methodologies and information related to the SOFTWARE or ABC. In order for any information provided verbally by ABC to CUSTOMER to come within the definition of ABC Information, it shall be identified as confidential at the time of disclosure and within five (5) business days after verbal disclosure thereof by ABC, such information shall be documented in writing specifying that ABC considers such information confidential.

(4.3) As used herein, "Confidential Information" shall include the CUSTOMER Information and the ABC Information, individually and collectively.

Notwithstanding anything to the contrary contained in this Agreement, Confidential Information shall not include information: (a) in the public domain (other than as a result of a breach of this Agreement); (b) generally known and disclosed to CUSTOMER or ABC by persons or entities engaged in a comparable business (other than as a result of a breach of this Agreement or any other agreement to which such persons or entities are parties); (c) in CUSTOMER or ABC's possession prior to its receipt from the other pursuant to this Agreement or (d) independently developed by CUSTOMER or ABC.

(4.4) CUSTOMER and ABC agree to use procedures no less rigorous than those used to protect and preserve the confidentiality of their own proprietary information to maintain the confidentiality of the Confidential Information of the other and shall not, directly or indirectly, (a) transfer or disclose any Confidential Information to a third party (other than to their respective employees); (b) use any Confidential Information other than as contemplated under this Agreement or (c) take any other action with respect to the Confidential Information inconsistent with the confidential and proprietary nature of such information. CUSTOMER and ABC further agree to return all Confidential Information (and all copies thereof) to the other upon termination of this Agreement, except as set forth to the contrary in Section 10 of this Agreement.

(4.5) CUSTOMER and ABC shall be permitted to disclose the Confidential Information to their respective employees having a need for access thereto in connection with their employment and who have executed confidentiality agreements containing provisions similar to those contained in this Agreement and specifying that other parties are third party beneficiaries thereof entitled to enforce the provisions thereof as though a party thereto. CUSTOMER and ABC shall each take steps, no less rigorous than those it takes to protect and preserve its own proprietary information, to prevent their respective employees from acting in a manner inconsistent with the terms of this Agreement.

(4.6) ABC acknowledges and agrees that CUSTOMER is engaged in the business of securities trading, and as such currently possesses knowledge and information relating to the functionality and capabilities required for computer systems in support thereof. Therefore, nothing contained in this Agreement shall prevent CUSTOMER from, on its own or through third parties, designing, developing or acquiring computer systems similar to the SOFTWARE so long as CUSTOMER does not make use of any ABC Information in connection therewith.

(4.7) The SOFTWARE, its logos, product names and other support materials, if any, are either patented, copyrighted, trademarked, or otherwise proprietary to ABC . Customer agrees never to remove any such notices and product identification. A copyright notice on the SOFTWARE shall not be deemed in and of itself to constitute or evidence a publication or public disclosure.

5. LICENSE FEE AND OTHER REQUIRED PAYMENTS

(5.1) Customer shall pay ABC one hundred fifty thousand United States dollars ($150,000) for the SOFTWARE License Fee, payable as follows:

(a) fifteen thousand dollars ($15,000) upon execution of this Agreement;

(b) twenty thousand dollars ($20,000) upon delivery and Installation of the SOFTWARE and confirmation by Customer that the SOFTWARE's program files listed in **Schedule "B"** attached to this Agreement and made a part hereof reside on the Hardware's program libraries;

(c) fifteen thousand dollars ($15,000) upon delivery of all Documentation to Customer;

(d) eighty thousand dollars ($80,000) upon Acceptance of the SOFTWARE; and

(e) twenty thousand dollars ($20,000) upon the later of (i) expiration of the warranty period specified in Section 7 of this Agreement, or (ii) all warranty claims having been properly satisfied by ABC.

(5.2) The Customer shall pay any sales or use tax imposed by the New York State and/or New York City government(s) in connection with the SOFTWARE.

(5.3) The Customer shall pay all reasonable expenses incurred by ABC in performing its obligations hereunder. Expenses which: (a) individually are in excess of two hundred fifty dollars ($250) or (b) during any calendar month, would cause total expenses incurred in such month to exceed five hundred dollars ($500), shall not be incurred without Customer's prior written consent.

(5.4) Invoices shall be payable within thirty (30) days after Customer's receipt of ABC's invoice, so long as the amounts stated therein are not reasonably in dispute.

(5.5) ABC warrants that the terms of this Agreement are comparable to or better than the terms offered by ABC to any of its present commercial customers of equal or lesser size for comparable deliverables and/or services. If ABC offers more favorable terms to its commercial customers during the period commencing on the date hereof and expiring one year thereafter, such terms shall also be made available to Customer together with any resulting refund within thirty (30) days from the execution of such agreement.

6. ACCEPTANCE TESTING

(6.1) Customer shall prepare Test Plans consistent with the Documentation and the RFP on or before the date which is thirty (30) calendar days prior to the date the SOFTWARE is scheduled for Installation. The Test Plans shall include procedures required to demonstrate that the SOFTWARE operates in all material respects in accordance with the Documentation and the RFP. In the event of an inconsistency between the RFP and the Documentation, the RFP shall prevail. Customer shall prepare the data necessary for performing the Acceptance Test and shall perform the Acceptance Test within ten (10) business days after Installation is complete.

(6.2) Within five (5) business days after completion of the Acceptance Test, Customer shall either give its Acceptance of the SOFTWARE or disapprove such results and provide detailed written reasons for such disapproval.

(6.3) If the SOFTWARE or any portion thereof fails to pass the Acceptance Test, ABC will correct all Error(s) not later than fourteen (14) calendar days after receipt of Customer's notice describing the Error(s). Within fourteen (14) calendar days after such corrections have been made,

Customer will retest the SOFTWARE. If the SOFTWARE still fails the Acceptance Test after corrections having been made in accordance with this paragraph 6.3, Customer may in its sole discretion: (a) grant ABC additional time to correct the outstanding Error(s) or (b) terminate this Agreement in which event ABC shall refund all amounts paid by Customer to ABC hereunder and, as liquidated damages for its failure, pay Customer ten thousand dollars ($10,000).

(6.4) Acceptance of the SOFTWARE shall be deemed to have occurred upon execution of the an Acceptance Certificate, the form of which is attached hereto as **Schedule "E"**.

7. LIMITED WARRANTY

(7.1) ABC warrants that the SOFTWARE, upon Acceptance and for a period of one hundred eighty (180) calendar days thereafter, will operate without an Error. ABC also warrants that it has inspected the SOFTWARE for computer viruses and that the SOFTWARE shall be free of all viruses when delivered. Furthermore, ABC warrants that the SOFTWARE shall be compatible and able to support date calculations for the years 2000 and beyond and have all of the capabilities and functions required by Customer as defined in Customer's RFP. EXCEPT FOR THE FOREGOING, ABC MAKES NO OTHER WARRANTY, EXPRESS OR IMPLIED, INCLUDING WITHOUT LIMITATION, THE IMPLIED WARRANTIES OF MERCHANTABILITY OR FITNESS FOR A PARTICULAR PURPOSE.

(7.2) ABC shall respond to service requests within one (1) hour of Customer's notice and shall have completed all necessary corrections not later than three (3) hours after Customer's notice. In the event that that, during any ninety (90) day period, ABC shall fail two (2) times to correct an Error within the time periods aforesaid, without prejudice to any of its other rights and remedies under this Agreement, Customer shall be entitled to receive access to the Deposit and shall further be entitled, at ABC's cost and expense, to employ its own personnel or a third party contractor of its own choosing to correct Errors occurring thereafter, if ABC shall again fail to correct an Error within the prescribed time period.

(7.3) In the event that an Error which prevents production use of the SOFT-WARE in any material respect, as reasonably determined by the Customer, is not corrected by ABC within seventy two (72) hours after notice (by telephone) thereof is given by Customer to ABC, Customer may terminate this Agreement in which case ABC shall promptly refund all amounts paid by Customer to ABC hereunder and, as liquidated damages for its failure, pay Customer fifteen thousand dollars ($15,000).

(7.4) ABC shall perform warranty services at the Installation Site at no additional charge to Customer. Alternatively, with Customer's prior consent, ABC shall be entitled to log-in to Customer's computer system and access the SOFTWARE for the purposes of Error diagnosis, correction and installation.

(7.5) During the term of the warranty period, ABC shall at no additional charge provide Customer with all technical enhancements to the SOFTWARE.

8. INTELLECTUAL PROPERTY INDEMNIFICATION

(8.1) ABC agrees to defend and/or handle at its own expense, any claim or action against Customer for actual or alleged infringement of any intellectual or industrial property right, including without limitation, trademarks, service marks, patents, copyrights, misappropriation of trade secrets or any similar property rights, based upon the SOFTWARE or Customer's use thereof. ABC further agrees to indemnify and hold Customer harmless from and against any and all liabilities, costs, losses, damages and expenses (including reasonable attorney's fees) associated with such claim or action. Customer shall reasonably cooperate with ABC in the defense of such claim or action to the extent that such cooperation is given at times and in a manner that does not negatively affect Customer's business, in Customer's sole discretion, and further, ABC reimburses Customer's expenses and pays Customer at Customer's hourly billing rate for all such assistance.

(8.2) ABC shall have the sole right to conduct the defense of any such claim or action and all negotiations for its settlement or compromise.

Notwithstanding the foregoing, in the event that ABC shall fail to appoint an attorney within ten (10) calendar days after the claim having first been made or action commenced or the attorney appointed by ABC is, in Customer's reasonable judgment not suitably qualified to represent Customer, Customer shall have the right to select and appoint an alternative attorney and the reasonable cost and expense thereof shall be paid by ABC.

(8.3) If the SOFTWARE becomes or in ABC's reasonable opinion is likely to become the subject of any such claim or action, then, ABC shall use best efforts at its sole expense to either: (a) procure for Customer the right to continue Using the SOFTWARE as contemplated hereunder; (b) modify the SOFTWARE to render same non-infringing (provided such modification does not adversely affect Customer's use as described in the RFP) or (c) replace same with equally suitable, functionally equivalent, compatible non-infringing SOFTWARE. If none of the foregoing is possible, ABC shall have the right to terminate this Agreement upon: (i) payment to Customer of all monies paid by Customer for the SOFTWARE under Section 5 of this Agreement and (ii) if this Agreement is terminated in accordance with this paragraph 8.3 within the first twenty four (24) months after Acceptance, ABC shall in addition pay Customer an amount equal to twenty percent (20%) of the License Fee as liquidated damages.

9. LIMITED REMEDIES & LIABILITY

(9.1) In all cases involving performance or non-performance of the SOFTWARE, Customer's primary remedy shall be correction of the Error(s). For all other failure(s) by ABC to perform in accordance with this Agreement, including without limitation, if the SOFTWARE is not Accepted by Customer (due to no fault of the Customer) or an Error cannot be corrected within the time periods specified in Section 7 of this Agreement, the Customer shall be entitled to terminate this Agreement in accordance with Section 10 and/or recover damages subject to the limits stated in paragraph 9.2.

(9.2) ABC's liability to Customer shall be limited to: (a) the amount of the License Fee and other amounts payable by Customer under Section 5 of this Agreement plus (b) the amount of any liquidated damages payable by ABC pursuant to the various sections of this Agreement. The foregoing limitation of liability shall not apply to the: (a) payment of costs, damages and attorney's fees referred to in Section 8 for ABC's indemnity obligation; (b) claims for personal injury or damage to real or personal property caused by willful or negligent acts of ABC, its employees or contractors or (c) damages resulting from violation of Section 4 of this Agreement for breach of confidentiality and non-disclosure obligations.

(9.3) IN NO EVENT SHALL ABC OR THE CUSTOMER BE LIABLE FOR INCIDENTAL, SPECIAL OR CONSEQUENTIAL DAMAGES (INCLUDING WITHOUT LIMITATION LOST PROFITS) EVEN IF EITHER PARTY HAS BEEN ADVISED OF THE POSSIBILITY OF SUCH DAMAGES.

10. TERMINATION

(10.1) If a party (the "Defaulting Party") is in material breach of or default under this Agreement, and the Defaulting Party does not remedy that breach or default within thirty (30) calendar days after receipt from the other party of written notice of that default or breach (provided that if the breach or default is one that cannot be remedied within such thirty (30) day period, this Agreement may be terminated effective immediately upon written notice to the Defaulting Party), the other party shall after the expiry of such thirty (30) calendar day period have the right to terminate this Agreement effective immediately upon written notice to the Defaulting Party.

(10.2) Either party may terminate this Agreement, at any time, by written notice in the event that the other: (a) files a voluntary petition in bankruptcy or under any similar insolvency law; (b) makes an assignment for the benefit of creditors; (c) has filed against it any involuntary petition in bankruptcy or under any similar insolvency law if any such petition is not dismissed within sixty (60) days after filing or (d) a receiver is appointed for, or a levy or attachment is made against, substantially all of its assets, if any such petition is not dismissed or such receiver or levy or attachment is not discharged within sixty (60) days after the filing or appointment.

(10.3) If the Defaulting Party is Customer, the termination of this Agreement by ABC shall (subject to paragraphs 10.5 and 10.6) terminate the License and Customer shall return to ABC all copies of the SOFTWARE in Customer's possession or control.

(10.4) If the Defaulting Party is ABC, the termination of this Agreement by Customer shall not terminate the License and Customer shall, in addition to all of Customer's other rights and remedies, be entitled to retain and Use all copies of the SOFTWARE in Customer's possession or control.

(10.5) For the purposes of paragraph 10.1 and 10.2, Customer shall be in material breach of or default under this Agreement and ABC may terminate this Agreement only if the breach or default relates to Customer's obligation to pay ABC an amount payable hereunder when due and the breach or default is not remedied within the applicable time period specified therefor. ABC's rights and remedies in respect of any other breach of or default under this Agreement shall be limited to such rights and remedies other than termination of this Agreement and the License, it being acknowledged and agreed by ABC that the License is irrevocable and not terminable except if Customer is in material breach of or default under this Agreement as provided in this paragraph.

(10.6) If this Agreement is terminated by ABC for a material default or breach of Customer as described in paragraph 10.5, Customer shall be entitled to retain possession of the SOFTWARE and to Use the SOFTWARE in the ordinary course of its business for the period of time, not to exceed six (6) months, required for Customer to wind down its current use of the SOFTWARE or to make a transition to alternate software or facilities.

11. TRAINING

(11.1) ABC shall provide thirty (30) hours of training to Customer in the use, operation and maintenance of the SOFTWARE. The training curriculum and ABC's instructors assigned thereto is identified in **Schedule "G"** attached hereto and made a part hereof. Training will be conducted in not less than two or greater than three (3) hour sessions per day at Customer's offices in New York. ABC shall assume and be responsible for the payment of all transportation, room and board expenses of its employees in furnishing such training.

12. INSTALLATION

(12.1) Installation of the SOFTWARE shall be the responsibility of ABC and shall be completed by the dates set forth in the Implementation Schedule. As a condition to Installation, Customer shall prepare the Installation Site. Installation shall be deemed complete when each of the data screens identified in **Schedule "J"** attached hereto and made a part hereof, can be displayed on the Hardware's terminal devices.

(12.2) If through no fault of the Customer, Installation is not complete by the date specified therefor in the Implementation Schedule, without limiting any other rights and remedies available to the Customer at law and under this Agreement, ABC shall pay Customer one thousand dollars ($1,000) for each business day after the fourth business day that completion of Installation is delayed.

13. SITE PREPARATION

(13.1) Customer shall be responsible for preparation of the Installation Site in accordance with the specifications set forth in **Schedule "I"**. At such time that the Installation Site has been prepared, Customer shall give written notice thereof to ABC and within five (5) business days after receipt of Customer's notice by ABC, ABC shall inspect the Installation Site and either give its approval or disapproval. In the event ABC does not approve the Installation Site, it shall provide detailed reasons therefor within three (3) business days after its inspection in which case Customer shall correct the deficiencies identified by ABC and the inspection process shall be repeated.

14. GENERAL

(14.1) Not later than fifteen (15) calendar days after the date of Installation, ABC shall deliver a full and complete set of the Deposit to the escrow agent in accordance with the Escrow Agreement.

(14.2) The professional personnel provided by ABC shall be appropriately trained in the technical skills necessary to perform their duties. Customer may require ABC to replace any person who is performing services pursuant to this Agreement, if Customer in Customer's sole but reasonable discretion determines that such person is unfit or otherwise unsatisfactory.

(14.3) The personnel of each party, when on the premises of the other, shall comply with the security and other personnel regulations of the party on whose premises such person is on.

(14.4) ABC recognizes that its employees identified in **Schedule "M"** are particularly qualified to perform the services under this Agreement and ABC agrees not to remove such personnel from the performance of services hereunder until such time that their respective tasks have been satisfactorily completed.

(14.5) Neither party shall assign its rights or obligations under this Agreement without the prior written consent of the other party. Notwithstanding the forgoing and anything to the contrary in Section 3.1 of this Agreement, the Customer shall be entitled to assign its rights and obligations hereunder to any one of Customer's subsidiaries without any further consent from ABC. For purposes of this paragraph 14.5, a " subsidiary" shall be any entity in which Customer owns or controls at least fifty percent (50%) of such entity's stock or other evidence of ownership.

(14.6) No modifications of this Agreement shall be valid or binding on either party unless acknowledged in writing and signed by the duly authorized officer of each party. All notices or other communications given under this Agreement shall be in writing, sent to the address hereinbefore set forth as the principal place of business or such other addresses as ABC or the Customer may designate in writing by certified mail (return receipt requested) or personal delivery. Notice shall be deemed given upon receipt.

(14.7) Both parties understand and agree that violation of Section 4 of this Agreement may cause damage to the other party in an amount which is impossible or extremely difficult to ascertain. Accordingly, without limitation to any other remedy available at law, the injured party may be entitled to injunctive relief restraining the other party from continuing to violate the terms and provisions of said section.

(14.8) Neither party shall be liable to the other for any delay or failure to perform its obligations under this Agreement if such delay or failure arises from a cause beyond the reasonable control of such party, including but not limited to labor disputes, strikes, other labor or industrial disturbances, acts of God, floods, lightning, utility or communication failures, earthquakes or other casualty.

If a delay or failure that ABC anticipates will cause an excusable delay, ABC by written notice shall inform Customer of the anticipated effect of such delay as soon as possible and in any event shall give written notice within ten (10) calendar days. Such notice shall contain a description of the steps ABC is taking to alleviate the problem. Anything in this Agreement to the contrary notwithstanding, Customer may, if the SOFTWARE has not been Accepted due to a problem described in this paragraph 14.8, by a date which is seventy five (75) calendar days after Acceptance Testing is to commence, terminate this Agreement upon fourteen (14) calendar days notice to ABC; in such event, ABC shall refund all payments made by Customer and Customer shall return all portions of the SOFTWARE delivered prior to termination.

(14.9) The parties acknowledge that each has read all the terms of this Agreement, is authorized to enter into it, agrees to be bound by its terms and conditions and that it is the complete and exclusive statement of the agreement between the parties which supersedes all prior communications and agreements between the parties relating to the subject matter of this Agreement.

(14.10) Any forbearance or delay on the part of either party in enforcing any provision of this Agreement or any of its rights hereunder shall not be construed as a waiver of such provision or of a right to enforce same.

(14.11) The provisions of Sections 4, 8, 10 and 14.6 through 14.14 shall survive termination of this Agreement or any portion thereof.

(14.12) The parties shall use all reasonable efforts to amicably resolve any dispute or controversy arising directly out of this Agreement by referring such dispute or controversy to a senior management executive of each party who was not directly involved in the procurement and day to day management of the SOFTWARE. The management executive selected by each party shall have the authority to bind its company to the terms of any settlement agreed to. If the parties, after good faith efforts, fail to resolve the dispute or controversy, the matter shall be referred to and settled by arbitration in accordance with the rules of XYZ Dispute Resolution Services.

In connection with any breach or threatened breach by either party of the confidential information obligations of this Agreement, the non-breaching party may, at any time seek by application to the United States District Court for the Southern District of New York or the Supreme Court of the State of New York for the County of New York any such temporary or provisional relief or remedy ("provisional remedy") provided for by the laws of the United States of America or the laws of the State of New York as would be available in an action based upon such dispute or controversy in the absence of this Section 14.12. No such application to either said Court for a provisional remedy, nor any act or conduct by either party in furtherance of or in opposition to such application, shall constitute a relinquishment or waiver of any right to have the underlying dispute or controversy with respect to which such application is made settled by arbitration.

In any arbitration proceeding, each party shall select one arbitrator who has technical software systems knowledge of real time trading systems. The two arbitrators so selected shall appoint a third so qualified arbitrator. A majority decision of the arbitrators shall be binding. Each party shall bear its own costs associated with such arbitration. The arbitration proceeding shall be kept confidential.

(14.13) Pending resolution of any dispute or controversy as provided in Section 14.12, each of the parties shall continue to perform its obligations under this Agreement and a failure to perform its obligations by either party pending the resolution process shall be deemed a separate breach of this Agreement.

(14.14) Any dispute arising under this Agreement shall be governed by the laws of the State of New York.

IN WITNESS WHEREOF, the parties have caused this Agreement to be executed and do each hereby warrant and represent that their respective signatory whose signature appears below has been and is on the date of this Agreement duly authorized by all necessary and appropriate corporate action to execute this Agreement.

CUSTOMER   ABC SYSTEMS, INC.

By: _____   By: _____

Name: _____   Name: _____

Title: _____   Title: _____

Date: _____   Date: _____

ABC SYSTEMS, INC.
SOFTWARE DEVELOPMENT AGREEMENT

AGREEMENT made as of the 28th day of August, 1996 by and between ABC Systems, Inc., with its office at 50 Main Street, White Plains, NY 11477 ("ABC") and Professional Trading Company, Ltd. with an office located at 100 Park Avenue, New York, NY 10017 ("Customer").

The Customer and ABC agree that ABC shall perform software development services for the Customer and that such work shall be provided in accordance with the following terms and conditions:

1. DEFINITIONS

As used in this document the following terms shall have the meanings set forth below:

(1.1) "Acceptance" shall have the meaning stated in Section 8 of this Agreement.

(1.2) "Acceptance Test" shall mean the testing process for the COMPUTER PROGRAM performed in accordance with the Test Plans, as specified in Section 8 of this Agreement.

(1.3) "Agreement" shall mean this agreement, any attached exhibits or schedules and any amendments to this agreement which are in writing and signed by both parties.

(1.4) "COMPUTER PROGRAM" shall mean the computer software program and Documentation identified in Sections 2.1 (c) and 3, respectively, of this Agreement individually or collectively, together with all amendments enhancements and modifications thereto which have been accepted by Customer.

(1.5) "Documentation" shall mean the documents identified in Section 3 of this Agreement.

(1.6) "Error" shall mean an error in the code of the COMPUTER PROGRAM which prevents the COMPUTER PROGRAM from operating in all material respects in accordance with the Documentation and the RFP.

(1.7) "Functional Specification" shall have the meaning given it in Section 3.1 (a) of this Agreement.

(1.8) "Hardware" shall mean the computer equipment identified in **Schedule "G"** to this Agreement.

(1.9) "Installation" shall have the meaning given it in Section 7.3 of this Agreement.

(1.10) "Installation Site" shall mean Customer's office above stated.

(1.11) "System Design Specification" shall have the meaning given it in Section 3.1 (b) of this Agreement.

(1.12) "Source Listings" shall mean the human-readable instructions together with annotations thereto which comprise the source code of the COMPUTER PROGRAM.

(1.13) "Test Plans" shall mean the procedures and objectives of the Acceptance Test for the COMPUTER PROGRAM, as specified in Section 8 of this Agreement.

(1.14) "RFP" shall mean Customer's Request for Proposal dated July 7, 1996, a copy of which is attached hereto as **Schedule "D"** and made a part hereof.

(1.15) "Work" shall mean the computer consulting and programming services performed by ABC for Customer hereunder.

2. STATEMENT OF WORK

(2.1) On or before the dates set forth in the Implementation Schedule attached hereto as **Schedule "A"** and made a part hereof, ABC shall deliver to Customer:

(a) the Functional Specification to be attached to this Agreement as **Schedule "B"** and made a part hereof upon its Acceptance;

(b) the System Design Specification to be attached to this Agreement as **Schedule "C"** and made a part hereof upon its Acceptance;

(c) computer software programs, in source code format, to be developed by ABC consistent with the System Design Specification and which have the capabilities described in the Functional Specification (the "COMPUTER PROGRAM"). However, to avoid doubt, the COMPUTER PROGRAM shall have all of the functions, features, performance, compatibility and enhancement characteristics described in the RFP. In the event of any inconsistency between the Functional Specification and the RFP, the RFP shall prevail; and

(d) Documentation in addition to the System Design and Functional Specification, as identified in Section 3.1(c) of this Agreement.

3. <u>DOCUMENTATION</u>

(3.1) ABC shall provide Customer with the following Documentation by the dates set forth in the Implementation Schedule:

(a) ABC shall prepare the Functional Specification describing each business function to be performed by the COMPUTER PROGRAM. The Functional Specification shall include: (i) all of the business functions identified in the RFP and (ii) Customer's current procedures for the purchase and sale of securities in the over the counter market;

(b) ABC shall prepare a System Design Specification for each business function described in the Functional Specification, which shall include (by way of example and not limitation): (i) data inputs and outputs, including codes and acronyms; (ii) program descriptions; (iii) file descriptions, formats and layouts; (iv) report descriptions and layouts; (v) screen descriptions and layouts; (vi) interface requirements and descriptions; (vii) processing flow charts; (viii) programming standards; (ix) processing narratives; (x) editing rules; (xi) error detection procedures; (xii) performance and response time requirements; (xiii) hardware and communication requirements and (ivx) RDBMS requirements; and

(c) user, operations and training manuals for the COMPUTER PROGRAM.

(3.2) All Documentation shall be produced in accordance and compliance with the standards identified in **Schedule "E"** attached hereto and made a part hereof. Two (2) copies of all Documentation shall be provided in printed form and one copy in electronic form compatible with Microsoft Word, version 6.0.

4. CHARGES

(4.1) Subject to paragraph 4.2, Customer shall pay ABC one hundred thousand United States dollars ($100,000) for the Work, payable as follows:

(a) ten thousand dollars ($10,000) upon execution of this Agreement;

(b) five thousand dollars ($5,000) upon Acceptance of the Functional Specifications;

(c) five thousand dollars ($5,000) upon Acceptance of the System Design Specifications;

(d) ten thousand dollars ($10,000) upon delivery and Installation of the COMPUTER PROGRAM and confirmation by Customer that the COMPUTER PROGRAM's program files listed in **Schedule "F"** attached hereto and made a part hereof reside on the Hardware's program libraries;

(e) twenty thousand dollars ($20,000) upon Acceptance of the COMPUTER PROGRAM;

(f) fifteen thousand dollars ($15,000) upon Acceptance of the user, operations and training Documentation to Customer; and

(g) thirty five thousand dollars ($35,000) upon the later of (i) expiration of the warranty period or (ii) all warranty claims having been properly satisfied by ABC .

(4.2) In the event that: (a) the Customer does not give its Acceptance of the Functional Specification or the System Design Specification within the time frames specified in Section 8 of this Agreement or (b) Customer and ABC fail to reach agreement with respect to a fixed charge for development of the COMPUTER PROGRAM within ten (10) business days after the last date by which the System Design Specification can be Accepted, either party may terminate this Agreement upon ten (10) business days prior written notice. This Agreement shall terminate automatically five (5) business days after the receipt of such notice by the receiving party if an agreement on the Functional Specification, System Design Specification or fixed charge, as applicable, has not been reached in writing by the expiration of such five (5) day period. In the event that this Agreement is terminated in accordance with this paragraph 4.2, within five (5) business days after the effective date of termination, ABC shall refund all monies paid by Customer to ABC in accordance with this Section.

(4.3) The Customer shall pay any sales or use tax imposed by the New York State and/or New York City government(s) in connection with the COMPUTER PROGRAM.

(4.4) The Customer shall pay all reasonable expenses incurred by ABC in performing its obligations hereunder. Expenses which: (a) individually are in excess of two hundred fifty dollars ($250) or (b) during any calendar month, would cause total expenses incurred in such month to exceed five hundred dollars ($500), shall not be incurred without Customer's prior written consent.

(4.5) Invoices shall be payable within thirty (30) days after Customer's receipt of ABC's invoice, so long as the amounts stated therein are not reasonably in dispute.

(4.6) ABC warrants that the terms of this Agreement are comparable to or better than the terms offered by ABC to any of its present commercial customers of equal or lesser size for comparable Work. If ABC offers more favorable terms to its commercial customers during the period commencing upon execution hereof and expiring one (1) year thereafter, such terms shall also be made available to Customer together with any resulting refund within thirty (30) days from the execution of such agreement.

5. OWNERSHIP

(5.1) ABC acknowledges that Customer shall have exclusive, unlimited ownership rights to all Work performed hereunder, to all materials and/or deliverables prepared for the Customer hereunder and all ideas, concepts, inventions, designs, techniques conceived by Customer or jointly with ABC hereunder, as a combination of components and/or individually, and whether or not this Agreement is satisfactorily completed, all of which shall be deemed work made for hire and made in the course of services rendered and shall belong exclusively to the Customer with the Customer having the right to obtain, hold and render, in its own name patents, copyrights and registrations therefor. In the event that certain other ownership rights do not originally vest in Customer as contemplated hereunder, ABC agrees to irrevocably assign, transfer and convey to the Customer all rights, title and interest therein. ABC and its personnel shall give Customer, and any person designated by Customer, all reasonable assistance and shall execute all necessary documents to assist and/or enable Customer to perfect, preserve, register and/or record its rights in all such Work, deliverables or material.

6. **CONFIDENTIALITY**

(6.1) As used herein, "Confidential Information" shall include all information and data furnished by CUSTOMER to ABC, whether in oral, written, graphic or machine-readable form, including without limitation, specifications, user, operations or systems manuals, diagrams, graphs, models, sketches, technical data, research, business or financial information, plans, strategies, forecasts, forecast assumptions, business practices, marketing information and material, customer names, proprietary ideas, concepts, know-how, methodologies and all other information related to CUSTOMER's business. Confidential Information shall also include the COMPUTER PROGRAM and confidential information received by CUSTOMER from a third party. In order for any information provided verbally by CUSTOMER to ABC to come within the definition of Confidential Information, it shall be identified as confidential at the time of disclosure and within five (5) business days after verbal disclosure thereof by CUSTOMER, such information shall be documented in writing specifying that CUSTOMER considers such information confidential.

(6.2) Notwithstanding anything to the contrary contained in this Agreement, Confidential Information shall not include information: (a) in the public domain (other than as a result of a breach of this Agreement); (b) generally known and disclosed to ABC by persons or entities engaged in a comparable business (other than as a result of a breach of this Agreement or any other agreement to which such persons or entities are parties); (c) in ABC's possession prior to its receipt from Customer pursuant to this Agreement or (d) independently developed by ABC.

(6.3) ABC agrees to maintain the confidentiality of the Confidential Information using procedures no less rigorous than those used to protect and preserve the confidentiality of its own proprietary information and shall not, directly or indirectly: (a) transfer or disclose any Confidential Information to any third party; (b) use any Confidential Information other than as contemplated under this Agreement or (c) take any other action with respect to the Confidential Information inconsistent with the confidential and proprietary nature of such information. ABC further agrees to return all Confidential Information (and all copies thereof) to the Customer upon termination of this Agreement.

(6.4) ABC shall be permitted to disclose the Confidential Information to its employees having a need for access thereto in connection with performance of the Work and who have executed confidentiality agreements containing provisions similar to those contained in this Agreement and specifying that the Customer is a third party beneficiary thereunder entitled to enforce the provisions thereof as though a party thereto. ABC shall take steps, no less rigorous than those it takes to protect its own proprietary information, to prevent its employees from acting in a manner inconsistent with the terms of this Agreement.

7. DELIVERY, INSTALLATION & SITE PREPARATION

(7.1) The COMPUTER PROGRAM shall be developed, delivered and implemented in accordance with Implementation Schedule attached hereto as **Schedule "A"**. ABC understands that that Customer has contracted for the licensing and/or purchase and delivery of other items of computer software and/or hardware comprising a major computer system to be implemented for Customer and therefore it is vital that the dates stated in the Implementation Schedule be met otherwise Customer will incur substantial additional expense and injury. In the event that ABC fails to perform in accordance with the Implementation Schedule, ABC shall assign additional qualified staff to the development, delivery and implementation, as applicable, of the COMPUTER PROGRAM. Without limiting any of its rights under this Agreement and at law, ABC shall pay Customer one thousand dollars ($1,000), as liquidated damages, for each business day after the fourth business day that it fails to complete a task, milestone or other delivery required to be made or performed in accordance with this Agreement and/or terminate this Agreement in accordance with Section 15.

(7.2) Installation of the COMPUTER PROGRAM shall be the responsibility of ABC. As a condition to such installation, Customer shall prepare the Installation Site in accordance with the site preparation requirements identified in **Schedule "H"** attached hereto and made a part hereof. At such time that the Installation Site has been prepared, Customer shall give written notice thereof to ABC and within five (5) business days after receipt of Customer's notice by ABC, ABC shall inspect the Installation Site and either give its approval or disapproval. In the event ABC does not approve the site, it shall provide detailed reasons therefor within three (3) business days after its inspection in which case Customer shall correct the deficiencies identified by ABC and the inspection process shall be repeated.

(7.3) Installation shall be deemed complete when each of the data screens identified in **Schedule "I"** attached hereto and made a part hereof, can be displayed on the Hardware's terminal devices.

(7.4) The Customer agrees to reasonably cooperate with ABC with respect to this Agreement including without limitation, providing all information and access to key personnel needed to develop and/or implement the COMPUTER PROGRAM.

8. ACCEPTANCE

(8.1) The Documentation developed by ABC pursuant to Section 3 of this Agreement shall be delivered for Customer's Acceptance not later than the dates specified in the Implementation Schedule. Customer shall have thirty (30) calendar days (the "Review Period) to review each item of Documentation and either approve or reject such Documentation in accordance with this Section.

(8.2) If an item of Documentation is unsatisfactory in any material respect, Customer shall prepare a detailed written description of its objections and deliver them to ABC not later than seven (7) business after expiration of the Review Period. ABC shall thereupon undertake to modify the Documentation to respond to such objections and shall do so within ten (10) business days of receipt of Customer's objections.

(8.3) If any item of Documentation continues to be unsatisfactory after the revisions made in accordance with paragraph 8.2 of this Section, Customer may, in sole discretion, grant ABC additional time to modify the Documentation so that it is conforming or terminate this Agreement. In such an event ABC shall refund to Customer all amounts paid hereunder and, as liquidated damages for its failure, pay Customer five thousand dollars ($5,000).

(8.4) Customer shall prepare Test Plans consistent with the Documentation on or before the date which is thirty (30) calendar days prior to the date the COMPUTER PROGRAM is scheduled for Installation. The Test Plans shall include procedures required to demonstrate that the COMPUTER PROGRAM operates in all material respects in accordance with the Documentation and RFP. In the event of an inconsistency between the RFP and the Documentation, the RFP shall prevail. Customer shall prepare the data necessary for performing the Acceptance Test. Customer shall perform the Acceptance Test within ten (10) business days after Installation is complete.

(8.5) Within five (5) business days after completion of the Acceptance Test, Customer shall either give its Acceptance of the COMPUTER PROGRAM or disapprove such results and provide detailed written reasons for such disapproval.

(8.6) If the COMPUTER PROGRAM or any portion thereof fails to pass the Acceptance Test, ABC will correct all Error(s) not later than fourteen (14) calendar days after receipt of Customer's notice describing the Error(s). Within fourteen (14) calendar days after such corrections have been made, Customer will retest the COMPUTER PROGRAM. If the COMPUTER PROGRAM still fails the Acceptance Test after corrections having been made in accordance with this paragraph (8.6), Customer may at its option, grant ABC additional time in Customer's sole discretion to correct the outstanding Error(s) or terminate this Agreement in which event ABC shall refund to Customer all amounts paid hereunder and, as liquidated damages for its failure, pay Customer ten thousand dollars ($10,000).

(8.7) Acceptance of the COMPUTER PROGRAM shall be deemed to have occurred upon execution of an Acceptance Certificate, the form of which is attached hereto as **Schedule "J"** .

9. LIMITED WARRANTY

(9.1) ABC warrants that the COMPUTER PROGRAM, upon Acceptance and for a period of one (1) year thereafter, will operate without an Error. ABC also warrants that it has inspected the SOFTWARE for computer viruses and that the SOFTWARE shall be free of all viruses when delivered. Furthermore, ABC warrants that the SOFTWARE shall be compatible and able to support date calculations for the years 2000 and beyond and have all of the capabilities and functions required by Customer as defined in Customer's RFP. In the event of an inconsistency between the RFP and the Documentation, the RFP shall prevail. EXCEPT FOR THE FOREGOING, ABC MAKES NO OTHER WARRANTY, EXPRESS OR IMPLIED, INCLUDING WITHOUT LIMITATION, THE IMPLIED WARRANTIES OF MERCHANTABILITY OR FITNESS FOR A PARTICULAR PURPOSE.

(9.2) ABC shall respond to service requests within one (1) hour of Customer's notice and shall have completed all necessary corrections not later than three (3) hours after Customer's notice. In the event that that, during any ninety (90) day period, ABC shall fail two (2) times to correct an Error within the time periods aforesaid, Customer shall be entitled, at ABC's cost and expense, to employ its own personnel or a third party contractor of its own choosing to correct Errors occurring thereafter if ABC shall again fail to correct an Error within the prescribed time period.

(9.3) In the event that an Error which prevents production use of the COMPUTER PROGRAM in any material respect as reasonably determined by the Customer is not corrected by ABC within seventy two (72) hours after notice (by telephone) thereof is given by Customer to ABC, Customer may terminate this Agreement in which case ABC shall promptly refund all amounts paid by Customer to ABC hereunder and, as liquidated damages for its failure, pay Customer fifteen thousand dollars ($15,000).

(9.4) ABC shall perform services at the Installation Site during the warranty period at no additional charge to Customer. Alternatively, with Customer's prior consent, ABC shall be entitled to log-in to Customer's computer system and access the COMPUTER PROGRAM for the purposes of Error diagnosis, correction and installation.

10. INTELLECTUAL PROPERTY INDEMNIFICATION

(10.1) ABC agrees to defend and/or handle at its own expense, any claim or action against Customer for actual or alleged infringement of any intellectual or industrial property right, including without limitation, trademarks, service marks, patents, copyrights, misappropriation of trade secrets or any similar property rights, based upon the COMPUTER PROGRAM or Customer's use thereof. ABC further agrees to indemnify and hold Customer harmless from and against any and all liabilities, costs, losses, damages and expenses (including reasonable attorney's fees) associated with such claim or action. Customer shall reasonably cooperate with ABC in the defense of such claim or action to the extent that such cooperation is given at such times and in a manner that does not negatively affect Customer's business in Customer's sole discretion and further, ABC reimburses Customer's expenses and pays Customer at Customer's hourly billing rate for all such assistance.

(10.2) ABC shall have the sole right to conduct the defense of any such claim or action and all negotiations for its settlement or compromise. Notwithstanding the foregoing, in the event that ABC shall fail to appoint an attorney within ten (10) calendar days after the claim having first been made or action commenced or the attorney appointed by ABC is, in Customer's reasonable judgment not suitably qualified to represent Customer, Customer shall have the right to select and appoint an alternative attorney and the reasonable cost and expense thereof shall be paid by ABC.

(10.3) If the COMPUTER PROGRAM becomes or in ABC's reasonable opinion is likely to become the subject of any such claim or action, then, ABC shall use best efforts at its sole expense to either: (a) procure for Customer the right to continue using the COMPUTER PROGRAM as contemplated hereunder; (b) modify the COMPUTER PROGRAM to render same non-infringing (provided such modification does not adversely affect Customer's use as described in the RFP) or (c) replace same with equally suitable, functionally equivalent, compatible non-infringing COMPUTER PROGRAM. If none of the foregoing is possible, ABC shall have the right to terminate this Agreement upon: (i) payment to Customer of all monies paid by Customer for the Work and (ii) if this Agreement is terminated in accordance with this paragraph within the first twenty four (24) months after Acceptance, ABC shall in addition pay Customer an amount equal to twenty percent (20%) of all monies payable by Customer to ABC for the Work as liquidated damages.

11. LIMITED REMEDIES & LIABILITY

(11.1) In all cases involving performance or non-performance of the COMPUTER PROGRAM, Customer's primary remedy shall be correction of the Error(s). For all other failure(s) by ABC to perform in accordance with this Agreement, including without limitation, if the COMPUTER PROGRAM is not Accepted by Customer (due to no fault of the Customer) or an Error cannot be corrected within the time periods specified in Section 9 of this Agreement, the Customer shall be entitled to terminate this Agreement in accordance with Section 15 and/or recover damages subject to paragraph 11.2.

(11.2) ABC's liability to Customer shall be limited to: (a) the charges payable by Customer under Section 4 of this Agreement plus (b) the amount of any liquidated damages payable by ABC pursuant to the various sections of this Agreement. The foregoing limitation of liability shall not apply to the: (a) payment of costs, damages and attorney's fees referred to in Section 10 for ABC's indemnity obligation; (b) claims for personal injury or damage to real or personal property caused by willful or negligent acts of ABC, its employees or contractors or (c) damages resulting from violation of Section 6 of this Agreement for breach of confidentiality and non-disclosure obligations.

(11.3) IN NO EVENT SHALL ABC OR THE CUSTOMER BE LIABLE FOR INCIDENTAL, SPECIAL OR CONSEQUENTIAL DAMAGES (INCLUDING WITHOUT LIMITATION LOST PROFITS) EVEN IF EITHER PARTY HAS BEEN ADVISED OF THE POSSIBILITY OF SUCH DAMAGES.

12. CHANGE IN SCOPE

(12.1) ABC and the Customer recognize that it may be desirable for the Customer to make changes to the Functional and/or System Design

Specifications (a "Revision") during the performance of this Agreement. Customer may request Revision by giving notice thereof to ABC specifying the nature of the change(s) desired (the "Revision Notice").

(12.2) Within ten (10) calendar days after ABC has received the Revision Notice, it shall provide Customer with a proposal identifying: (a) any addition or reduction in the cost associated with performing the Work; (b) the effect, if any, to the payment schedule identified in Section 4; (c) the revisions required and to be made to the Documentation; (d) the effect, if any, with respect to the delivery and implementation milestones identified in **Schedule "A"** attached hereto; and (e) any other change which would be required to any of the other sections or schedules to this Agreement (the "Revision Proposal").

(12.3) Upon Customer's written approval of the Revision Proposal, ABC shall, within ten (10) calendar days thereafter, revise the Functional and/or System Design Specification(s) (the "Revised Specifications") and submit them for Customer's approval. ABC shall not develop or implement any Revision until such time that the Customer has approved the Revised Specification(s) in writing. Upon Customer's approval of the Revised Specification(s), this Agreement shall be deemed amended to reflect the terms and conditions of the Revision Proposal.

13. PROJECT MANAGERS & MEETINGS

(13.1) The Customer and ABC shall each designate prior to the commencement of Work under this Agreement a project manager to whom all communications may be addressed, and who shall have complete responsibility and authority for the Customer and ABC, respectively, in all aspects of this Agreement.

(13.2) The project mangers shall meet at least weekly. ABC's project manager shall render a written status report as of the middle and end of each calendar month, such report to be delivered to Customer's project manager within three (3) business days after the end of such half month.

(13.3) ABC's project manager shall be available upon five (5) business day's notice to attend meetings of the Customer's management.

14. <u>TRAINING</u>

(14.1) ABC shall provide thirty (30) hours of training to Customer in the use, operation and maintenance of the COMPUTER PROGRAM. The training curriculum and ABC's instructors assigned thereto is identified in **Schedule "K"** attached hereto and made a part hereof. Training will be conducted in not less than two or greater than three (3) hour sessions per day at Customer's offices in New York. ABC shall assume and be responsible for the payment of all transportation, room and board expenses of its employees in furnishing such training.

15. <u>TERMINATION</u>

(15.1) If a party (the "Defaulting Party") is in material breach of or default under this Agreement, and the Defaulting Party does not remedy that breach or default within thirty (30) calendar days after receipt from the other party of written notice of that default or breach (provided that if the breach or default is one that cannot be remedied within such thirty (30) day period, this Agreement may be terminated effective immediately upon written notice to the Defaulting Party), the other party shall after the expiry of such thirty (30) calendar day period have the right to terminate this Agreement effective immediately upon written notice to the Defaulting Party.

(15.2) Either party may terminate this Agreement, at any time, by written notice in the event that the other: (a) files a voluntary petition in bankruptcy or under any similar insolvency law; (b) makes an assignment for the benefit of creditors; (c) has filed against it any involuntary petition in bankruptcy or under any similar insolvency law if any such petition is not dismissed within sixty (60) days after filing or (d) a receiver is appointed for, or a levy or attachment is made against, substantially all of its assets, if any such petition is not dismissed or such receiver or levy or attachment is not discharged within sixty (60) days after the filing or appointment.

(15.3) For the purposes of paragraph 15.1 and 15.2, Customer shall be in material breach of or default under this Agreement and ABC may terminate this Agreement only if the breach or default relates to Customer's obligation to pay ABC any amount payable hereunder when due and the breach or default is not remedied within the applicable time period specified therefor. ABC's rights and remedies in respect of any other breach of or default under this Agreement shall be limited to such rights and remedies other than termination of this Agreement.

16. GENERAL

(16.1) The professional personnel provided by ABC shall be appropriately trained in the technical skills to perform their duties. Customer may require ABC to replace any person who is performing Work pursuant to this Agreement, if Customer in Customer's sole but reasonable discretion determines that such person is unfit or otherwise unsatisfactory. The personnel of each party, when on the premises of the other, shall comply with the security and other personnel regulations of the party on whose premises such person is on.

ABC recognizes that its employees identified in **Schedule "L"** are particularly qualified to perform the services under this Agreement and ABC agrees not to remove such personnel from the performance of Work hereunder until such time that their respective tasks have been satisfactorily completed.

(16.2) Neither party shall assign its rights or obligations under this Agreement without the prior written consent of the other party. Notwithstanding the forgoing, the Customer shall be entitled to assign its rights and obligations hereunder to any one of Customer's subsidiaries without any further consent from ABC. For purposes of this paragraph 16.2, a " subsidiary" shall be any entity in which Customer owns or controls at least fifty percent (50%) of such entity's stock or other evidence of ownership.

(16.3) No modifications of this Agreement shall be valid or binding on either party unless acknowledged in writing and signed by the duly authorized officer of each party. All notices or other communications given under this Agreement shall be in writing, sent to the address hereinbefore set forth as the principal place of business or such other addresses as ABC or the Customer may designate in writing by certified mail (return receipt requested) or personal delivery. Notice shall be deemed given upon receipt.

(16.4) ABC understands and agrees that violation of Section 6 of this Agreement may cause damage to the Customer in an amount which is impossible or extremely difficult to ascertain. Accordingly, without limitation to any other remedy available at law, the Customer may be entitled to injunctive relief restraining ABC from continuing to violate the terms and provisions of said section.

(16.5) Neither party shall be liable to the other for any delay or failure to perform its obligations under this Agreement if such delay or failure arises from any cause beyond the reasonable control of such party, including but not limited to labor disputes, strikes, other labor or industrial disturbances, acts of God, floods, lightning, utility or communication failures, earthquakes or other casualty.

If a delay or failure that ABC anticipates will cause an excusable delay, ABC by written notice shall inform Customer of the anticipated effect of such delay as soon as possible and in any event shall give written notice within ten (10) calendar days. Such notice shall contain a description of the steps ABC is taking to alleviate the problem. Anything in this Agreement to the contrary notwithstanding, Customer may, if the COMPUTER PROGRAM has not been Accepted due to a problem described in this paragraph 16.5, by a date which is seventy five (75) calendar days after Acceptance Testing is to commence, terminate this Agreement upon fourteen (14) calendar days notice to ABC; in such event, Customer may return all portions of the COMPUTER PROGRAM delivered prior to termination in which case ABC shall refund all payments made by Customer.

(16.6) The parties acknowledge that each has read all the terms of this Agreement, is authorized to enter into it, agrees to be bound by its terms and conditions and that it is the complete and exclusive statement of the agreement between the parties which supersedes all prior communications and agreements between the parties relating to the subject matter of this Agreement.

(16.7) Any forbearance or delay on the part of either party in enforcing any provision of this Agreement or any of its rights hereunder shall not be construed as a waiver of such provision or of a right to enforce same.

(16.8) ABC is an independent contractor in performance of the Work and shall not be considered to be or permitted to be an agent, employee, joint venturer or partner of the Customer. All persons furnished, used, retained or hired by or on behalf of ABC, are and shall be considered employees or agents of ABC. ABC assumes sole and full responsibility for their acts. ABC shall at all times during the term of this Agreement maintain such supervision, direction and control over its employees and agents as is consistent with and necessary to preserve its independent contractor status.

(16.9) The provisions of Sections 5, 6, 10, 11, 15 and 16.3 through 16.12 shall survive termination of this Agreement or any portion thereof.

(16.10) The parties shall use all reasonable efforts to amicably resolve any dispute or controversy arising directly out of this Agreement by referring such dispute or controversy to a senior management executive of each party who was not directly involved in the procurement and day to day management of the COMPUTER PROGRAM. The management executive selected by each party shall have the authority to bind its company to the terms of any settlement agreed to. If the parties, after good faith efforts, fail to resolve the dispute or controversy, the matter shall be referred to mediation in accordance with the rules of XYZ Dispute Resolution Services.

In connection with any breach or threatened breach by either party of the confidential information obligations of this Agreement, the non-breaching party may, at any time seek by application to the United States District Court for the Southern District of New York or the Supreme Court of the State of New York for the County of New York any such temporary or provisional relief or remedy ("provisional remedy") provided for by the laws of the United States of America or the laws of the State of New York as would be available in an action based upon such dispute or controversy in the absence of this Section 16.10. No such application to either said Court for a provisional remedy, nor any act or conduct by either party in furtherance of or in opposition to such application, shall constitute a relinquishment or waiver of any right to have the underlying dispute or controversy with respect to which such application is made settled by mediation.

In any mediation proceeding, the parties shall select one mediator who has technical software systems knowledge of real time trading systems. In the event that the parties fail to agree upon a mediator, XYZ Dispute Resolution Services shall be entitled to appoint a mediator with the required qualifications. Each party shall bear its own costs associated with such mediation. The mediation proceeding shall be kept confidential.

In the event that the mediation proceeding does not result in the resolution of the dispute, the parties shall submit the dispute to binding arbitration in accordance with the procedures set forth in **Schedule "M"** attached hereto an made a part hereof.

(16.11) Pending resolution of any dispute or controversy as provided in Section 16.10, each of the parties shall continue to perform its obligations under this Agreement and a failure to perform its obligations by either party pending the resolution process shall be deemed a separate breach of this Agreement.

(16.12) Any dispute arising under this Agreement shall be governed by the laws of the State of New York.

IN WITNESS WHEREOF, the parties have caused this Agreement to be executed and do each hereby warrant and represent that their respective signatory whose signature appears below has been and is on the date of this Agreement duly authorized by all necessary and appropriate corporate action to execute this Agreement.

CUSTOMER   ABC SYSTEMS, INC.

By: _____   By: _____

Name: _____   Name: _____

Title: _____   Title: _____

Date: _____   Date: _____

ABC SYSTEMS, INC.
CUSTOMIZED SOFTWARE SERVICES AGREEMENT

AGREEMENT made as of the 28th day of August, 1996 by and between ABC Systems, Inc., with its office at 50 Main Street, White Plains, NY 11477 ("ABC") and Professional Trading Company, Ltd. with an office located at 100 Park Avenue, New York, NY 10017 ("Customer").

The Customer and ABC agree that ABC shall perform software development services for the Customer and that such work shall be provided in accordance with the following terms and conditions:

1. **DEFINITIONS**

   As used in this document the following terms shall have the meanings set forth below:

   (1.1) "Acceptance" shall have the meaning stated in Section 8 of this Agreement.

   (1.2) "Acceptance Test" shall mean the testing process for the COMPUTER PROGRAM performed in accordance with the Test Plans as specified in Section 8 of this Agreement.

   (1.3) "Agreement" shall mean this agreement, any attached exhibits or schedules and any amendments to this Agreement which are in writing and signed by both parties.

   (1.4) "COMPUTER PROGRAM" shall mean the SOFTWARE, as modified and/or enhanced by performance of the Work and Documentation, collectively or individually, together with all amendments enhancements and modifications thereto which have been accepted by Customer.

   (1.5) "Documentation" shall mean the documents identified in Section 3 of this Agreement.

   (1.6) "Error" shall mean an error in the code of the COMPUTER PROGRAM which prevents the COMPUTER PROGRAM from operating in all material respects in accordance with the Documentation and RFP.

   (1.7) "Functional Specification" shall have the meaning given it in Section 3.1(a) of this Agreement.

(1.8) "Hardware" shall mean the computer equipment identified in **Schedule "G"** to this Agreement.

(1.9) "Installation" shall have the meaning given it in Section 7.3 of this Agreement.

(1.10) "Installation Site" shall mean Customer's principal place of business located at 100 Park Avenue, New York, NY 10017.

(1.11) "License Agreement" shall mean the license agreement between Customer and ABC for the SOFTWARE of even date herewith.

(1.12) "License Fee" shall mean the license fee payable by Customer to ABC under Section 5 of the License Agreement.

(1.13) "RFP" shall mean Customer's Request for Proposal dated July 7, 1996, a copy of which is attached hereto as **Schedule "D"** and made a part hereof.

(1.14) "SOFTWARE" shall mean the computer software program products more particularly described in paragraph 1.13 of the License Agreement.

(1.15) "Software Documentation" shall mean version 4 of the SOFTWARE's user, operations and training manuals.

(1.16) "Source Listings" shall mean the human-readable instructions together with annotations thereto which comprise the source code of the COMPUTER PROGRAM.

(1.17) "System Design Specification" shall have the meaning given it in Section 3.1(b) of this Agreement.

(1.18) "Test Plans" shall mean the procedures and objectives of the Acceptance Test for the COMPUTER PROGRAM as specified in Section 8 of this Agreement.

(1.19) "Work" shall mean the computer consulting and programming services performed by ABC for Customer hereunder.

2. STATEMENT OF WORK

(2.1) On or before the dates set forth in the Implementation Schedule attached as **Schedule "A"** hereto and made a part hereof, ABC shall deliver to Customer:

(a) the Functional Specification to be attached to this Agreement as **Schedule "B"** and made a part hereof upon its Acceptance;

(b) the System Design Specification to be attached to this Agreement as **Schedule "C"** and made a part hereof upon its Acceptance;

(c) computer software programs, in source code format, to be developed by ABC consistent with the System Design Specification and which have the capabilities described in the Functional Specification. To avoid doubt, the COMPUTER PROGRAM shall have all of the functions, features, performance, compatibility and enhancement characteristics described in the RFP. In the event of an inconsistency between the Documentation, Software Documentation and the RFP, the RFP shall prevail; and

(d) Documentation in addition to the System Design and Functional Specification, as identified in Section 3.1(c) of this Agreement.

3. DOCUMENTATION

(3.1) ABC shall provide Customer with the following Documentation by the dates set forth in the implementation schedule attached hereto as **Schedule "A"**:

(a) ABC shall prepare the Functional Specification describing each business function to be performed by the COMPUTER PROGRAM. The Functional Specification shall include: (i) all of the business functions identified in the Software Documentation and the RFP and (ii) Customer's current procedures for the purchase and sale of securities in the over the counter market;

(b) ABC shall prepare a System Design Specification for each business function described in the Functional Specification which shall include (by way of example and not limitation): (i) data inputs and outputs, including codes and acronyms; (ii) program descriptions; (iii) file descriptions, formats and layouts; (iv) report descriptions and layouts; (v) screen descriptions and layouts; (vi) interface requirements and descriptions; (vii) processing flow charts; (viii) programming standards; (ix) processing narratives; (x) editing rules; (xi) error detection procedures; (xii) performance and response time requirements; (xiii) hardware and communication requirements and (ivx) RDBMS requirements; and

(c) user, operations and training manuals for the COMPUTER PROGRAM.

(3.2) All Documentation shall be produced in accordance and compliance with the standards identified in **Schedule "E"** attached hereto and made a part hereof. Two (2) copies of all Documentation shall be provided in printed form and one copy in electronic form compatible with Microsoft Word, version 6.0.

4. CHARGES

(4.1) Subject to paragraph 4.2, Customer shall pay ABC seventy five thousand United States dollars ($75,000) for the Work, payable as follows:

(a) ten thousand dollars ($10,000) upon execution of this Agreement;

(b) five thousand dollars ($5,000) upon Acceptance of the Functional Specification;

(c) five thousand dollars ($5,000) upon Acceptance of the System Design Specification;

(d) ten thousand dollars ($10,000) upon delivery and Installation of the COMPUTER PROGRAM and confirmation by Customer that the COMPUTER PROGRAM's program files listed in **Schedule "F"** attached hereto and made a part hereof reside on the Hardware's program libraries;

(e) twenty thousand dollars ($20,000) upon Acceptance of the COMPUTER PROGRAM;

(f) five thousand dollars ($5,000) upon Acceptance of the user, operations and training Documentation to Customer; and

(g) twenty thousand dollars ($20,000) upon the later of: (i) expiration of the warranty period or (ii) all warranty claims having been properly satisfied by ABC.

(4.2) In the event that: (a) the Customer does not give its Acceptance of the Functional Specification or the System Design Specification within the time frames specified in Section 8 of this Agreement or (b) Customer and ABC fail to reach agreement with respect to a fixed charge for the Work within ten (10) business days after the last date by which the System Design Specification can be Accepted, either party may terminate this Agreement upon ten (10) business days prior written notice. This Agreement shall terminate automatically five (5) business days after the receipt of such notice by the receiving party if an agreement on the Functional Specification, System Design Specification or the fixed charge, as applicable, has not been reached in writing by the expiration of such five (5) day period. In the event that this Agreement is terminated in accordance with this paragraph 4.2, within five (5) business days after the effective date of termination, ABC shall refund all monies paid by Customer in accordance with this Article, the License Fee and other amounts payable by Customer under Section 5 of the License Agreement.

(4.3) The Customer shall pay any sales or use tax imposed by the New York State and/or New York City government(s) in connection with the Work.

(4.4) The Customer shall pay all reasonable expenses incurred by ABC in performing its obligations hereunder. Expenses which: (a) individually are in excess of two hundred fifty dollars ($250) or (b) during any calendar month, would cause total expenses incurred in such month to exceed five hundred dollars ($500), shall not be incurred without Customer's prior written consent.

(4.5) Invoices shall be payable within thirty (30) days after Customer's receipt of ABC's invoice, so long as the amounts stated therein are not reasonably in dispute.

(4.6) ABC warrants that the terms of this Agreement are comparable to or better than the terms offered by ABC to any of its present commercial customers of equal or lesser size for comparable Work. If ABC offers more favorable terms to its commercial customers during the period commencing upon the date hereof and expiring one (1) year thereafter, such terms shall also be made available to Customer together with any resulting refund within thirty (30) days from the execution of such agreement.

5. OWNERSHIP

(5.1) ABC acknowledges that Customer shall have exclusive, unlimited owner-ship rights to all Work performed hereunder, to all materials and/or deliverables prepared for the Customer hereunder and all ideas, concepts, inventions, designs, techniques conceived by Customer or jointly with ABC hereunder, as a combination of components and/or individually, and whether or not this Agreement is satisfactorily completed, all of which shall be deemed work made for hire and made in the course of services rendered and shall belong exclusively to the Customer with the Cus-tomer having the right to obtain, hold and render, in its own name pat-ents, copyrights and registrations therefor. In the event that certain other ownership rights do not originally vest in Customer as contemplated here-under, ABC agrees to irrevocably assign, transfer and convey to the Cus-tomer all rights, title and interest therein. ABC and its personnel shall give Customer, and any person designated by Customer, all reasonable assistance and shall execute all necessary documents to assist and/or en-able Customer to perfect, preserve, register and/or record its rights in all such Work, deliverables or material.

6. CONFIDENTIALITY

(6.1) As used herein, "Confidential Information" shall include all information and data furnished by CUSTOMER to ABC, whether in oral, written, graphic or machine-readable form, including without limitation, specifi-cations, user, operations or systems manuals, diagrams, graphs, models, sketches, technical data, research, business or financial information, plans, strategies, forecasts, forecast assumptions, business practices, marketing information and material, customer names, proprietary ideas, concepts, know-how, methodologies and all other information related to Customer's business. Confidential Information shall also include the Work and con-fidential information received by CUSTOMER from a third party. In or-der for any information provided verbally by CUSTOMER to ABC to come within the definition of Confidential Information, it shall be identified as confidential at the time of disclosure and within five (5) business days after verbal disclosure thereof by CUSTOMER, such information shall be documented in writing specifying that CUSTOMER considers such in-formation confidential.

(6.2) Notwithstanding anything to the contrary contained in this Agreement, Confidential Information shall not include information: (a) in the public domain (other than as a result of a breach of this Agreement); (b) generally known and disclosed to ABC by persons or entities engaged in a comparable business (other than as a result of a breach of this Agreement or any other agreement to which such persons or entities are parties); (c) in ABC's possession prior to its receipt from Customer pursuant to this Agreement or (d) independently developed by ABC.

(6.3) ABC agrees to maintain the confidentiality of the Confidential Information using procedures no less rigorous than those used to protect and preserve the confidentiality of its own proprietary information and shall not, directly or indirectly: (a) transfer or disclose any Confidential Information to any third party; (b) use any Confidential Information other than as contemplated under this Agreement or (c) take any other action with respect to the Confidential Information inconsistent with the confidential and proprietary nature of such information. ABC further agrees to return all Confidential Information (and all copies thereof) to the Customer upon termination of this Agreement.

(6.4) ABC shall be permitted to disclose the Confidential Information to its employees having a need for access thereto in connection with performance of the Work and who have executed confidentiality agreements containing provisions similar to those contained in this Agreement and specifying that the Customer is a third party beneficiary thereunder entitled to enforce the provisions thereof as though a party thereto. ABC shall take steps, no less rigorous than those it takes to protect its own proprietary information, to prevent its employees from acting in a manner inconsistent with the terms of this Agreement.

7. **DELIVERY, INSTALLATION & SITE PREPARATION**

(7.1) The COMPUTER PROGRAM shall be developed, delivered and implemented in accordance with Implementation Schedule. ABC understands that that Customer has contracted for the licensing and/or purchase and delivery of other items of computer software and/or hardware comprising a major computer system to be implemented for Customer and therefore it is vital that the dates stated in the Implementation Schedule be met otherwise Customer will incur substantial additional expense and injury. In the event that ABC fails to perform in accordance with the Implementation Schedule, ABC shall assign additional qualified staff to the development, delivery and implementation, as applicable, of the COMPUTER PROGRAM. Without limiting any of its rights under this Agreement and at law, ABC shall pay Customer one thousand dollars ($1,000), as liquidated damages, for each business day after the fourth business day that it fails to complete a task, milestone or other delivery required to be made or performed in accordance with this Agreement and/or terminate this Agreement in accordance with Section 15.

(7.2) Installation of the COMPUTER PROGRAM shall be the responsibility of ABC. As a condition to such installation, Customer shall prepare the Installation Site in accordance with the site preparation requirements identified in **Schedule "H"** attached hereto and made a part hereof. At such time that the Installation Site has been prepared, Customer shall give written notice thereof to ABC and within five (5) business days after receipt of Customer's notice by ABC, ABC shall inspect the Installation Site and either give its approval or disapproval. In the event ABC does not approve the site, it shall provide detailed reasons therefor within three (3) business days after its inspection in which case Customer shall correct the deficiencies identified by ABC and the inspection process shall be repeated.

(7.3) Installation shall be deemed complete when each of the data screens identified in **Schedule "I"** attached hereto and made a part hereof, can be displayed on the Hardware's terminal devices.

(7.4) The Customer agrees to reasonably cooperate with ABC with respect to this Agreement including without limitation, providing all information and access to key personnel needed to develop and/or implement the COMPUTER PROGRAM.

8. ACCEPTANCE

(8.1) The Documentation developed by ABC pursuant to Section 3 of this Agreement shall be delivered for Customer's Acceptance not later than the dates specified in the Implementation Schedule attached hereto as **Schedule**

"A". Customer shall have thirty (30) calendar days (the "Review Period") to review each item of Documentation and either accept or reject such Documentation in accordance with this Section.

(8.2) If any item of Documentation is unsatisfactory in any material respect, Customer shall prepare a detailed written description of its objections and deliver them to ABC not later than seven (7) business days after expiration of the Review Period. ABC shall thereupon undertake to modify the Documentation to respond to such objections and shall do so within ten (10) business days of receipt of Customer's objections.

(8.3) If any item of Documentation continues to be unsatisfactory in any material respect after the revisions having been made in accordance with paragraph 8.2, Customer, may in its sole discretion, grant ABC additional time to modify the Documentation so that it is conforming or terminate this Agreement. In such an event ABC shall refund to Customer all amounts paid by Customer to ABC hereunder and under Section 5 of the License Agreement and, as liquidated damages for its failure, pay Customer five thousand dollars ($5,000).

(8.4) Customer shall prepare Test Plans consistent with the Documentation and the RFP on or before the date which is thirty (30) calendar days prior to the date the COMPUTER PROGRAM is scheduled for Installation. The Test Plans shall include procedures required to demonstrate that the COMPUTER PROGRAM operates in all material respects in accordance with the Documentation and RFP. In the event of an inconsistency between the RFP and the Documentation, the RFP shall prevail. Customer shall prepare the data necessary for performing the Acceptance Test. Customer shall perform the Acceptance Test within ten (10) business days after Installation is complete.

(8.5) Within five (5) business days after completion of the Acceptance Test, Customer shall either give its Acceptance of the COMPUTER PROGRAM or disapprove such results and provide detailed written reasons for such disapproval.

(8.6) If the COMPUTER PROGRAM or any portion thereof fails to pass the Acceptance Test, ABC will correct all Error(s) not later than fourteen (14) calendar days after receipt of Customer's notice describing the Error(s). Within fourteen (14) calendar days after such corrections have been made, Customer will retest the COMPUTER PROGRAM. If the COMPUTER PROGRAM still fails the Acceptance Test after corrections having been made in accordance with this paragraph 8.6, Customer may at its option, grant ABC additional time in Customer's sole discretion to correct the outstanding Error(s) or terminate this Agreement in which event ABC shall: (a) refund to Customer all amounts paid to ABC hereunder together with the License Fee and all other amounts paid by Customer to ABC in accordance with Section 5 of the License Agreement and (b) pay Customer liquidated damages in the amount of ten thousand dollars ($10,000).

(8.7) Acceptance of the COMPUTER PROGRAM shall be deemed to have occurred upon execution of an Acceptance Certificate, the form of which is attached hereto as **Schedule "J"** .

9.   LIMITED WARRANTY

(9.1) ABC warrants that the COMPUTER PROGRAM, upon Acceptance and for a period of one (1) year thereafter, will operate without an Error. ABC also warrants that it has inspected the SOFTWARE for computer viruses and that the SOFTWARE shall be free of all viruses when delivered. Furthermore, ABC warrants that the SOFTWARE shall be compatible and able to support date calculations for the years 2000 and beyond and have all of the capabilities and functions required by Customer as defined in Customer's RFP. In the event of an inconsistency between Documentation and the RFP, the RFP shall prevail. EXCEPT FOR THE FOREGOING, ABC MAKES NO OTHER WARRANTY, EXPRESS OR IMPLIED, INCLUDING WITHOUT LIMITATION, THE IMPLIED WARRANTIES OF MERCHANTABILITY OR FITNESS FOR A PARTICULAR PURPOSE.

(9.2) ABC shall respond to service requests within one (1) hour of Customer's notice of an Error and shall have completed all necessary corrections not later than three (3) hours after Customer's notice. In the event that, that during any ninety (90) day period, ABC shall fail two (2) times to correct any Error within the time periods aforesaid, Customer shall be entitled, at ABC's cost and expense, to employ its own personnel or a third party contractor of its own choosing to correct Errors occurring thereafter if

ABC shall again fail to correct an Error within the prescribed time period.

(9.3) In the event that an Error which prevents production use of the COM-
PUTER PROGRAM in any material respect as reasonably determined by
the Customer is not corrected by ABC within seventy two (72) hours
after notice (by telephone) thereof is given by Customer to ABC, Customer may terminate this Agreement in which case ABC shall: (a) refund
to Customer all amounts paid to ABC hereunder together with the License Fee and all other amounts paid by Customer to ABC in accordance
with Section 5 of the License Agreement and (b) pay Customer liquidated
damages in the amount of ten thousand dollars ($10,000).

(9.4) ABC shall perform services at the Installation Site during the warranty
period at no additional charge to Customer. Alternatively, with Customer's
prior consent, ABC shall be entitled to log-in to Customer's computer
system and access the COMPUTER PROGRAM for the purposes of Error
diagnosis, correction and installation.

10. INTELLECTUAL PROPERTY INDEMNIFICATION

(10.1) ABC agrees to defend and/or handle at its own expense, any claim or
action against Customer for actual or alleged infringement of any intellectual or industrial property right, including without limitation, trademarks, service marks, patents, copyrights, misappropriation of trade secrets or any similar property rights, based upon the COMPUTER PRO-
GRAM or Customer's use thereof. ABC further agrees to indemnify and
hold Customer harmless from and against any and all liabilities, costs,
losses, damages and expenses (including reasonable attorney's fees) associated with such claim or action. Customer shall reasonably cooperate
with ABC in the defense of such claim or action to the extent that such
cooperation is given at such times and in a manner that does not negatively affect Customer's business in Customer's sole discretion and further, ABC reimburses Customer's expenses and pays Customer at
Customer's hourly billing rate for all such assistance.

(10.2) ABC shall have the sole right to conduct the defense of any such claim or
action and all negotiations for its settlement or compromise. Notwithstanding the foregoing, in the event that ABC shall fail to appoint an

attorney within ten (10) calendar days after the claim having first been made or action commenced or the attorney appointed by ABC is, in Customer's reasonable judgment not suitably qualified to represent Customer, Customer shall have the right to select and appoint an alternative attorney and the reasonable cost and expense thereof shall be paid by ABC.

(10.3) If the COMPUTER PROGRAM becomes or in ABC's reasonable opinion is likely to become the subject of any such claim or action, then, ABC shall use best efforts at its sole expense to either: (a) procure for Customer the right to continue using the COMPUTER PROGRAM as contemplated hereunder; (b) modify the COMPUTER PROGRAM to render same non-infringing (provided such modification does not adversely affect Customer's use as described in the RFP) or (c) replace same with equally suitable, functionally equivalent, compatible non-infringing COMPUTER PROGRAM. If none of the foregoing is possible, ABC shall have the right to terminate this Agreement upon: (i) payment to Customer of all monies paid by Customer for the Work together with the License Fee and all other amounts paid by Customer to ABC in accordance with Section 5 of the License Agreement and (ii) if this Agreement is terminated in accordance with this paragraph within the first twenty four (24) months after Acceptance, ABC shall in addition pay Customer an amount equal to twenty thousand dollars ($20,000) as liquidated damages.

11. LIMITED REMEDIES & LIABILITY

(11.1) In all cases involving performance or non-performance of the COMPUTER PROGRAM, Customer's primary remedy shall be correction of the Error(s). For all other failure(s) by ABC to perform in accordance with this Agreement, including without limitation, if the COMPUTER PROGRAM is not Accepted by Customer (due to no fault of the Customer) or an Error cannot be corrected within the time periods specified in Section 9 of this Agreement, the Customer shall be entitled to terminate this Agreement in accordance with Section 15 and/or recover damages subject to paragraph 11.2.

(11.2) ABC's liability to Customer shall be limited to: (a) the charges payable by Customer under Section 4 of this Agreement; plus (b) the License Fee and all other amounts paid by Customer to ABC under the License Agreement plus (c) the amount of any liquidated damages payable by ABC pursuant to the various sections of this Agreement. The foregoing limitation of liability shall not apply to the: (a) payment of costs, damages and attorney's fees referred to in Section 10 of this Agreement or Section 5 of the License Agreement for ABC's indemnity obligation; (b) claims for personal injury or damage to real or personal property caused by willful or negligent acts of ABC, its employees or contractors or (c) damages resulting from violation of Section 6 of this Agreement or Section 4 of the License Agreement for breach of confidentiality and non-disclosure obligations.

(11.3) IN NO EVENT SHALL ABC OR THE CUSTOMER BE LIABLE FOR INCIDENTAL, SPECIAL OR CONSEQUENTIAL DAMAGES (INCLUDING WITHOUT LIMITATION LOST PROFITS) EVEN IF EITHER PARTY HAS BEEN ADVISED OF THE POSSIBILITY OF SUCH DAMAGES.

12. CHANGE IN SCOPE

(12.1) ABC and the Customer recognize that it may be desirable for the Customer to make changes to the Functional and/or System Design Specifications (a "Revision") during the performance of this Agreement. Customer may request Revision by giving notice thereof to ABC specifying the nature of the change(s) desired (the "Revision Notice").

(12.2) Within ten (10) calendar days after ABC has received the Revision Notice, it shall provide Customer with a proposal identifying: (a) any addition or reduction in the cost associated with performing the Work; (b) the effect, if any, to the payment schedule identified in Section 4; (c) the revisions required and to be made to the Documentation; (d) the effect, if any, with respect to the delivery and implementation milestones identified in **Schedule "A"** attached hereto and (e) any other change which would be required to any of the other Sections or Schedules to this Agreement (the "Revision Proposal").

(12.3) Upon Customer's written approval of the Revision Proposal, ABC shall, within ten (10) calendar days thereafter, revise the Functional and/or System Design Specifications (the "Revised Specifications") and submit them for Customer's approval. ABC shall not develop or implement any Revision until such time that the Customer has approved the Revised Specifications in writing. Upon Customer's approval of the Revised Specifications, this Agreement shall be deemed amended to reflect the terms and conditions of the Revision Proposal.

13. PROJECT MANAGERS & MEETINGS

(13.1) The Customer and ABC shall each designate prior to the commencement of Work under this Agreement a project manager to whom all communications may be addressed, and who shall have complete responsibility and authority for the Customer and ABC, respectively, in all aspects of this Agreement.

(13.2) The project mangers shall meet at least weekly. ABC's project manager shall render a written status report as of the middle and end of each calendar month, such report to be delivered to Customer's project manager within three (3) business days after the end of such half month.

(13.3) ABC's project manager shall be available upon five (5) business day's notice to attend meetings of the Customer's management.

14. TRAINING

(14.1) ABC shall provide thirty (30) hours of training to Customer in the use, operation and maintenance of the COMPUTER PROGRAM. The training curriculum and ABC's instructors assigned thereto is identified in **Schedule "K"** attached hereto and made a part hereof. Training will be conducted in not less than two or greater than three (3) hour sessions per day at Customer's offices in New York. ABC shall assume and be responsible for the payment of all transportation, room and board expenses of its employees in furnishing such training.

15. TERMINATION

(15.1) If a party (the "Defaulting Party") is in material breach of or default under this Agreement, and the Defaulting Party does not remedy that breach or default within thirty (30) calendar days after receipt from the other party of written notice of that default or breach (provided that if the breach or default is one that cannot be remedied within such thirty

(30) day period, this Agreement may be terminated effective immediately upon written notice to the Defaulting Party), the other party shall after the expiry of such thirty (30) calendar day period have the right to terminate this Agreement effective immediately upon written notice to the Defaulting Party.

(15.2) Either party may terminate this Agreement, at any time, by written notice in the event that the other: (a) files a voluntary petition in bankruptcy or under any similar insolvency law; (b) makes an assignment for the benefit of creditors; (c) has filed against it any involuntary petition in bankruptcy or under any similar insolvency law if any such petition is not dismissed within sixty (60) days after filing or (d) a receiver is appointed for, or a levy or attachment is made against, substantially all of its assets, if any such petition is not dismissed or such receiver or levy or attachment is not discharged within sixty (60) days after the filing or appointment.

(15.3) For the purposes of paragraph 15.1 and 15.2, Customer shall be in material breach of or default under this Agreement and ABC may terminate this Agreement only if the breach or default relates to Customer's obligation to pay ABC any amount payable hereunder when due and the breach or default is not remedied within the applicable time period specified therefor. ABC's rights and remedies in respect of any other breach of or default under this Agreement shall be limited to such rights and remedies other than termination of this Agreement.

(15.4) Either party may terminate this Agreement to take effect immediately upon termination of the License Agreement. In the event the License Agreement is terminated due to default thereunder by ABC, in addition to all other rights and remedies available to Customer, ABC shall immediately refund to Customer all monies paid by Customer to ABC under the License Agreement.

16. GENERAL

(16.1) The professional personnel provided by ABC shall be appropriately trained in the technical skills to perform their duties. Customer may require ABC to replace any person who is performing Work pursuant to this Agreement, if Customer in Customer's sole but reasonable discretion determines that such person is unfit or otherwise unsatisfactory. The personnel of each party, when on the premises of the other, shall comply with the security and other personnel regulations of the party on whose premises such person is on.

ABC recognizes that its employees identified in **Schedule "L"** are particularly qualified to perform the services under this Agreement and ABC agrees not to remove such personnel from the performance of Work hereunder until such time that their respective tasks have been satisfactorily completed.

(16.2) Neither party shall assign its rights or obligations under this Agreement without the prior written consent of the other party. Notwithstanding the forgoing, the Customer shall be entitled to assign its rights and obligations hereunder to any one of Customer's subsidiaries without any further consent from ABC. For purposes of this paragraph 16.2, a "subsidiary" shall be any entity in which Customer owns or controls at least fifty percent (50%) of such entity's stock or other evidence of ownership.

(16.3) No modifications of this Agreement shall be valid or binding on either party unless acknowledged in writing and signed by the duly authorized officer of each party. All notices or other communications given under this Agreement shall be in writing, sent to the address hereinbefore set forth as the principal place of business or such other addresses as ABC or the Customer may designate in writing by certified mail (return receipt requested) or personal delivery. Notice shall be deemed given upon receipt.

(16.4) ABC understands and agrees that violation of Section 6 of this Agreement may cause damage to the Customer in an amount which is impossible or extremely difficult to ascertain. Accordingly, without limitation to any other remedy available at law, the Customer may be entitled to injunctive relief restraining ABC from continuing to violate the terms and provisions of said section.

(16.5) Neither party shall be liable to the other for any delay or failure to perform its obligations under this Agreement if such delay or failure arises from any cause beyond the reasonable control of such party, including but not limited to labor disputes, strikes, other labor or industrial disturbances, acts of God, floods, lightning, utility or communication failures, earthquakes or other casualty.

If a delay or failure that ABC anticipates will cause an excusable delay, ABC by written notice shall inform Customer of the anticipated effect of such delay as soon as possible and in any event shall give written notice within ten (10) calendar days. Such notice shall contain a description of the steps ABC is taking to alleviate the problem. Anything in this Agreement to the contrary notwithstanding, Customer may, if the COMPUTER PROGRAM has not been Accepted due to a problem described in this paragraph 16.5, by a date which is seventy five (75) calendar days after Acceptance Testing is to commence, terminate this Agreement upon fourteen (14) calendar days notice to ABC; in such event, Customer may return all portions of the COMPUTER PROGRAM delivered prior to termination in which case ABC shall refund all payments made by Customer.

(16.6) The parties acknowledge that each has read all the terms of this Agreement, is authorized to enter into it, agrees to be bound by its terms and conditions and that it is the complete and exclusive statement of the agreement between the parties which supersedes all prior communications and agreements between the parties relating to the subject matter of this Agreement.

(16.7) Any forbearance or delay on the part of either party in enforcing any provision of this Agreement or any of its rights hereunder shall not be construed as a waiver of such provision or of a right to enforce same.

(16.8) ABC is an independent contractor in performance of the Work and shall not be considered to be or permitted to be an agent, employee, joint venturer or partner of the Customer. All persons furnished, used, retained or hired by or on behalf of ABC, are and shall be considered employees or agents of ABC. ABC assumes sole and full responsibility for their acts. ABC shall at all times during the term of this Agreement maintain such supervision, direction and control over its employees and agents as is consistent with and necessary to preserve its independent contractor status.

(16.9) The provisions of Sections 5, 6, 10, 11 15 and 16.3 through 16.12 shall survive termination of this Agreement or any portion thereof.

(16.10) The parties shall use all reasonable efforts to amicably resolve any dispute or controversy arising directly out of this Agreement by referring such dispute or controversy to a senior management executive of each party who was not directly involved in the procurement and day to day management of the COMPUTER PROGRAM. The management executive selected by each party shall have the authority to bind its company to the terms of any settlement agreed to. If the parties, after good faith efforts, fail to resolve the dispute or controversy, the matter shall be submitted for resolution in accordance with the "mini-trial" resolution process provided through XYZ Dispute Resolution Services.

In connection with any breach or threatened breach by either party of the confidential information obligations of this Agreement, the non-breaching party may, at any time seek by application to the United States District Court for the Southern District of New York or the Supreme Court of the State of New York for the County of New York any such temporary or provisional relief or remedy ("provisional remedy") provided for by the laws of the United States of America or the laws of the State of New York as would be available in an action based upon such dispute or controversy in the absence of this Section 16.10. No such application to either said Court for a provisional remedy, nor any act or conduct by either party in furtherance of or in opposition to such application, shall constitute a relinquishment or waiver of any right to have the underlying dispute or controversy with respect to which such application is made settled through the mini-trial process.

In the mini-trial proceeding, the parties shall select an individual who has technical software systems knowledge of real time trading systems to serve as judge. In the event that the parties fail to agree upon an individual who can serve as a judge, XYZ Dispute Resolution Services shall be entitled to appoint a judge who has the required qualifications. The mini-trial proceeding shall be kept confidential and each party shall bear its own costs and expenses.

In the event that the mini-trial proceeding does not result a resolution of the dispute, the parties shall submit the dispute to binding arbitration in accordance with the procedures set forth in **Schedule "M"** attached hereto an made a part hereof.

(16.11) Pending resolution of any dispute or controversy as provided in Section 16.10, each of the parties shall continue to perform its obligations under this Agreement and a failure to perform its obligations by either party pending the resolution process shall be deemed a separate breach of this Agreement.

(16.12) Any dispute arising under this Agreement shall be governed by the laws of the State of New York.

IN WITNESS WHEREOF, the parties have caused this Agreement to be executed and do each hereby warrant and represent that their respective signatory whose signature appears below has been and is on the date of this Agreement duly authorized by all necessary and appropriate corporate action to execute this Agreement.

CUSTOMER   ABC SYSTEMS, INC.

By: _____   By: _____

Name: _____   Name: _____

Title: _____   Title: _____

Date: _____   Date: _____

ABC SYSTEMS, INC.
SOFTWARE LICENSE AGREEMENT

[For Use In Connection With Customized Software Services Agreement]

CUSTOMER: Professional Trading Company, Ltd.
ADDRESS: 100 Park Avenue
CITY: New York
STATE: NY ZIP: 10017
CONTACT: John Smith
DATE: September 28, 1996

1. <u>DEFINITIONS</u>

As used in this document the following terms shall have the meanings set forth below:

(1.1) "ABC " shall mean ABC Systems, Inc. 50 Main Street, White Plains, NY 11477.

(1.2) "Acceptance" shall have the meaning stated in Section 8 of the Development Agreement.

(1.3) "Acceptance Test" shall mean the testing process described in and performed in accordance with Section 8 of the Development Agreement.

(1.4) "Agreement" shall mean this agreement, any attached exhibits or schedules and any amendments to this Agreement which are in writing and signed by both parties.

(1.5) "COMPUTER PROGRAM" shall mean the computer software programs described in Section 2.1(c) of the Development Agreement.

(1.6) "Deposit" shall mean the material to be deposited into escrow by ABC in accordance with the Escrow Agreement attached hereto as **Schedule "G"**.

(1.7) "Development Agreement" shall mean the agreement for Customized Software Services between the parties of even date herewith.

(1.8) "Documentation" shall mean the user, operations and training manuals for version 4 of the "STOCK" software program.

(1.9) "Hardware" shall mean the computer equipment identified in **Schedule "B"** to this Agreement or any replacement of such computer equipment in accordance with Section 3.2 hereof.

(1.10) "Installation" shall have the meaning given it in Section 8 of this Agreement.

(1.11) "Installation Site" shall mean Customer's address above stated.

(1.12) "License Fee" shall mean the license fee for the SOFTWARE as specified in Section 5.1 of this Agreement.

(1.13) "SOFTWARE" shall mean the version 4 of the Stock computer software program product in object code format as described by the Documentation. Throughout this Agreement, "SOFTWARE" shall include version 4 of the Stock computer program and the Documentation, individually and/ or collectively, together with all amendments enhancements and modifications thereto which have been accepted by Customer.

(1.14) "Use" shall mean to load, execute and display the SOFTWARE on the Hardware.

2. DELIVERABLES

(2.1) On or before the dates set forth in the Implementation Schedule attached hereto as **Schedule "A"** and made a part hereof, ABC shall deliver to Customer the: (a) SOFTWARE which shall have all of the functions, features, performance, compatibility and enhancement characteristics described in the documentation and (b) two (2) copies of the Documentation in printed form and one copy in electronic form compatible with Microsoft Word, version 6.0.

3. LICENSE

(3.1) ABC hereby grants the Customer a personal, nontransferable, non-exclusive, paid-up and irrevocable license to Use the SOFTWARE, in object code format, to process its own data. In no event shall Customer have the right to Use the SOFTWARE to process the data of any other entity. One copy of the SOFTWARE may also be Used on a back-up computer during a reasonable, temporary period of inoperability of the Hardware.

(3.2) Upon thirty (30) days prior written notice, Customer may transfer the SOFTWARE to: (a) other Hardware of comparable processing power or (b) Hardware of greater processing power upon payment of an additional license fee calculated in accordance with **Schedule "E"** attached to this Agreement and made a part hereof. Such notice shall specify the date of the transfer and thereafter the Hardware shall be the hardware designated in such notice.

(3.3) Customer shall be entitled to make up to two (2) copies of the SOFTWARE for back-up or archival purposes. Customer shall keep a record of each copy made, where such copy is located and in whose custody it is in.

(3.4) Customer shall not reverse engineer, decompile, disassemble, re-engineer or otherwise attempt to discover the source code or the structural framework of the SOFTWARE.

(3.5) Customer agrees that the SOFTWARE shall not be exported directly or indirectly, separately or as part of a system. Diversion of Products contrary to U.S. law is prohibited.

4. <u>DISCLOSURE & OWNERSHIP</u>

(4.1) As used herein, "CUSTOMER Information" shall include all information and data furnished by CUSTOMER to ABC, whether in oral, written, graphic or machine-readable form, including without limitation, the COMPUTER PROGRAM, specifications, user, operations or systems manuals, diagrams, graphs, models, sketches, technical data, research, business or financial information, plans, strategies, forecasts, forecast assumptions, business practices, marketing information and material, customer names, proprietary ideas, concepts, know-how, methodologies and all other information related to CUSTOMER's business. CUSTOMER Information shall also include confidential information received by CUSTOMER from a third party. In order for any information provided verbally by CUSTOMER to ABC to come within the definition of CUSTOMER Information, it shall be identified as confidential at the time of disclosure and within five (5) business days after verbal disclosure thereof by CUSTOMER, such information shall be documented in writing specifying that CUSTOMER considers such information confidential.

(4.2) As used herein, "ABC Information" shall include all information and data furnished by ABC to CUSTOMER, whether in oral, written, graphic or machine-readable form, in connection with the SOFTWARE, including, without limitation, object code, source code, source listings, computer programs, specifications, user, operations or systems manuals, diagrams, graphs, technical data, research, business or financial information, plans, strategies, forecasts, forecast assumptions, business practices, procedures, marketing information, trade secrets and other proprietary ideas, concepts, know-how, methodologies and information related to the SOFTWARE or ABC. In order for any information provided verbally by ABC to CUSTOMER to come within the definition of ABC Information, it shall be identified as confidential at the time of disclosure and within five (5) business days after verbal disclosure thereof by ABC, such information shall be documented in writing specifying that ABC considers such information confidential.

(4.3) As used herein, "Confidential Information" shall include the CUSTOMER Information and the ABC Information, individually and collectively. Notwithstanding anything to the contrary contained in this Agreement, Confidential Information shall not include information: (a) in the public domain (other than as a result of a breach of this Agreement); (b) generally known and disclosed to CUSTOMER or ABC by persons or entities engaged in a comparable business (other than as a result of a breach of this Agreement or any other agreement to which such persons or entities are parties); (c) in CUSTOMER or ABC's possession prior to its receipt from the other pursuant to this Agreement or (d) independently developed by CUSTOMER or ABC.

(4.4) CUSTOMER and ABC agree to use procedures no less rigorous than those used to protect and preserve the confidentiality of their own proprietary information to maintain the confidentiality of the Confidential Information of the other and shall not, directly or indirectly: (a) transfer or disclose any Confidential Information to a third party (other than to their respective employees); (b) use any Confidential Information other than as contemplated under this Agreement or (c) take any other action with respect to the Confidential Information inconsistent with the confidential and proprietary nature of such information. CUSTOMER and ABC further agree to return all Confidential Information (and all copies thereof) to the other upon termination of this Agreement, except as set forth to the contrary in Section 10 of this Agreement.

(4.5) CUSTOMER and ABC shall be permitted to disclose the Confidential Information to their respective employees having a need for access thereto in connection with their employment and who have executed confidentiality agreements containing provisions similar to those contained in this Agreement and specifying that other parties are third party beneficiaries thereof entitled to enforce the provisions thereof as though a party thereto. CUSTOMER and ABC shall each take steps, no less rigorous than those it takes to protect and preserve its own proprietary information, to prevent their respective employees from acting in a manner inconsistent with the terms of this Agreement.

(4.6) ABC acknowledges and agrees that CUSTOMER is engaged in the business of securities trading, and as such currently possesses knowledge and information relating to the functionality and capabilities required for computer systems in support thereof. Therefore, nothing contained in this Agreement shall prevent CUSTOMER from, on its own or through third parties, designing, developing or acquiring computer systems similar to the SOFTWARE so long as CUSTOMER does not make use of any ABC Information in connection therewith.

(4.7) The SOFTWARE, its logos, product names and other support materials, if any, are either patented, copyrighted, trademarked, or otherwise proprietary to ABC. Customer agrees never to remove any such notices and product identification. A copyright notice on the SOFTWARE shall not be deemed in and of itself to constitute or evidence a publication or public disclosure.

5. **LICENSE FEE AND OTHER REQUIRED PAYMENTS**

(5.1) Customer shall pay ABC fifty thousand United States dollars ($50,000) for the SOFTWARE License Fee, payable as follows:

(a) ten thousand dollars ($10,000) upon execution of this Agreement;

(b) ten thousand dollars ($10,000) upon delivery and Installation of the

COMPUTER PROGRAM and confirmation by Customer that the COM-PUTER PROGRAM's program files listed in **Schedule "D"** attached to this Agreement and made a part hereof reside on the Hardware's program libraries;

(c) fifteen thousand dollars ($15,000) upon Acceptance of the COMPUTER PROGRAM; and

(d) fifteen thousand dollars ($15,000) upon the later of: (i) expiration of the warranty period specified in Section 9 of the Development Agreement or (ii) all warranty claims under the Development Agreement having been properly satisfied by ABC.

(5.2) The Customer shall pay any sales or use tax imposed by the New York State and/or New York City government(s) in connection with the SOFT-WARE.

(5.3) Invoices shall be payable within thirty (30) days after Customer's receipt of ABC's invoice, so long as the amounts stated therein are not reasonably in dispute.

(5.4) ABC warrants that the terms of this Agreement are comparable to or better than the terms offered by ABC to any of its present commercial customers of equal or lesser size for comparable deliverables and/or services. If ABC offers more favorable terms to its commercial customers during the period commencing on the date hereof and expiring one year thereafter, such terms shall also be made available to Customer together with any resulting refund within thirty (30) days from the execution of such agreement.

6. INTELLECTUAL PROPERTY INDEMNIFICATION

(6.1) ABC agrees to defend and/or handle at its own expense, any claim or action against Customer for actual or alleged infringement of any intellectual or industrial property right, including without limitation, trademarks, service marks, patents, copyrights, misappropriation of trade secrets or any similar property rights, based upon the SOFTWARE or Customer's use thereof. ABC further agrees to indemnify and hold Customer harmless from and against any and all liabilities, costs, losses, damages and expenses (including reasonable attorney's fees) associated with such claim or action. Customer shall reasonably cooperate with ABC in the defense of such claim or action to the extent that such cooperation is given at times and in a manner that does not negatively affect Customer's business, in Customer's sole discretion, and further, ABC reimburses Customer's expenses and pays Customer at Customer's hourly billing rate for all such assistance.

(6.2) ABC shall have the sole right to conduct the defense of any such claim or action and all negotiations for its settlement or compromise. Notwithstanding the foregoing, in the event that ABC shall fail to appoint an attorney within ten (10) calendar days after the claim having first been made or action commenced or the attorney appointed by ABC is, in Customer's reasonable judgment not suitably qualified to represent Customer, Customer shall have the right to select and appoint an alternative attorney and the reasonable cost and expense thereof shall be paid by ABC.

(6.3) If the SOFTWARE becomes or in ABC's reasonable opinion is likely to become the subject of any such claim or action, then, ABC shall use best efforts at its sole expense to either: (a) procure for Customer the right to continue Using the SOFTWARE as contemplated hereunder; (b) modify the SOFTWARE to render same non-infringing (provided such modification does not adversely affect Customer's use as described in the RFP) or (c) replace same with equally suitable, functionally equivalent, compatible non-infringing SOFTWARE. If none of the foregoing is possible, ABC shall have the right to terminate this Agreement upon: (i) payment to Customer of all monies paid by Customer for the SOFTWARE under Section 5 of this Agreement and (ii) if this Agreement is terminated in accordance with this paragraph 6.3 within the first twenty four (24) months after Acceptance, ABC shall in addition pay Customer an amount equal to twenty percent (20%) of the License Fee as liquidated damages.

7. <u>TERMINATION</u>

(7.1) If a party (the "Defaulting Party") is in material breach of or default under this Agreement, and the Defaulting Party does not remedy that breach or default within thirty (30) calendar days after receipt from the other party of written notice of that default or breach (provided that if the breach or default is one that cannot be remedied within such thirty (30) day period, this Agreement may be terminated effective immediately upon written notice to the Defaulting Party), the other party shall after the expiry of such thirty (30) calendar day period have the right to terminate this Agreement effective immediately upon written notice to the Defaulting Party.

(7.2) Either party may terminate this Agreement, at any time, by written notice in the event that the other: (a) files a voluntary petition in bankruptcy or under any similar insolvency law; (b) makes an assignment for the benefit of creditors; (c) has filed against it any involuntary petition in bankruptcy or under any similar insolvency law if any such petition is not dismissed within sixty (60) days after filing or (d) a receiver is appointed for, or a levy or attachment is made against, substantially all of its assets, if any such petition is not dismissed or such receiver or levy or attachment is not discharged within sixty (60) days after the filing or appointment.

(7.3) If the Defaulting Party is Customer, the termination of this Agreement by ABC shall (subject to paragraphs 7.5 and 7.6) terminate the License and Customer shall return to ABC all copies of the SOFTWARE in Customer's possession or control.

(7.4) If the Defaulting Party is ABC, the termination of this Agreement by Customer shall not terminate the License and Customer shall, in addition to all of Customer's other rights and remedies, be entitled to retain and Use all copies of the SOFTWARE in Customer's possession or control.

(7.5) For the purposes of paragraph 7.1 and 7.2, Customer shall be in material breach of or default under this Agreement and ABC may terminate this Agreement only if the breach or default relates to Customer's obligation to pay ABC an amount payable hereunder when due and the breach or default is not remedied within the applicable time period specified therefor. ABC's rights and remedies in respect of any other breach of or default under this Agreement shall be limited to such rights and remedies other than termination of this Agreement and the License, it being acknowledged and agreed by ABC that the License is irrevocable and not terminable except if Customer is in material breach of or default under this Agreement as provided in this paragraph.

(7.6) If this Agreement is terminated by ABC for a material default or breach of Customer as described in paragraph 7.5, Customer shall be entitled to retain possession of the SOFTWARE and to Use the SOFTWARE in the ordinary course of its business for the period of time, not to exceed six (6) months, required for Customer to wind down its current use of the SOFTWARE or to make a transition to alternate software or facilities.

(7.7) Customer shall have the right to terminate this Agreement to be effective upon the effective date of termination of the Development Agreement.

8. INSTALLATION

(8.1) Installation of the SOFTWARE shall be the responsibility of ABC and shall be completed by the dates set forth in the Implementation Schedule. As a condition to Installation, Customer shall prepare the Installation Site as described in Section 7.2 of the Development Agreement. Installation shall be deemed complete when each of the data screens identified in **Schedule "C"** attached hereto and made a part hereof, can be displayed on the Hardware's terminal devices.

(8.2) If through no fault of the Customer, Installation is not complete by the date specified therefor in the Implementation Schedule, without limiting any other rights and remedies available to the Customer at law and under this Agreement, ABC shall pay Customer one thousand dollars ($1,000) for each business day after the fourth business day that completion of Installation is delayed.

9. GENERAL

(9.1) Not later than fifteen (15) calendar days after the date of Installation, ABC shall deliver a full and complete set of the Deposit to the escrow agent in accordance with the Escrow Agreement.

(9.2) The professional personnel provided by ABC shall be appropriately trained in the technical skills necessary to perform their duties. Customer may require ABC to replace any person who is performing services pursuant to this Agreement, if Customer in Customer's sole but reasonable discretion determines that such person is unfit or otherwise unsatisfactory.

(9.3) The personnel of each party, when on the premises of the other, shall comply with the security and other personnel regulations of the party on whose premises such person is on.

(9.4) ABC recognizes that its employees identified in **Schedule "F"** are particularly qualified to perform the services under this Agreement and ABC agrees not to remove such personnel from the performance of services hereunder until such time that their respective tasks have been satisfactorily completed.

(9.5) Neither party shall assign its rights or obligations under this Agreement without the prior written consent of the other party. Notwithstanding the forgoing and anything to the contrary in Section 3.1 of this Agreement, the Customer shall be entitled to assign its rights and obligations hereunder to any one of Customer's subsidiaries without any further consent from ABC. For purposes of this paragraph 9.5, a "subsidiary" shall be any entity in which Customer owns or controls at least fifty percent (50%) of such entity's stock or other evidence of ownership.

(9.6) No modifications of this Agreement shall be valid or binding on either party unless acknowledged in writing and signed by the duly authorized officer of each party. All notices or other communications given under this Agreement shall be in writing, sent to the address hereinbefore set forth as the principal place of business or such other addresses as ABC or the Customer may designate in writing by certified mail (return receipt requested) or personal delivery. Notice shall be deemed given upon receipt.

(9.7) Both parties understand and agree that violation of Section 4 of this Agreement may cause damage to the other party in an amount which is impossible or extremely difficult to ascertain. Accordingly, without limitation to any other remedy available at law, the injured party may be entitled to injunctive relief restraining the other party from continuing to violate the terms and provisions of said section.

(9.8) Neither party shall be liable to the other for any delay or failure to perform its obligations under this Agreement if such delay or failure arises from a cause beyond the reasonable control of such party, including but not limited to labor disputes, strikes, other labor or industrial disturbances, acts of God, floods, lightning, utility or communication failures, earthquakes or other casualty.

If a delay or failure that ABC anticipates will cause an excusable delay, ABC by written notice shall inform Customer of the anticipated effect of such delay as soon as possible and in any event shall give written notice within ten (10) calendar days. Such notice shall contain a description of the steps ABC is taking to alleviate the problem. Anything in this Agreement to the contrary notwithstanding, Customer may, if the SOFTWARE has not been Accepted due to a problem described in this paragraph 9.8, by a date which is seventy five (75) calendar days after Acceptance Testing is to commence, terminate this Agreement upon fourteen (14) calendar days notice to ABC; in such event, ABC shall refund all payments made by Customer and Customer shall return all portions of the SOFTWARE delivered prior to termination.

(9.9) The parties acknowledge that each has read all the terms of this Agreement, is authorized to enter into it, agrees to be bound by its terms and conditions and that it is the complete and exclusive statement of the agreement between the parties which supersedes all prior communications and agreements between the parties relating to the subject matter of this Agreement.

(9.10) Any forbearance or delay on the part of either party in enforcing any provision of this Agreement or any of its rights hereunder shall not be construed as a waiver of such provision or of a right to enforce same.

(9.11) The provisions of Sections 4, 6, 9.6, 9.7, 9.8, 9.10 and 9.12 shall survive termination of this Agreement or any portion thereof.

(9.12) The parties shall use all reasonable efforts to amicably resolve any dispute or controversy arising directly out of this Agreement in the same manner as under the Development Agreement.

IN WITNESS WHEREOF, the parties have caused this Agreement to be executed and do each hereby warrant and represent that their respective signatory whose signature appears below has been and is on the date of this Agreement duly authorized by all necessary and appropriate corporate action to execute this Agreement.

CUSTOMER   ABC SYSTEMS, INC.

By: _____   By: _____

Name: _____   Name: _____

Title: _____   Title: _____

Date: _____   Date: _____

ABC SYSTEMS, INC.
MAINTENANCE SERVICES AGREEMENT

AGREEMENT made this 28th day of September, 1996 by and between ABC Systems, Inc. ("ABC") having its principal place of business at 50 Main Street, White Plains, NY 11477 and Professional Trading Company, Ltd. with its principal place of at 100 Park Avenue, New York, NY 10017 ("Customer").

WHEREAS, ABC has licensed to the Customer that certain computer software program specified in the Software License Agreement ("License Agreement"), executed on even date herewith as more particularly identified in Schedule A annexed thereto ("SOFTWARE") and the Customer wishes to have ABC perform Maintenance Services with respect to the SOFTWARE pursuant to the following terms and conditions:

1. **SOFTWARE COVERED**

    (1.1) The software covered in this Agreement is limited to the SOFTWARE as the same may be enhanced, amended or otherwise modified from time to time.

2. **MAINTENANCE SERVICES**

The maintenance services to be provided hereunder (the "Maintenance Services") shall consist of the following:

    (2.1) ABC will provide an individual at ABC's office in New York City who shall be available by telephone between the hours of 9:00 A.M. through 5:00 P.M. during business days, in New York City, ("Business Hours") for the purpose of receiving "Error" (as defined in Section 1.7 of the License Agreement) reports from the Customer.

    (2.2) In response to a reported Error, ABC shall:

    (a) if the Error is a Critical Error, ABC shall dial into Customer's computer "Hardware" (as defined in Section 1.9 of the License Agreement) and attempt to correct the Error remotely. If a site visit to Customer's office is required, a qualified ABC staff member will be dispatched immediately. If the Error has not been corrected within one (1) hour after ABC has been notified thereof, a ABC project manager, vice president or director will be notified. Status reports will be provided to the Customer every sixty (60) minutes until the Error is corrected. For purposes of this Section a "Critical Error" means an Error which prevents production use of the SOFTWARE.

(b) if the Error is not a Critical Error, ABC shall complete all necessary corrections not later than twenty four (24) hours after Customer's notice.

(c) as long as the Error is reported during Business Hours, ABC shall continue to perform Maintenance Services until the Error condition has been corrected, even after Business Hours.

(d) In the event that a Critical Error is not corrected by ABC within thirty six (36) hours after notice (by telephone) thereof is given by Customer to ABC, Customer may terminate this Agreement in which case ABC shall: (a) refund to Customer all amounts paid to ABC hereunder during the immediately preceding twelve (12) months; and (b) pay Customer liquidated damages in the amount of ten thousand dollars ($10,000).

(2.3) Corrections to Error(s) will be integrated with the SOFTWARE and installed by ABC onto Customer's Hardware.

(2.4) In the event that that during any ninety (90) day period, ABC shall fail two (2) times to correct any Error within the time periods aforesaid, without prejudice to any of its other rights and remedies under this Agreement, Customer shall be entitled to receive access to the "Deposit" (as defined in Section 1.5 the License Agreement) and shall further be entitled, at ABC's cost and expense, to employ its own personnel or a third party contractor of its own choosing to correct Errors occurring thereafter if ABC shall again fail to correct the Error within the prescribed time period.

(2.5) ABC shall perform Maintenance Services at Customer's "Installation Site" (as defined in Section 1.11) of the License Agreement during the Term of this Agreement at no additional charge to Customer. Alternatively, with Customer's prior consent, ABC shall be entitled to log-in to Customer's Hardware and access the SOFTWARE for the purposes of Error diagnosis, correction and installation.

(2.6) ABC shall provide and install for the Customer all updated versions of the SOFTWARE which contain corrections to Errors, whether or not reported by the Customer or Technical Enhancements which Customer shall be entitled to use in accordance with the License granted under Section 3 of the License Agreement. As used herein "Technical Enhancements" shall mean any improvement or modification to the functions licensed to Customer as described in the Documentation. Technical Enhancements shall be provided to and installed for the Customer at no charge. ABC shall provide to Customer all updates to the Documentation reflecting corrections to all Errors and Technical Enhancements.

(2.7) ABC warrants that it has inspected all software delivered and/or installed for Customer in connection with the Maintenance Services for computer viruses and that they shall be free of all viruses.

3. TERM

(3.1) The Term of this Agreement shall be one (1) year commencing upon expiration of the warranty period specified in Section 6 of the License Agreement, and shall automatically continue for at least four (4) successive one year periods thereafter unless written notice of non-renewal is given by Customer to ABC at least ninety (90) days prior to the scheduled expiration of the then current Term.

4. MAINTENANCE FEES

(4.1) During the first full year of the Term of this Agreement, ABC shall provide Maintenance Services to Customer for a yearly fee of twenty two thousand five hundred dollars ($22,500). The annual maintenance fee for successive years during the Term hereof shall be subject to mutual agreement but shall not be increased by more than six percent (6%) of the immediately preceding year's maintenance fee. Maintenance fees shall be payable in four (4) quarterly installments on the first day of each calendar quarter in advance.

(4.2) In the event that an Error is due to modifications made by the Customer (other than modifications resulting from Customer's exercise of its rights under Section 2.4), Customer shall pay ABC, ABC's then current time and material charges for time spent in the correction of such Error.

(4.3) In the event Customer requests and ABC performs Maintenance Services outside of Business Hours (except where such Maintenance Services are performed in accordance with Section 2.2 (c)), Customer shall pay ABC , ABC's then current time and material consulting charges for such work performed by ABC.

(4.4) The Customer shall pay all reasonable expenses incurred by ABC in performing its obligations hereunder. Expenses which: (a) individually are in excess of two hundred fifty dollars ($250) or (b) during any calendar month, would cause total expenses incurred in such month to exceed five hundred dollars ($500), shall not be incurred without Customer's prior written consent.

(4.5) The Customer shall pay any sales or use tax imposed by the New York State and/or New York City government(s) in connection with the SOFTWARE.

(4.6) Invoices shall be payable within thirty (30) days after Customer's receipt of ABC's invoice, so long as the amounts stated therein are not reasonably in dispute.

(4.7) ABC warrants that the terms of this Agreement are comparable to or better than the terms offered by ABC to any of its present commercial customers of equal or lesser size for comparable Maintenance Services. If ABC offers more favorable terms to its commercial customers during the period expiring one year from the date this Agreement is executed, such terms shall also be made available to Customer together with any resulting refund within thirty (30) days from the execution of such agreement.

5. TITLE & CONFIDENTIALITY

(5.1) Any changes, additions, and enhancements in the form of new or partial programs or Documentation as may be provided under this Agreement shall be governed by the same terms and conditions as contained in Section 4 of the License Agreement which is incorporated herein by reference.

6. INTELLECTUAL PROPERTY INDEMNIFICATION

(6.1) ABC agrees to indemnify Customer and defend and/or handle at its own expense, any claim or action against Customer for actual or alleged infringement of any intellectual or industrial property right, including without limitation, trademarks, service marks, patents, copyrights, misappropriation of trade secrets or any similar property rights, based upon the Maintenance Services or Customer's use thereof in accordance with the same terms and conditions as contained in Section 8 of the License Agreement which is incorporated herein by reference.

7. LIMITED REMEDIES & LIABILITY

(7.1) In all cases where an Error cannot be corrected within the time periods specified in Section 2 of this Agreement, the Customer shall be entitled to recover actual damages up to the amounts specified in Section 7.2 plus liquidated damages as specified in Section 2.2(d).

(7.2) ABC's liability to Customer shall be limited to two (2) times the annual Maintenance Fees then payable by Customer to ABC. The foregoing limitation of liability shall not apply to the: (a) payment of costs, damages and attorney's fees referred to in Section 6 for ABC's indemnity obligation; (b) claims for personal injury or damage to real or personal property caused by willful or negligent acts of ABC, its employees or contractors or (c) damages resulting from violation of Section 5 for breach of confidentiality obligations.

(7.3) IN NO EVENT SHALL ABC OR THE CUSTOMER BE LIABLE FOR INCIDENTAL, SPECIAL OR CONSEQUENTIAL DAMAGES (INCLUDING WITHOUT LIMITATION LOST PROFITS) EVEN IF EITHER PARTY HAS BEEN ADVISED OF THE POSSIBILITY OF SUCH DAMAGES.

8. TERMINATION

(8.1) If a party (the "Defaulting Party") is in material breach of or default under this Agreement, and the Defaulting Party does not remedy that breach or default within fifteen (15) calendar days after receipt from the other party of written notice of that default or breach (provided that if the breach or default is one that cannot be remedied within such fifteen (15) day period, this Agreement may be terminated effective immediately upon written notice to the Defaulting Party), the other party shall after the expiry of such fifteen (15) calendar day period have the right to terminate this Agreement effective immediately upon written notice to the Defaulting Party.

(8.2) Either party may terminate this Agreement, at any time, by written notice in the event that the other: (a) files a voluntary petition in bankruptcy or under any similar insolvency law; (b) makes an assignment for the benefit of creditors; (c) has filed against it any involuntary petition in bankruptcy or under any similar insolvency law if any such petition is not dismissed within sixty (60) days after filing; (d) a receiver is appointed for, or a levy or attachment is made against, substantially all of its assets, if any such petition is not dismissed or such receiver or levy or attachment is not discharged within sixty (60) days after the filing or appointment or (e) upon termination of the License Agreement.

(8.3) For the purposes of paragraph 8.1 and 8.2, Customer shall be in material breach of or default under this Agreement and ABC may terminate this Agreement only if the breach or default relates to Customer's obligation to pay ABC any amount payable hereunder when due and the breach or default is not remedied within the applicable time period specified therefor. ABC's rights and remedies in respect of any other breach of or default under this Agreement shall be limited to such rights and remedies other than termination of this Agreement.

(8.4) Either party may terminate this Agreement to take effect immediately upon termination of the of the wind-down period specified in Section 10.6 of the License Agreement.

9. <u>GENERAL</u>

(9.1) Not later than fifteen (15) calendar days after the date of each Error correction, Technical Enhancement or modification made by ABC to the SOFTWARE, ABC shall deliver a full and complete set of the source code and all "Documentation" (as defined in Section 1.6) of the License Agreement) to the Escrow Agent for purposes of updating the Deposit under the "Escrow Agreement" (attached to the License Agreement as **Schedule "L"**).

(9.2) Neither party shall assign its rights or obligations under this Agreement without the prior written consent of the other party. Notwithstanding the forgoing, the Customer shall be entitled to assign its rights and obligations hereunder to any one of Customer's subsidiaries without any further consent from ABC. For purposes of this paragraph 9.2, a " subsidiary" shall be any entity in which Customer owns or controls at least fifty percent (50%) of such entity's stock or other evidence of ownership.

(9.3) No modifications of this Agreement shall be valid or binding on either party unless acknowledged in writing and signed by the duly authorized officer of each party. All notices or other communications given under this Agreement shall be in writing, sent to the address hereinbefore set forth as the principal place of business or such other addresses as ABC or the Customer may designate in writing by certified mail (return receipt requested) or personal delivery. Notice shall be deemed given upon receipt.

(9.4) Neither party shall be liable to the other for any delay or failure to perform its obligations under this Agreement if such delay or failure arises from any cause beyond the reasonable control of such party, including but not limited to labor disputes, strikes, other labor or industrial disturbances, acts of God, floods, lightning, utility or communication failures, earthquakes or other casualty.

If a delay or failure that ABC anticipates will cause an excusable delay, ABC by written notice shall inform Customer of the anticipated effect of such delay as soon as possible and in any event shall give written notice within ten (10) calendar days. Such notice shall contain a description of the steps ABC is taking to alleviate the problem. Anything in this Agreement to the contrary notwithstanding, Customer may, if the problem described in this paragraph 9.4 continues for a period in excess of thirty (30) calendar days, terminate this Agreement upon seven (7) calendar days notice to ABC; in such event, ABC shall refund all advance payments made by Customer and Customer shall be entitled to receive access to the Deposit in accordance with the Escrow Agreement..

(9.5) The parties acknowledge that each has read all the terms of this Agreement, is authorized to enter into it, agrees to be bound by its terms and conditions and that it is the complete and exclusive statement of the agreement between the parties which supersedes all prior communications and agreements between the parties relating to the subject matter of this Agreement.

(9.6) Any forbearance or delay on the part of either party in enforcing any provision of this Agreement or any of its rights hereunder shall not be construed as a waiver of such provision or of a right to enforce same.

(9.7) The provisions of Sections 2.2(d), 5, 6, 7, 8, and 9.2 through 9.10 shall survive termination of this Agreement or any portion thereof.

(9.8) The parties shall use all reasonable efforts to amicably resolve any dispute or controversy arising directly out of this Agreement by referring such dispute or controversy to a senior management executive of each party who was not directly involved in the procurement and day to day management of the Maintenance Services. The management executive selected by each party shall have the authority to bind its company to the terms of any settlement agreed to. If the parties, after good faith efforts, fail to resolve the dispute or controversy, the matter shall be referred to and settled by arbitration in accordance with the rules of XYZ Dispute Resolution Services.

In connection with any breach or threatened breach by either party of the confidential information obligations of this Agreement, the non-breaching party may, at any time seek by application to the United States District Court for the Southern District of New York or the Supreme Court of the State of New York for the County of New York any such temporary or provisional relief or remedy ("provisional remedy") provided for by the laws of the United States of America or the laws of the State of New York as would be available in an action based upon such dispute or controversy in the absence of this Section 9.8. No such application to either said Court for a provisional remedy, nor any act or conduct by either party in furtherance of or in opposition to such application, shall constitute a relinquishment or waiver of any right to have the underlying dispute or controversy with respect to which such application is made settled by arbitration.

In any arbitration proceeding, each party shall select one arbitrator who has technical software systems knowledge of real time trading systems. The two arbitrators so selected shall appoint a third so qualified arbitrator. A majority decision of the arbitrators shall be binding. Each party shall bear its own costs associated with such arbitration. The arbitration proceeding shall be kept confidential.

(9.9) Pending resolution of any dispute or controversy as provided in Section 9.8, each of the parties shall continue to perform its obligations under this Agreement and a failure to perform its obligations by either party pending the resolution process shall be deemed a separate breach of this Agreement.

(9.10) Any dispute arising under this Agreement shall be governed by the laws of the State of New York.

IN WITNESS WHEREOF, the parties have caused this Agreement to be executed and do each hereby warrant and represent that their respective signatory whose signature appears below has been and is on the date of this Agreement duly authorized by all necessary and appropriate corporate action to execute this Agreement.

CUSTOMER   ABC SYSTEMS, INC.

By: _____   **By:** _____

Name: _____   Name: _____

Title: _____   Title: _____

Date: _____   Date: _____

ABC SYSTEMS, INC.
END USER PURCHASE AND LICENSE AGREEMENT

AGREEMENT made as of the 28th day of August, 1996 by and between ABC Systems, Inc., with its office at 50 Main Street, White Plains, NY 11477 ("ABC") and Professional Trading Company, Ltd. with an office located at 100 Park Avenue, New York, NY 10017 ("Customer").

ABC and Customer agree that the following terms & conditions shall apply to Customer's purchase of the Products.

1. DEFINITIONS

As used in this document the following terms shall have the following meanings:

(1.1) "Acceptance" shall have the meaning stated in Section 8 of this Agreement.

(1.2) "Acceptance Test" shall mean the testing process for the Products performed in accordance with the test objectives specified in Section 8 of this Agreement.

(1.3) "Agreement" shall mean this agreement, any attached exhibits or schedules and any amendments to this Agreement which are in writing and signed by both parties.

(1.4) "Documentation" shall have the meaning given it in Section 2.2 of this Agreement.

(1.5) "Error" shall mean an error in the code of the Software, Network Link and/or a malfunction of the Hardware which prevents the Products from operating in all material respects in accordance with the Documentation or the RFP.

(1.6) "Hardware" shall mean the computer equipment identified in **Schedule "A"** attached hereto and made a part hereof.

(1.7) "Installation" shall have the meaning given it in Section 7.3 of this Agreement.

(1.8) "Installation Site" shall mean Customer's principal place of business located at 100 Park Avenue, New York, NY 10017.

(1.9) "Installation Tests" shall mean the tests described in **Schedule "F"** attached hereto and made a part hereof demonstrating Installation of the Products is complete.

(1.10) "NetWork Link" shall mean the network operating system software in object code format as more particularly identified in **Schedule "B'** attached hereto and made a part hereof.

(1.11) "Processing Module" shall mean a single, integrated operating unit consisting of at least a central processing unit, internal memory, intelligent controller(s), internal disk or tape unit, and internal power supply.

(1.12) "Products" shall mean the Hardware, Software and NetWork Link, together with all amendments enhancements and modifications thereto which have been accepted by Customer.

(1.13) "Software" shall mean the operating system software program in object code format as more particularly identified in **Schedule "C"** attached hereto and made a part hereof.

(1.14) "RFP" shall mean Customer's Request for Proposal dated July 7, 1996, a copy of which is attached hereto as **Schedule "D"** and made a part hereof.

2. DELIVERABLES

(2.1) ABC hereby sells and Customer agrees to purchase the Hardware together with a personal, nontransferable, non-exclusive, paid-up and irrevocable license to use the SOFTWARE and NetWork Link, in object code format, in connection with the Hardware.

(2.2) ABC shall provide Customer with two (2) copies of user, operations and training manuals for the Hardware, Software and NetWork Link in printed form and one (1) copy in electronic form which is compatible with Microsoft Word version 6.0..

3. LICENSE

(3.1) The Software and NetWork Link, including improvements, enhancements, revisions or updates provided by ABC, are furnished to Customer under a nonexclusive, nontransferable license solely for Customer's own use. The Software shall only be used by Customer in connection with the

Hardware. Notwithstanding the foregoing, the Software may be installed and executed on any number of Processing Modules interconnected with the Hardware and with each other into a network, using the NetWork Link software, but only for so long as such interconnection via NetWork Link exists. The Software and NetWork Link may only be copied, in whole or in part (with the proper inclusion of existing copyright notice(s) and any other proprietary notice(s) thereon), as may be necessary and incidental to use on the Hardware, for archival and back-up purposes or to replace a worn or defective copy.

(3.2) If Customer is unable to operate the Software on the Hardware due to an equipment malfunction, the Software may be transferred temporarily to another single Processing Module during the period of the equipment malfunction. Should the Hardware be upgraded and/or replaced by another ABC Processing Module, the Software may be used on the replacement Processing Module upon payment of an additional license fee calculated in accordance with **Schedule "E"** attached to this Agreement and made a part hereof. Thereafter the Hardware shall be the upgraded and/or replacement Processing Module.

(3.3) No title to nor ownership to the Software or NetWork Link or any of their parts, nor in any applicable rights therein such as patents, copyrights and trade secrets, is transferred to Customer, all of which shall continue to remain with ABC.

(3.4) Customer shall not reverse engineer, decompile, disassemble, re-engineer or otherwise attempt to discover the source code or the structural framework of the SOFTWARE or NetWork Link.

4. **PRICES AND TAXES**

(4.1) Customer shall pay ABC one hundred fifty thousand United States dollars ($150,000) for the Software and NetWork Link license fee and Hardware, payable as follows:

(a) fifteen thousand dollars ($15,000) upon execution of this Agreement;

(b) twenty thousand dollars ($20,000) upon: (i) delivery of the Hardware, (ii) Installation of the Software and NetWork Link and (iii) confirmation by

Customer that the Software and NetWork Link program files listed in **Schedule "E"** attached to this Agreement and made a part hereof reside on the Hardware's program libraries;

(c) fifteen thousand dollars ($15,000) upon delivery of: all Documentation to Customer;

(d) eighty thousand dollars ($80,000) upon Acceptance of the Hardware, Software and NetWork Link; and

(e) twenty thousand dollars ($20,000) upon the later of: (i) expiration of the warranty period or (ii) all warranty claims having been properly satisfied by ABC.

(4.2) The Customer shall pay any sales or use tax imposed by the New York State and/or New York City government(s) in connection with the Products.

(4.3) The Customer shall pay all transportation charges associated with shipment and delivery of the Products to the Installation Site together with reasonable expenses incurred by ABC in performing its obligations hereunder. Expenses which: (a) individually are in excess of two hundred fifty dollars ($250) or (b) during any calendar month, would cause total expenses incurred in such month to cxcccd fivc hundred dollars ($500) shall not be incurred without Customer's prior written consent.

(4.4) Invoices shall be payable within thirty (30) days after Customer's receipt of ABC's invoice, so long as the amounts stated therein are not reasonably in dispute.

(4.5) ABC warrants that the terms of this Agreement are comparable to or better than the terms offered by ABC to any of its present commercial customers of equal or lesser size for comparable products and services. If ABC offers more favorable terms to its commercial customers during the period expiring one year from the date this Agreement is executed, such terms shall also be made available to Customer together with any resulting refund within thirty (30) days from the execution of such agreement.

5. DELIVERY, TITLE & RISK OF LOSS

(5.1) All Products shall be delivered to Customer FOB Installation Site.

(5.2) Title to Hardware and risk of loss for the Products shall pass to Customer upon receipt by Customer at the Installation Site. ABC shall maintain insurance for loss or damage to the Products until receipt by Customer at the Installation Site.

6. SECURITY INTEREST

(6.1) ABC reserves a security interest in all Products, all additions, replacements and proceeds thereof to secure Customer's payment obligations. Such security interest is retained until Customer's payment obligations are satisfied in full. ABC may file this Agreement or financing statements pursuant to the Uniform Commercial Code or other applicable law to evidence or perfect ABC's security interest. Customer agrees to execute any additional agreements ABC reasonably deems necessary to perfect any such security interest.

7. INSTALLATION & SITE PREPARATION

(7.1) Installation of the Products shall be the responsibility of ABC and shall be completed by the dates set forth in the Implementation Schedule attached as **Schedule "H"** hereto and made a part hereof. As a condition to Installation, Customer shall prepare the Installation Site in accordance with the site preparation requirements identified in **Schedule "F"** attached hereto and made a part hereof.

(7.2) Customer shall be responsible for preparation of the Installation Site in accordance with the specifications attached to this Agreement as **Schedule "F"** attached hereto and made a part hereof. At such time that the Installation Site has been prepared, Customer shall give written notice thereof to ABC and within five (5) business days after receipt of Customer's notice by ABC, ABC shall inspect the Installation Site and either give its approval or disapproval. In the event ABC does not approve the Installation

Site, it shall provide detailed reasons therefor within three (3) business days after its inspection in which case Customer shall correct the deficiencies identified by ABC and the inspection process shall be repeated.

(7.3) Installation of the Products shall be deemed complete when the Products are ready for live production use as evidenced by successful completion of the Installation Tests.

(7.4) If through no fault of the Customer, Installation is not complete by the date specified therefor in the Implementation Schedule, in addition to all of Customer's other rights and remedies under this Agreement and at law, ABC shall pay Customer one thousand dollars ($1,000) for each business day beyond the fourth business day that completion of Installation is delayed.

8. ACCEPTANCE

(8.1) Customer shall prepare and, with the assistance of ABC, execute the Acceptance Test which include those procedures required to demonstrate that the Products are: (a) compatible with and can execute version 3.1 of the "Stock" computer software program yielding response times for each process identified in **Schedule "G"** attached hereto and made a part hereof no greater than the times set forth alongside each process in said schedule; (b) capable of executing Stock on a continuous basis without an Error or Product related service interruption at least ninety percent **(90%)** of the time during the acceptance test period of forty five (45) consecutive calendar days; (c) perform in all respects in accordance with the Documentation and (d) support Customer's requirements as defined in Customer's RFP. The RFP shall prevail in the event of any inconsistencies between the RFP and the standards or documents referred to in this paragraph. Customer shall commence Acceptance Testing within ten (10) business days after the Products have been Installed.

(8.2) If the Products fail to pass the Acceptance Test within sixty (60) calendar days from commencement thereof, Customer may at its option, request a replacement of the applicable Product or terminate this Agreement, in which event ABC shall refund to Customer all amounts paid by Customer to ABC hereunder and, as liquidated damages for its failure, pay Customer an amount equal to ten thousand dollars ($10,000). Notwithstanding the foregoing, unless the Products were rejected due to lack of compatibility with the Stock computer software program, and in the event ABC substitutes hardware, operating and network software acceptable to Customer with greater processing capability at no additional cost, Customer's right to terminate this Agreement shall be suspended for a period of forty five (45) calendar days during which the Acceptance Test will be repeated in accordance with the criteria set forth in paragraph 8.1.

(8.3) Upon Acceptance of the Products by Customer, Customer shall execute an Acceptance Certificate, the form of which is attached hereto as **Schedule "I"**.

9. <u>WARRANTIES</u>

(9.1) ABC warrants that Customer shall acquire good and clear title to the Hardware being purchased hereunder free and clear of all liens and encumbrances except as set forth in Section 6. ABC also warrants that it has inspected the Products for computer viruses and that the Products shall be free of all viruses when delivered.

(9.2) ABC further warrants that the Products delivered hereunder shall for a period of one hundred eighty (180) calendar days from date of Customer's Acceptance as set forth in Section 8 be: (a) free from defects in material and workmanship; (b) compatible with and can execute version 3.1 of the "Stock" computer software program, yielding response times for each process identified in **Schedule "G"** attached hereto no greater than the times set forth alongside each process in said schedule; (c) capable of executing Stock on a continuous basis without an Error or Product related service interruption at least ninety percent (90%) of the time during the warranty period; (d) perform in all respects in accordance with the Documentation; (e) compatible and able to support date calculations for the years 2000 and beyond and (f) support Customer's requirements as defined in Customer's RFP. The RFP shall prevail in the event of any inconsistencies between the RFP and the standards or documents referred to in this paragraph. ABC shall continue to provide warranty services to correct any Error notwithstanding expiration of the one hundred eighty (180) day warranty period so long as notice of such Error was given to

ABC prior thereto. EXCEPT FOR THE FOREGOING WARRANTY, ABC MAKES NO OTHER WARRANTY, EXPRESS OR IMPLIED, INCLUDING WITHOUT LIMITATION, THE IMPLIED WARRANTIES OF MERCHANT-ABILITY OR FITNESS FOR A PARTICULAR PURPOSE.

(9.3) ABC shall respond to warranty service requests within one (1) hour of Customer's notice and shall have completed all necessary corrections not later than three (3) hours after Customer's notice. In the event that that, during any ninety (90) day period, ABC shall fail two (2) times to correct an Error within the time periods aforesaid, Customer shall be entitled, at ABC's cost and expense, to employ its own personnel or a third party contractor of its own choosing to correct Errors occurring thereafter if ABC shall again fail to correct an Error within the prescribed time period.

(9.4) In the event that an Error which prevents production use of any one of the Products in any material respect as reasonably determined by the Customer is not corrected by ABC within seventy two (72) hours after notice (by telephone) thereof is given by Customer to ABC, Customer may terminate this Agreement in which case ABC shall: (a) refund to Customer all amounts paid to ABC hereunder and (b) pay Customer liquidated damages in the amount of ten thousand dollars ($10,000).

(9.5) ABC shall perform warranty services at the Installation Site during the warranty period at no additional charge to Customer.

10. <u>CANCELLATION AND RESCHEDULING CHARGES</u>

(10.1) Should Customer terminate this Agreement through no fault of ABC or portion thereof or request, and ABC accept, a rescheduling or reconfiguration of ordered Products, Customer agrees to pay to ABC cancellation/rescheduling charges as a percentage of the purchase price of the Product(s) (as itemized in **Schedule "K"** attached hereto and made a part hereof) canceled, rescheduled or reconfigured, not as a penalty, but as an agreed to amount based on the difficulty of computing actual charges. Such charges are as follows:

Customer Notice Received	Reschedule/ Reconfiguration Charges	Cancellation Charges
1 Prior to scheduled shipment month		
a. More than 60 days prior to:	0%	0%
b. 31-60 days prior to:	5%	10%
c. 30 or less days prior to:	10%	15%
2. During scheduled shipment month	15%	20%

Products shall not be subject to cancellation, rescheduling or reconfiguration after shipment.

11. INTELLECTUAL PROPERTY INDEMNIFICATION

(11.1) ABC agrees to defend and/or handle at its own expense, any claim or action against Customer for actual or alleged infringement of any intellectual or industrial property right, including without limitation, trademarks, service marks, patents, copyrights, misappropriation of trade secrets or any similar property rights, based upon any individual item comprising the Products or Customer's use thereof. ABC further agrees to indemnify and hold Customer harmless from and against any and all liabilities, costs, losses, damages and expenses (including reasonable attorney's fees) associated with such claim or action. Customer shall reasonably cooperate with ABC in the defense of such claim or action to the extent that such cooperation is given at such times and in a manner that does not negatively affect Customer's business in Customer's sole discretion and further, ABC reimburses Customer's expenses and pays Customer at Customer's hourly billing rate for all such assistance.

(11.2) ABC shall have the sole right to conduct the defense of any such claim or action and all negotiations for its settlement or compromise. Notwithstanding the foregoing, in the event that ABC shall fail to appoint an attorney within ten (10) calendar days after the claim having first been made or action commenced or the attorney appointed by ABC is, in Customer's reasonable judgment not suitably qualified to represent Customer, Customer shall have the right to select and appoint an alternative attorney and the reasonable cost and expense thereof shall be paid by ABC.

(11.3) If the Products or any individual item comprising the Products becomes or in ABC's reasonable opinion are likely to become the subject of any such claim or action, then, ABC shall use best efforts at its sole expense to either: (a) procure for Customer the right to continue using the affected Product as contemplated hereunder; (b) modify the affected Product to render same non-infringing (provided such modification does not adversely affect Customer's use as described in the RFP) or (c) replace same with equally suitable, functionally equivalent, compatible non-infringing Product. If none of the foregoing is possible, ABC shall have the right to terminate this Agreement upon: (i) payment to Customer of all monies paid by Customer for the Products and (ii) if this Agreement is terminated in accordance with this paragraph within the first twenty four (24) months after Acceptance, ABC shall in addition pay Customer an amount equal to twenty thousand dollars ($20,000) as liquidated damages.

12. <u>LIMITED REMEDIES & LIABILITY</u>

(12.1) In all cases involving performance or non-performance of the Products, Customer's primary remedy shall be correction of the Error(s). For all other failure(s) by ABC to perform in accordance with this Agreement, including without limitation, if any individual item comprising the Products is not Accepted by Customer (due to no fault of the Customer) or an Error cannot be corrected within the time periods specified in Section 9 of this Agreement, the Customer shall be entitled to terminate this Agreement in accordance with Section 15 and/or recover damages subject to the limits stated in paragraph 12.2.

(12.2) ABC's liability to Customer shall be limited to: (a) the amount of the charges payable by Customer under Section 4 of this Agreement plus (b) the amount of any liquidated damages payable by ABC pursuant to the various sections of this Agreement. The foregoing limitation of liability shall not apply to the: (a) payment of costs, damages and attorney's fees referred to in Section 11 for ABC's indemnity obligation; (b) claims for personal injury or damage to real or personal property caused by willful or negligent acts of ABC, its employees or contractors or (c) damages resulting from violation of Section 13 of this Agreement for breach of confidentiality and non-disclosure obligations.

(12.3) IN NO EVENT SHALL ABC OR THE CUSTOMER BE LIABLE FOR INCI-DENTAL, SPECIAL OR CONSEQUENTIAL DAMAGES (INCLUDING WITHOUT LIMITATION LOST PROFITS) EVEN IF EITHER PARTY HAS BEEN ADVISED OF THE POSSIBILITY OF SUCH DAMAGES.

13. <u>CONFIDENTIALITY</u>

(13.1) As used herein, "CUSTOMER Information" shall include all information and data furnished by CUSTOMER to ABC, whether in oral, written, graphic or machine-readable form, including without limitation, specifications, user, operations or systems manuals, diagrams, graphs, models, sketches, technical data, research, business or financial information, plans, strategies, forecasts, forecast assumptions, business practices, marketing information and material, customer names, proprietary ideas, concepts, know-how, methodologies and all other information related to Customer's business. CUSTOMER Information shall also include confidential information received by CUSTOMER from a third party. In order for any information provided verbally by CUSTOMER to ABC to come within the definition of CUSTOMER Information, it shall be identified as confidential at the time of disclosure and within five (5) business days after verbal disclosure thereof by CUSTOMER, such information shall be documented in writing specifying that CUSTOMER considers such information confidential.

(13.2) As used herein, "ABC Information" shall include all information and data furnished by ABC to CUSTOMER, whether in oral, written, graphic or machine-readable form, in connection with the Products, including, without limitation, object code, source code, source listings, computer programs, specifications, user, operations or systems manuals, diagrams, graphs, technical data, research, business or financial information, plans, strategies, forecasts, forecast assumptions, business practices, procedures, marketing information, trade secrets and other proprietary ideas, concepts, know-how, methodologies and information related to the Products or ABC. In order for any information provided verbally by ABC to CUS-TOMER to come within the definition of ABC Information, it shall be identified as confidential at the time of disclosure and within five (5) business days after verbal disclosure thereof by ABC, such information

shall be documented in writing specifying that ABC considers such information confidential.

(13.3) As used herein, "Confidential Information" shall include the CUSTOMER
Information and the ABC Information, individually and collectively. Notwithstanding anything to the contrary contained in this Agreement, Confidential Information shall not include information: (i) in the public domain (other than as a result of a breach of this Agreement); (ii) generally
known and disclosed to CUSTOMER or ABC by persons or entities engaged in a comparable business (other than as a result of a breach of this
Agreement or any other agreement to which such persons or entities are
parties); (iii) in CUSTOMER or ABC's possession prior to its receipt from
the other pursuant to this Agreement or (d) independently developed by
CUSTOMER or ABC.

(13.4) CUSTOMER and ABC agree to use steps no less rigorous than those used
to protect and preserve their own confidential information to maintain
the confidentiality of the Confidential Information of the other and shall
not, directly or indirectly: (a) transfer or disclose any Confidential Information to any third party (other than to their respective employees); (b)
use any Confidential Information other than as contemplated under this
Agreement or (c) take any other action with respect to the Confidential
Information inconsistent with the confidential and proprietary nature of
such information. CUSTOMER and ABC further agree to return all Confidential Information (and all copies thereof) to the other upon termination of this Agreement, subject to Section 15.3 of this Agreement.

(13.5) CUSTOMER and ABC shall be permitted to disclose the Confidential Information to their respective employees having a need for access thereto
in connection with their employment and who have executed confidentiality agreements containing provisions similar to those contained in this
Agreement and specifying that other parties are third party beneficiaries
thereof entitled to enforce the provisions thereof as though a party thereto.
CUSTOMER and ABC shall each take steps, no less rigorous than those it
takes to protect its own proprietary information, to prevent their respective employees from acting in a manner inconsistent with the terms of
this Agreement.

(13.6) ABC acknowledges and agrees that CUSTOMER is engaged in the business of securities trading, and as such currently possesses knowledge and information relating to the functionality and capabilities required for computer systems in support thereof. Therefore, nothing contained in this Agreement shall prevent CUSTOMER from, on its own or through third parties, designing, developing or acquiring computer systems similar to the any individual item comprising the Products so long as CUSTOMER does not make use of any ABC Information in connection therewith.

14. TRAINING

(14.1) ABC shall provide thirty (30) hours of training to Customer in the use, operation and maintenance of the Products. The training curriculum and ABC's instructors assigned thereto is identified in **Schedule "J"** attached hereto and made a part hereof. Training will be conducted in not less than two or greater than three (3) hour sessions per day at the Installation Site. ABC shall assume and be responsible for the payment of all transportation, room and board expenses of its employees in furnishing such training.

15. TERMINATION

(15.1) If a party (the "Defaulting Party") is in material breach of or default under this Agreement, and the Defaulting Party does not remedy that breach or default within thirty (30) calendar days after receipt from the other party of written notice of that default or breach (provided that if the breach or default is one that cannot be remedied within such thirty (30) day period, this Agreement may be terminated effective immediately upon written notice to the Defaulting Party), the other party shall after the expiry of such thirty (30) calendar day period have the right to terminate this Agreement effective immediately upon written notice to the Defaulting Party.

(15.2) Either party may terminate this Agreement, at any time, by written notice in the event that the other: (a) files a voluntary petition in bankruptcy or under any similar insolvency law; (b) makes an assignment for the benefit of creditors; (c) has filed against it any involuntary petition in bankruptcy or under any similar insolvency law if any such petition is not dismissed within sixty (60) days after filing or (d) a receiver is appointed for, or a levy or attachment is made against, substantially all of its assets, if any such petition is not dismissed or such receiver or levy or attachment is not discharged within sixty (60) days after the filing or appointment.

(15.3) For the purposes of paragraphs 15.1 and 15.2, Customer shall be in material breach of or default under this Agreement and ABC may terminate this Agreement only if the breach or default relates to Customer's obligation to pay ABC any amount payable hereunder when due and the breach or default is not remedied within the applicable time period specified therefor. ABC's rights and remedies in respect of any other breach of or default under this Agreement shall be limited to such rights and remedies other than termination of this Agreement.

16. <u>EXPORT</u>

(16.1) Customer agrees that the Products purchased hereunder shall not be exported directly or indirectly, separately or as part of a system, without first obtaining a license from the U.S. Department of Commerce or any other appropriate agency of the U.S. Government, as required. Diversion of Products contrary to U.S. law is prohibited.

17. <u>GENERAL</u>

(17.1) Neither party shall assign its rights or obligations under this Agreement without the prior written consent of the other party. Notwithstanding the forgoing, the Customer shall be entitled to assign its rights and obligations hereunder to any one of Customer's subsidiaries without any further consent from ABC. For purposes of this paragraph 17.1, a " subsidiary" shall be any entity in which Customer owns or controls at least fifty percent (50%) of such entity's stock or other evidence of ownership.

(17.2) No modifications of this Agreement shall be valid or binding on either party unless acknowledged in writing and signed by the duly authorized officer of each party. All notices or other communications given under this Agreement shall be in writing, sent to the address hereinbefore set forth as the principal place of business or such other addresses as

ABC or the Customer may designate in writing by certified mail (return receipt requested) or personal delivery. Notice shall be deemed given upon receipt.

(17.3) Both parties understand and agree that violation of Section 13 of this Agreement may cause damage to the other party in an amount which is impossible or extremely difficult to ascertain. Accordingly, without limitation to any other remedy available at law, the injured party may be entitled to injunctive relief restraining the other party from continuing to violate the terms and provisions of said section.

(17.4) Neither party shall be liable to the other for any delay or failure to perform its obligations under this Agreement if such delay or failure arises from any cause beyond the reasonable control of such party, including but not limited to labor disputes, strikes, other labor or industrial disturbances, acts of God, floods, lightning, utility or communication failures, earthquakes or other casualty.

If a delay or failure that ABC anticipates will cause an excusable delay, ABC by written notice shall inform Customer of the anticipated effect of such delay as soon as possible and in any event shall give written notice within ten (10) calendar days. Such notice shall contain a description of the steps ABC is taking to alleviate the problem. Anything in this Agreement to the contrary notwithstanding, Customer may, if the Products have not been Accepted due to a problem described in this paragraph 17.4, by a date which is thirty (30) calendar days after Acceptance Testing is to commence, terminate this Agreement upon seven (7) calendar days notice to ABC; in such event, ABC shall refund all payments made by Customer and Customer shall return Products delivered prior to termination.

(17.5) The parties acknowledge that each has read all the terms of this Agreement, is authorized to enter into it, agrees to be bound by its terms and conditions and that it is the complete and exclusive statement of the agreement between the parties which supersedes all prior communications and agreements between the parties relating to the subject matter of this Agreement.

(17.6) Any forbearance or delay on the part of either party in enforcing any provision of this Agreement or any of its rights hereunder shall not be construed as a waiver of such provision or of a right to enforce same.

(17.7) The provisions of Sections 5.2, 6, 9.1, 11, 12, 13, 15, 16, and 17.2 through 17.10 shall survive termination of this Agreement or any portion thereof.

(17.8) The parties shall use all reasonable efforts to amicably resolve any dispute or controversy arising directly out of this Agreement by referring such dispute or controversy to a senior management executive of each party who was not directly involved in the procurement and day to day management of the Products. The management executive selected by each party shall have the authority to bind its company to the terms of any settlement agreed to. If the parties, after good faith efforts, fail to resolve the dispute or controversy, the matter shall be referred to and settled by arbitration in accordance with the rules of XYZ Dispute Resolution Services.

In connection with any breach or threatened breach by either party of the confidential information obligations of this Agreement, the non-breaching party may, at any time seek by application to the United States District Court for the Southern District of New York or the Supreme Court of the State of New York for the County of New York any such temporary or provisional relief or remedy ("provisional remedy") provided for by the laws of the United States of America or the laws of the State of New York as would be available in an action based upon such dispute or controversy in the absence of this Section 17.8. No such application to either said Court for a provisional remedy, nor any act or conduct by either party in furtherance of or in opposition to such application, shall constitute a relinquishment or waiver of any right to have the underlying dispute or controversy with respect to which such application is made settled by arbitration.

In any arbitration proceeding, each party shall select one arbitrator who has technical software systems knowledge of real time trading systems. The two arbitrators so selected shall appoint a third so qualified arbitrator.

A majority decision of the arbitrators shall be binding. Each party shall bear its own costs associated with such arbitration. The arbitration proceeding shall be kept confidential.

(17.9) Pending resolution of any dispute or controversy as provided in Section 17.8, each of the parties shall continue to perform its obligations under this Agreement and a failure to perform its obligations by either party pending the resolution process shall be deemed a separate breach of this Agreement.

(17.10) Any dispute arising under this Agreement shall be governed by the laws of the State of New York.

IN WITNESS WHEREOF, the parties have caused this Agreement to be executed and do each hereby warrant and represent that their respective signatory whose signature appears below has been and is on the date of this Agreement duly authorized by all necessary and appropriate corporate action to execute this Agreement.

CUSTOMER   ABC SYSTEMS, INC.

By: _____   By: _____

Name: _____   Name: _____

Title: _____   Title: _____

Date: _____   Date: _____

APPENDIX

REQUEST FOR INFORMATION

This Request for Information ("RFI") is being furnished by Professional Trading Company, Ltd., 100 Park Avenue, New York, NY 11477 ("PTC"). This RFI solicits information with respect to a fully automated computer software system for real time portfolio management.[72]

This RFI outlines various of PTC's functional requirements and will be used by PTC to select the vendors who will receive a more detailed Request for Proposal ("RFP"). The RFI and RFP shall comprise the totality of PTC's functional requirements.

A. General Information

A.1 Rights of PTC

PTC reserves and may exercise, at any time, any of the following rights and options with respect to this RFI:

(a) To reject any and all bids without incurring any cost, to seek additional bids, to enter into negotiations with and subsequently contract with more than one bidder, and/or to award a contract on the basis of criteria other than price. Even though your Proposal may be rejected, PTC reserves the right to use any of the concepts or ideas contained therein without incurring any liability (subject to Section A.2 hereof).

---

72. This Request For Information and the Request For Proposal contained in Appendix C have been provided through the courtesy of Joseph Rosen at Enterprise Technology Corporation of New York.

(b) To evaluate separately the individual components of each bid, such as any proposed subsystem, product or service, and to contract with such vendors for any individual component(s).

(c) To cancel or withdraw this RFI with or without substitution, to alter the terms or conditions of this RFI, and/or to alter, within reason, the proposed implementation schedule.

(d) To conduct investigations into the qualifications of any bidder prior to the time of contract award.

(e) The terms of PTC's attached Software License Agreement, Software Development Agreement, Customized Software Services Agreement and Maintenance Services Agreement, as applicable, ("Master Agreements") shall apply to any contract awarded. PTC has the option to reasonably incorporate and/or change any or all parts of the Master Agreements into the final agreement executed with the vendor.

(f) Through its signed response to this RFI, each bidder agrees that in the event it is selected for contract award by PTC pursuant to the RFI and RFP, it shall enter into a contractual arrangement with PTC and shall abide by the terms stated in this RFI, the RFP and the Master Agreements. The vendor's response to this RFI acknowledges that the PTC reserves the right to include any part or parts of the selected vendor's proposal in the final agreement.

A.2 Confidentiality

(a) The contents of this RFI are confidential. Access to or disclosure of the contents should be limited to those individuals directly involved in the preparation of vendor's response.

(b) In connection with this RFI, or PTC's proposed project, the vendor shall not use the name of PTC or any of its subsidiaries or affiliates in any publication or public relations document without the prior written consent of PTC prior to such publication or announcement. PTC reserves the right to review and approve all press-related copy and may withhold consent for release of such copy, with or without cause.

(c) It is the vendor's responsibility to identify any information contained in their proposal that is of a confidential or proprietary nature, so that this information will be treated accordingly.

A.3. Quality of Proposal & Completeness of Response

(a) The quality of the proposal submitted by the vendor is viewed as a basic indication of the vendor's general capability and technical competence. Quality is interpreted as: (i) completeness, (ii) thoroughness, (iii) accuracy, (iv) compliance with the RFI instructions, (v) timeliness and (vi) the organization and conciseness of the descriptive text material. Proposals which do not comply with the instructions may be eliminated from further consideration.

(b) By virtue of submitting a signed response, the vendor warrants that the requirements of this RFI have been read and understood and represents that the delivery and implementation of the products and services specified in the RFI shall in no way obligate PTC to pay any additional fees or costs to the vendor for services or products other than those presented in the response.

A.4 Non-Binding Effect

(a) This RFI represents a preliminary definition of specific requirements. It is not an offer to enter into an agreement with any vendor. Only execution of a written agreement by PTC will obligate PTC in accordance with the terms and conditions contained in such agreement.

(b) This RFI does not obligate PTC to pay any costs that the vendor incurs in the preparation of the response. All costs associated with the preparation of a response to this RFI shall be the responsibility and entirely borne by the vendor. Your response shall become the property of PTC.

A.5 Prime Contractor's Responsibility

Any vendor's response which includes equipment, software or services marketed, supported and/or sold by other companies, entities or individuals, must contain a statement indicating which party intends to act as the prime contractor for the delivery and implementation of the entire system.

A.6 Commitments

No commitment will be made to select a vendor's system solely on the basis of price nor on the basis of information contained in the vendor's response to this RFI.

A.7 Test Demonstrations

Test demonstrations may be requested of any of the programs proposed as a means of confirming the vendor's claims regarding the capabilities of the proposed system.

A.8 Performance Period

A performance period will be required to ascertain the effectiveness of the system and services prior to acceptance. The performance period shall be sufficient to verify that the application software performs in accordance with this RFI , the RFP and agreed specifications. Time allocated by the vendor for program testing or file conversion is not included in the performance time period.

A.9 Validity

All terms and quotations of the vendor's response, including but not limited to the vendor's price, shall be valid for a period of not less than one hundred eighty calendar days (180) following the date of submission.

A.10 Response Delivery

Responses must be received by PTC by the close of business on February 4, 1996. No extensions can be granted. Seven (7) bound copies of each response together with a an electronic copy in Microsoft Word for Windows version 6.0 format should be sent to:

Ms. Sharon K. Smith
MIS Director
Professional Trading Company, Ltd.
100 Park Avenue
New York. NY 11477

B. Please respond to the following questions which reflect PTC's requirement for the system to be implemented:

1. Company Name _____ Year Founded _____

2. Product Name _____ # Installations _____

3. Total # Employees _____ # Developers _____ # Support _____

4. Date current version first installed _____
   Date original version first installed _____

5. Joint venture with other software companies and/or vendors?
   _____

6. Can we review financial statements (if you are chosen as a finalist)?
   ____Yes ____ No

7. What platforms and operating systems does the system run on ? _____
   _____

8. Is it a true multi-user (shared database) system? ____Yes ____No

9. What is the database manager or file structure? _____
   _____

10. What is the programming language(s)? _____
    _____

11. Can it support 40 users on a reasonably configured LAN?
    ____Yes ____No Maximum? _____

12. Can it support 5,000 individual portfolios/accounts?
    ____Yes ____No Maximum? _____

13. Can it support 65,000 individual security positions (8,000 different issues)
    in those portfolios? ____Yes ____No Maximum? _____

14. What is a reasonable estimate of expected response time for an average
    Account Holdings on-line inquiry display, given these volume assump-
    tions? _____
    For an average single-portfolio full-year performance report?
    _____

15. What configuration (clients and server) would you recommend given all of these assumptions? _____

16. What are the provisions for using the system remotely or as a stand-alone user? _____

17. Does the system include integrated Client Contact Management capabilities? (client personal data, free-form notes, tickler file, WP download, autodialing, shared calendar, etc.) ___Yes ___No

18. Does the system perform portfolio performance calculation and reporting? ___Yes ___No
    If Yes, is it *fully* AIMR-compliant? ___Yes___No

19. Please indicate whether your proposed system accommodates the following functions and features.

Security Types	Supported? Yes	No		Fully Automated Yes	No	Explanation
Domestic Equities						
Treasury Bonds						
Treasury Bills						
Corporate Bonds						
Convertible Bonds						
Convertible Preferred Stock						
Municipal Bonds						
Closed-End Mutual Funds						
Open-End Mutual Funds						
Cash/Money Funds						
Foreign Equities (in foreign currency)						
Open-End Foreign Funds (in foreign)						
Closed-End Foreign Funds (in foreign)						
Options						

Transaction Types	Supported? Yes	No		Fully Automated Yes	No	Explanation
Purchase						
Sale						
Cash Dividend						
Stock Split						
Stock Dividend						
Reverse Split						
Interest Accrual						
Bond/Preferred Conversions						
Bond Calls						
Tender Offers (cash and/or stock)						
Dividend as Stock of Another Company						
Spinoffs						
Cancel/Correct any of the above transactions						
Transfers Between Accounts (delivery-in, delivery-out)						

System Functions	Supported? Yes	No	Explanation
On-Line Inquiry Functions			
Display Account Holdings			
Display Account Transaction History			
Display Account Personal Data			
Display Accounts Holding a Security			
Display Accounts Not Holding a Security			
Reports			
Portfolio Appraisal			
Realized Gains/Losses			
Unrealized Gains/Losses			
Performance Report			
Ad-Hoc Reporting Capabilities			
Data Entry Functions			
Enter Trade			
Trade Correction			
Security Master Record Maintenance			
Account/Portfolio Maintenance			
Cash In/Out			
Features			
Down-Load Reports To A File			
Multiple Categories Of Account Types			
DTC Interface			
Portfolio Modeling/What-If Analysis			
Trade Order Management			
Automatic Order Generation			
Advisory Fee Billing			
Trade Date Accounting			
Tax Lots			
Addresses In Account Table			
Clearing Interface With Pershing			
Other Correspondent/Clearing Interfaces			
Clearing Firm Holdings Reconciliation			
Performance Calculations Net Of Fees			
Can Accounts Be Linked For Reporting/Performance			
Can Accounts Be Linked For Billing			

20. For what Pricing Services are there standard interfaces? Real-time? End-of-day? _____

21. Describe the facilities for extracting/downloading data from the system.

    _____

22. Interface with vendor of corporate action information? ___ Yes ___ No
    If Yes, which one(s) _____

23. What security features does the system have? _____

    _____

24. Do you have a continuously-staffed Hot-Line/Help Desk? ___Yes ___No

25. How long does system take to install? _____

26. What documentation is available? _____

    _____

27. What are the arrangements for training? How long does it take?

    _____

28. What are the provisions for the client to independently modify the system in order to enhance or extend its functionality? (e.g. source code availability, OLE 2, API's and/or user exits) _____

    _____

29. Pricing Basis: ❏ Single Price   ❏ per User
                       ❏ by Asset Size   ❏ per Module

    Other(describe) _____

30. What is the expected purchase price given the assumptions we have provided ?_____

31. Is there an extended "try before you buy" option? ___Yes ___No

32. What support/customization/conversion assistance is included with the purchase? _____

33. What are the options and pricing for ongoing maintenance, support and new versions? _____

REQUEST FOR PROPOSAL

This Request for Proposal ("RFP") is being furnished by Professional Trading Company, Ltd., 100 Park Avenue, New York, NY 11477 ("PTC"). This RFP solicits information with respect to an fully automated computer software system for real time portfolio management.

This RFP and the Request for Information dated January 4, 1996 ("RFI") previously submitted to the vendor outlines PTC's functional requirements and will be used by PTC to select the vendor(s) with whom to engage in negotiations for the procurement of the required system.

A. General Information

A.1 Rights of PTC

PTC reserves and may exercise, at any time, any of the following rights and options with respect to this RFP:

(a) To reject any and all bids without incurring any cost, to seek additional bids, to enter into negotiations with and subsequently contract with more than one bidder, and/or to award a contract on the basis of criteria other than price. Even though your Proposal may be rejected, PTC reserves the right to use any of the concepts or ideas contained therein without incurring any liability (subject to Section A.2 hereof).

(b) To evaluate separately the individual components of each bid, such as any proposed subsystem, product or service, and to contract with such vendors for any individual component(s).

(c) To cancel or withdraw this RFP with or without substitution, to alter the terms or conditions of this RFP, and/or to alter, within reason, the proposed implementation schedule.

(d) To conduct investigations into the qualifications of any bidder prior to the time of contract award.

(e) The terms of PTC's attached Software License Agreement, Software Development Agreement, Customized Software Services Agreement and Maintenance Services Agreement, as applicable, ("Master Agreements") shall apply to any contract awarded. PTC has the option to reasonably incorporate and/or change any or all parts of the Master Agreements into the final agreement executed with the vendor.

(f) Through its signed response to this RFP, each bidder agrees that in the event it is selected for contract award by PTC pursuant to the RFI and this RFP, it shall enter into a contractual arrangement with PTC and shall abide by the terms stated in the RFI, this RFP and the Master Agreements. By its response to the RFP, the vendor acknowledges that the PTC reserves the right to include any part or parts of the selected vendor's proposal in the final agreement.

A.2 Confidentiality

This RFP and vendor's response hereto shall be subject to the confidentiality agreement executed between the parties on January 20, 1996.

A.3 Quality of Proposal & Completeness of Response

(a) The quality of the proposal submitted by the vendor is viewed as a basic indication of the vendor's general capability and technical competence. Quality is interpreted as: (i) completeness, (ii) thoroughness, (iii) accuracy, (iv) compliance with the RFP instructions, (v) timeliness and (vi) the organization and conciseness of the descriptive text material. Proposals which do not comply with these instructions may be eliminated from further consideration.

(b) By virtue of submitting a signed response, the vendor warrants that the requirements of this RFP have been read and understood and represents that the delivery and implementation of the products and services specified in the RFP shall in no way obligate PTC to pay any additional fees or costs to the vendor for services or products other than those presented in the response.

A.4 Non-Binding Effect

This RFP represents a definition of specific requirements. It is not an offer to enter into an agreement with any vendor. Only execution of a written agreement by PTC will obligate PTC in accordance with the terms and conditions contained in such agreement.

This RFP does not obligate PTC to pay any costs that the vendor incurs in the preparation of the response. All costs associated with the preparation of a response to this RFP shall be the responsibility and entirely borne by the vendor. Your response shall become the property of PTC.

A.5 Prime Contractor's Responsibility

Any vendor's response which includes equipment, software or services marketed, supported and/or sold by other companies, entities or individuals, must contain a statement indicating which party intends to act as the prime contractor for the delivery and implementation of the entire system.

A.6 Commitments

No commitment will be made to select a vendor's system solely on the basis of price nor on the basis of information contained in the vendor's response to this RFP.

A.7 Test Demonstrations

Test demonstrations may be requested of any of the programs proposed as a means of confirming the vendor's claims regarding the capabilities of the proposed system.

A.8 Performance Period

A performance period will be required to ascertain the effectiveness of the system and services prior to acceptance. The performance period shall be sufficient to verify that the application software performs in accordance with this RFP and agreed specifications. Time allocated by the vendor for program testing or file conversion is not included in the performance time period.

A.9 Validity

All terms and quotations of the vendor's response, including but not limited to the vendor's price, shall constitute a firm offer by vendor which shall be valid for a period of not less than one hundred eighty calendar days (180) following the date of submission.

A.10 Response Delivery

Responses must be received by PTC by the close of business on March 10, 1996. No extensions can be granted. Seven (7) bound copies of each response together with a an electronic copy in Microsoft Word for Windows version 6.0 format should be sent to:

Ms. Sharon K. Smith

MIS Director

Professional Trading Company, Ltd.

100 Park Avenue

New York. NY 11477

A.11 Bidders' Conference

A bidders' conference will be mandatory for all bidders. The bidders' conference will be held at PTC's offices to answer any questions and to allow vendors to become familiar with the proposed project. The date and time of the conference will be March 17, 1996 at 10:00 A.M.

B. Please respond to the following questions which reflect PTC's requirement for the system to be implemented:

1. Vendor Information

    1.1 Company Name

    1.2 Product Name

    1.3 Please provide the release history for your product.

        1.3.1 Describe the initial release (dates, original client name, original scope, etc.).

        1.3.2 Describe all subsequent releases and major enhancements to each.

        1.3.3 What are the major features of next release planned? When is it expected?

    1.4 Describe the future product direction.

        1.4.1 New platforms

        1.4.2 New features

        1.4.3 Upgrades

    1.5 Provide a list of current users. Include the following items:

          - client company name, address and industry

          - contact name, title and phone number

          - operating environment

          - year system was purchased, installed and went into production

    1.6 Who are your most prestigious (recognizable) customers?

    1.7 What range of products do you offer?

    1.8 Please provide resumes/biographies of owners, senior management, designers and developers.

    1.9 Please provide the following financial information about your firm:

- supply a complete statement of financial condition for your firm, including an audited or certified statement of income, current assets, and liabilities with the name of the auditor or certifier clearly indicated

- provide year-end results for the three (3) previous fiscal years, including revenues, expenses, net income, and total assets and liabilities

- list insurance coverage applicable to the services to be performed, including carriers, limits and ratings

- indicate performance guarantees offered by your firm (e.g. performance bond)

- list any and all previous and pending lawsuits against your firm and previous and pending lawsuits your firm has or had against another firm, corporation or individual together with a brief description of each and the outcome, if any.

2. Competitive Considerations

2.1 What is the major product weakness (actual and/or perceived)? How is it addressed?

2.2 For what size/type of institution is your product most suitable?

2.3 How do you competitively distinguish your product from alternative solutions available (i.e. key strengths, operational efficiencies and effectiveness gains achieved by your clients, etc.) ? What are some special characteristics of your product?

2.4 Who are your major competition? What are their weaknesses? What are their strengths?

2.5 What industry trends are you particularly sensitive to?

3. Technology Issues

3.1 Product Size

3.1.1 How many programs does your system contain? How many are batch? How many are on-line?

3.2.2 What is the approximate number of lines of code?

3.2 Describe the network proposed/recommended. Address hardware, management, audit, data management and data integration/strategy issues. Provide performance capabilities and measurement techniques.

3.3 What OS version(s) is required?

3.4 Can we review the source code?

3.5 Is the source code included?

If Yes, what is the price?

If No, what are the escrow provisions?

3.6 What special features exist to facilitate data entry?

3.7 Describe the facilities available to system administrators for running batch, adding reports, users, connections, etc.

3.8 Are your end-of-day and beginning-of-day processes automated? Please describe them.

3.9 What facilities are available for integrating with E-Mail?

4. System Capacity, Configuration and Limitations

4.1 How much disk storage is consumed (based on statistics given in our description) ?

4.1.1 How much disk storage is required for 2 years of active data?

4.1.2 How much disk storage is required for 5 years of historical data?

4.2 Describe any system limitations with regards to the following:

4.2.1 Number and size of the portfolios

4.2.2 Data file limits and any critical field limits

4.2.3 Accuracy to decimal place of calculations

4.2.4 Field sizes for dollars, other currencies

4.2.5 Number of active users/connection limits

4.2.6. Transaction volume limits

4.2.7. Portfolio consolidation limits

4.2.8. Remote connections

4.2.9. Any other limitations of note

5. Query/Reporting

5.1 Describe the report writer, query language and/or on-line interface for report viewing and browsing that you are proposing or recommending. Disclose any report writer limits (number of files, fields, etc.). Indicate how the business user prepares ad hoc reports without the assistance of a developer, including multi-file(database) queries.

Specify if:

- output can be requested in spreadsheet format and/or to a printable disk file

- the user can define report calculations such as column and row totals

- there is report formatting for titles, headers, footers and page numbering

5.2 Describe the facilities for customizing existing reports.

5.3 Describe your compliance facilities. Do you provide reports to support 13D and 13G filings?

5.4 Please provide a complete list of standard reports.

5.5 Describe the facilities for extracting/downloading data from the package.

5.6 Describe your facilities for reporting on trading commissions.

6. Database Structure

6.1 Describe the files/tables and structure (data model) of the database.

6.2 Indicate the flexibility of the system's data architecture to store new data elements required to support client's business needs.

6.3 Provide a list of all system files/tables. Describe how and by whom (users, system administrator, analysts, programmers) they can be modified.

6.4 Is the data dictionary available?

    6.4.1 Is it integrated with the file structure/database (edits and referential integrity reside in the dictionary) ?

    6.4.2 Explain how the data dictionary is utilized to support report writing efforts.

6.5 Provide database documentation if possible.

6.6 Describe the system/software features addressing database locking, transaction rollback and reapplication of transactions.

7. Documentation and Support

7.1 Please provide samples of the following documentation:

    7.1.1 User manuals

    7.1.2 On-line Help screens

    7.1.3 Installation guides and technical documentation

    7.1.4 Samples of standard reports

    7.1.5 Operator manuals

7.2 Is there an 800 number for Hot-Line support?

8. Additional Security Types

Explanation	Supported? Yes	No		Fully Automated Yes	No	Explanation
Rights						
Warrants						
Units						

9. Additional Transaction Types

	Supported? Yes No		Fully Automated Yes No		Explanation
Security Deposit					
Cash Deposit					
Security Withdrawal					
Cash Withdrawal					
Expiration (option, warrant etc.)					
Exercise (option, warrant etc.)					
Assignments (option, warrant etc.)					
Conversions (bonds, preferred stock)					

9.1 Can any supported transaction types not be reversed with a simple cancel transaction?

If not, please explain.

9.2 Can canceled transactions and canceling transactions be suppressed from printing on client reports?

10. Additional Features

10.1 Does the package include support for proxy voting?

10.2 Does the package include integrated Client Contact Management capabilities?

Which of the following does it include? Please describe.

10.2.1 Client personal data

10.2.2 Free-form notes

10.2.3 Tickler file

10.2.4 Word Processing download

10.2.5 Autodialing

10.2.6 Shared calendar

10.2.7 Other

11.   **Security Data Maintenance**

Data Item	Supported? Yes	No	Explanation
Issuer Identification			
Issue Identification			
Currency			
Security Type			
Other Security Classifications			
Industry			
Quality Ratings			
Fixed Rates			
Variable Rates			
Call Schedules			
Put Schedules			
Multiple Prices Per Date			
Historical Prices			
Computed data (yields, duration, etc.)			
EPS			
Freeform Text			
Shares Outstanding			

11.1 Explain how EPS, shares outstanding, and quality ratings are loaded into the system.

11.2 Does your product accept CUSIPs and tickers interchangeably during data entry?

11.3 How does your product handle changes in ticker symbols, CUSIPs and company names?

12. Securities Pricing

12.1 How are OTC securities priced (bid, ask, last)? Is the method selectable by portfolio?

12.2 How are options priced?

12.3 How can we verify the accuracy and reliability of pricing?

12.4 What pricing exception reports are produced? Please provide a sample of each.

12.5 Do you check prices across multiple sources?

12.6 Can different portfolios use different pricing sources for the same security?

12.7 Valuation

	Supported?		
	Yes	No	Explanation
Manual Pricing			
Override Of Automated Pricing			
Price Change Tolerance Control			
Matrix Pricing			

13. Performance Measurement

	Supported?		
	Yes	No	Explanation
By Firm			
By Portfolio Manager			
By Portfolio, Including Cash			
By Portfolio, Excluding Cash			
By Security Type			
By Industry Classification			
By Quality			
By Maturity Category			
By User Defined Category			
Excluding Specified Assets			
Full AIMR Reporting Compliance			
Certified AIMR Compliance			
Can You Allocate Cash To The Equity And Fixed Segments Of A Balanced Account			
Time Weighted Rate Of Return			
Dollar Weighted Rate Of Return			
Principal Return			
Income Return			
Total Return			
Gross Of Fees			
Net Of Fees			
On Composite/Combined Portfolios			
On Hypothetical Portfolios			
"What-If" Analysis			
Returns On Indices			
Money Market Yield			
Multiple Periods			
Monthly			
Quarterly			
Year-To-Date			
Annual			
Multi-Year			
From Inception			
User Defined			

14. Trade Processing

	Supported?		
	Yes	No	Explanation
Block Trade Order Entry			
Position Not Owned Sale Prevention			
- Override			
Position On Covering Option Sale Prevention			
- Override			
Insufficient Cash Warning			
Trade Order Creation From "What-If"			
Write/Close Options			
Trade Order Processing			
Open Not Executed			
Partial Executions			
Filled Orders			
Block Trade Allocation			
Immediate Update Of Trade Date Position			
Automatic Link To Securities Accounting			
Freeform Comments On Trades			
Calculations			
Price Given Yield			
Yield Given Price			
Accrued Income			
Next Coupon Date			
Duration			

15. Settlement Processing

	Supported?		
	Yes	No	Explanation
Confirmation			
Affirmation			
Automatic Affirmation With DTC			
Normal Settlement			
Same Day Settlement			
Exception Reporting			

15.1 Are settlement dates calculated by security type?

15.2 How does the product handle holidays and leap years?

15.3 Can the user override a system-calculated settlement date?

16. Multicurrency Processing

	Supported?		
	Yes	No	Explanation
Securities Data Maintenance			
Portfolio Management			
Performance Measurement			
Trade Processing			
Settlement Processing			
Securities Accounting			
Reporting			

17. Securities Accounting

	Supported?		
	Yes	No	Explanation
Multiple Accounting Bases			
Trade Date			
Settlement Date			
Selectable			
Tax Lot Accounting			
Realized Gain/Loss			
Unrealized Gain/Loss			
Fifo			
Lifo			
High Cost			
Low Cost			
Average Cost			
Specific Lot Designation			
Tax Straddle Identification For Hedged Transactions			
Interest Accruals			
30/360 Basis			
Actual/360			
Actual/365			
Actual/Actual			
Step Coupons			
Deferred Interest			
Variable Rate			
Premium Amortization/Discount Accretion			
Straight Line			
Scientific			
Zero Coupons			
Deferred Interest			
Step Coupons			

18. Capital Changes/Corporate Actions

| | Supported? | | |
	Yes	No	Explanation
Automatic Maturities			
Stock Splits			
Stock Dividends			
Exchanges			
Mergers			
Tenders			
Spin-Offs Taxable			
Spin-Offs Nontaxable			

18.1 For each capital change listed above which your product supports please provide the following information:

18.1.1 How is each transaction accumulated and stored before and after ex-date?

18.1.2 How is each transaction applied?

18.1.3 How are reversals handled?

18.1.4 When is it processed (e.g. on ex-date)?

18.1.5 Does performance measurement require any special handling/processing?

18.2 Describe how options contracts and positions are adjusted in the event of a split in the underlying stock.

18.3 Are dividend accruals posted on ex-date?

18.4 Are cash dividend receipts posted on payable date?

19. DTC Interface

19.1 Describe (if it exists) your interface to DTC.

19.2 Do you provide auto-matching with DTC?

19.3 Describe the trade affirmation process.

19.4 Can DTC be used for trade entry? Please explain.

19.5 Are there any exception reports? Please describe.

19.6 How do you prevent duplicate posting?

20. Security

20.1 Describe how system security is administered and how it is applied. For instance, indicate if it is at the menu level, screen, record and/or field.

20.2 Describe capability to restrict access to certain information to certain personnel.

20.3 Describe the audit functions and system update logging. Address the preventative, detective and corrective controls built into the system. Indicate if the system keeps an audit log of all transactions by user and whether these are time-stamped.

21. Fee Billing

	Supported?		
	Yes	No	Explanation
Base Fees + Incremental Based On Assets			
Override Market Values For Billing Purposes			
Allow Adjustments To Fees			
Merge Accounts For Billing Only			
Bill Monthly In Advance			
Bill In Arrears At Calendar Quarter End			

21.1 How many fee schedules can be maintained in your system?

22. Conversion

22.1 Describe the typical system conversion process.

22.2 How long does conversion and parallel testing normally take?

23. Corrections/Changes to RFI

Please indicate any changes or corrections which you would like to make to your responses to the original Request for Information (RFI).

24. Cost Proposal

24.1 Please provide a complete cost proposal for acquisition of the product, maintenance and support over the initial 2-year period. Please specify everything that is included with the cost specified. If more information is needed please contact us.

24.2 What is the cost of the first year of support? When does it start?

24.3 Describe the procedure for testing or piloting the system before committing to a full-scale purchase.

24.4 What additional costs might we expect to incur?

24.5 Please list the per diem cost(s) of your personnel for software customization and additional training.

24.6 Is on-going system maintenance required? How many people are needed?

GLOSSARY

☐ **APPLICATION SOFTWARE:** A software program that performs a particular function other than management of the CPU or its related peripherals. Examples of application software include word processing, electronic mail and accounting programs.

☐ **BACKUP:** A copy of a file or data set that is kept for reference in case the original file or data set is damaged or destroyed.

☐ **BAUD:** A measure of speed in sending or receiving data by telephone wires. Baud equals binary units of information per second. For example, 9800 baud means 9800 bits of data can be sent per second.

☐ **BATCH PROCESSING:** Process whereby data is collected over a defined period of time for subsequent processing.

☐ **BIT:** The abbreviation for Binary digIT. It is the basic element of computer data.

☐ **CENTRAL PROCESSING UNIT (CPU):** Component of a computer which executes program instructions and controls data input and output.

☐ **COMPILE:** The process of translating source code into object code or machine language.

☐ **DIRECTORY:** An index that contains the names and addresses of each file in the data storage system.

☐ **DISTRIBUTED PROCESSING:** The manner in which processing functions and/or data is distributed over an integrated number of computers and/or peripheral devices.

☐ **GATEWAY:** A computer system that transfers data between normally incompatible applications or networks. It reformats the data before passing it on so that is acceptable for the new network.

☐ **HYPERTEXT:** Documents that contain links to other documents. Selecting a link automatically displays the second document.

☐ **INTERNET:** A world-wide network of computers and networks that are connected to each other. The internet provides file transfer, remote login, electronic mail, news and other services.

☐ **LOCAL AREA NETWORK (LAN):** A communication system within a limited geographic area designed to allow a number of computers and/or peripheral devices to communicate with each other.

☐ **MAINFRAME:** A multi-user computer system characterized by large storage capacity and much peripheral support.

☐ **MEMORY:** The storage component of a computer where program instructions and data reside.

☐ **MODEM:** A peripheral device that connects a computer to a data transmission line (usually a telephone line).

☐ **MULTIMEDIA:** Documents that include different kinds of data; for example, plain text, and audio, or text in several different languages, or text with embedded graphics.

☐ **MULTI-USER SYSTEM:** A system that allows more than one user to use the system at the same time.

☐ **NETWORK:** A combination of computer equipment and/or peripheral devices that are interconnected allowing for the sharing of data and/or programs.

☐ **OBJECT CODE:** The version of the software program which is compiled from source code and is understood by the computer.

☐ **ON-LINE PROCESSING:** Process whereby data is processed at the same time as it is entered.

☐ **OPERATING SYSTEM:** Program instructions which control and direct the internal operation of the computer's various components.

☐ **ORIGINAL EQUIPMENT MANUFACTURER (OEM):** A manufacturer of computer hardware that often bundles and sells the hardware with application software packages which it has either developed or has the right to license.

☐ **PARALLEL PROCESSING:** The method by which the same data is processed using two different computer systems for the purpose of identifying any discrepancies.

☐ **PORT:** One of the computer's physical input/output channels.

☐ **PROTOCOL:** Protocols define how computers will act when talking to each other. Standard protocols allow computers from different manufacturers to communicate; the computers can use completely different software, providing that the programs running on both ends agree on what the data means.

☐ **RAM:** An acronym for Random Access Memory in which data and computer programs can be recorded temporarily.

☐ **REVERSE ENGINEERING:** The process by which object code is dissected to uncover its structure, logic and the process by which the software program was developed.

☐ **SERVER HARDWARE:** The computer on which server software operates.

☐ **SERVER SOFTWARE:** Software that allows a computer to offer a service to another computer.

☐ **SOURCE CODE:** The computer program as the software programmer writes it and therefore is understood by humans.

☐ **SYSTEM INTEGRATOR:** A contractor who teams up with different vendors to create a system and usually does not manufacture its own equipment.

☐ **VIRUS:** A software program that attaches itself to another program in computer memory or on a disk, and spreads from one program to another. Viruses may damage data and other programs, cause the computer to malfunction, display error messages or lie dormant.

☐ **WIDE AREA NETWORK (WAN):** A communication system within an unlimited geographic area designed to allow a number of computers and/or peripheral devices to communicate with each other.

☐ **WORLD WIDE WEB:** A hypertext-based system for finding and accessing internet resources.

INDEX

ABOUT THE AUTHOR

Jeff Monassebian is a practicing attorney in New York City with more than 10 years specialized experience in computer technology transactions. Between 1985 and 1995, Jeff was a principal in, and general counsel to, TCAM Systems, an international software development and licensing company. There he was responsible for the negotiation of software development and licensing agreements with securities trading firms, investment banks, stock exchanges and central banks in the United States, Europe, Asia and Australia.

As TCAM's director of new business development, Jeff was directly responsible for designing and overseeing development of the first distributed database client-server multiple listing service in the United States and the establishment of a real time service bureau for trading and order routing of OTC, third market and listed securities.

Involvement in the management of TCAM's day to day business operation and formulation of tactical as well as strategic direction allows Jeff to bring a unique business perspective to the representation of clients in all aspects of computer technology development, licensing, procurement and dispute resolution. He is the founder and President of CADRE, Inc., a forum dedicated to the resolution of technology related disputes by means other than litigation. He is also a partner in the intellectual property law firm of Lieberman & Nowak in New York City, where he assists clients in connection with both their legal and investment banking activities.

Jeff has been interviewed on CBS News and his companies have been featured on CBS News and *Building America*. Jeff is a graduate of Georgetown University Law Center and is a member of the *Beta Gamma Sigma* and *Omicron Delta Epsilon* honor societies.

NOTES

ORDER FORM

Please send the following:

Item	Unit Price	Quantity	Cost
A Survival Guide to Computer Contracts	$24.95	_____	_____
Agreements on Disk	$19.95	_____	_____

		Tax:	_____
		Shipping:	_____
		Discounts:	(_____)
		Total:	_____

* Order both *A Survival Guide to Computer Contracts* and Agreements on Disk together and receive a 15% discount. That's $38.00 for both.

* Order three or more of any one item and take an additional 10% discount on your order.

**I understand that I may return any books
for a full refund—for any reason
—no questions asked.**

Name: _____ Company: _____

Title: _____ Address: _____

City: _____ State: _____ Zip: _____ - _____

Telephone: (_____) _____ Fax: (_____) _____

E-Mail: _____

Sales tax:
Please add 8.5% for books and disks shipped to New York State residents.

Shipping:
Book rate: $2.00 for the first book or disk and $.75 for each additional book or disk (surface shipping may take four to five weeks).
Air Mail: $3.50 per book or disk.

Payment method:

❒ Check   ❒ VISA   ❒ Master Card   ❒ AMEX   ❒ Discover

Card Number: _____ Exp. Date: _____

Name on Card: _____ Signature: _____

Fax orders to: (516) 773-4743

Telephone orders to: (516) 482-5796. Please have your credit card information ready.

Mail orders to: Application Publishing, Inc., PO Box 4124, Great Neck, NY 11023.